The Westminster Cardinals

The Westminster Cardinals

The Past and the Future

MICHAEL WALSH

burns & oates

Published by Continuum
The Tower Building, 11 York Road, London SE1 7NX
80 Maiden Lane, Suite 704, New York NY 10038

www.continuumbooks.com

First published 2008

British Library Cataloguing-in-Publication Data
A catalogue record for this book is available from the British Library.

ISBN 978-0-86012-459-7

Typeset by Kenneth Burnley, Wirral, Cheshire
Printed and bound by MPG Books, Bodmin, Cornwall

Contents

An Acknowledgement

This is something of an instant book, written at relatively short notice. I would therefore like to pay tribute to all those other scholars who have laboured far longer than I in the archives, or among the files of newspapers, to produce the scholarship upon which this volume has so liberally drawn. Wherever I have quoted directly I have, I think, always acknowledged my source. But to anyone who reads this book it will, I hope, be immediately obvious that my indebtedness goes far further than the occasional quotation. So, to all those who have gone before and whose publications are listed in the Bibliography, very many thanks indeed. I cannot hope to have done you justice, but I hope that I have in no way misrepresented the information that you have so sedulously gathered.

Like so many who live within the boundaries of the Diocese of Westminster I am an incomer, but I have now lived in London north of the Thames for the greater part of my life. I recall having to buy a black homburg to satisfy a whim of Cardinal Godfrey. I remember a priest colleague running into trouble with Cardinal Heenan for appearing on television wearing a tie rather than a clerical collar. Cardinal Hume landed me in an embarrassing situation, and never apologized. I have eaten cake and taken tea with Cardinal Murphy-O'Connor. The Diocese of Westminster has been the context within which much of my adult life has been lived. I hope I have been fair to it. It has not been dull.

Introduction

Popes do not retire – at least, not so far – but bishops are expected to do so. The retirement age is 75, at which birthday they are supposed to submit their resignation to the Holy See. It is not always accepted. It commonly happens that the incumbent prelate is asked to stay on for another year or so while a search is conducted for his successor. Just why it happens like this I could not say. It gives the rather endearing, but probably false, impression that the Congregation for Bishops, which oversees such things, had not noticed until Bishop So-and-So had drawn it to their attention that Bishop So-and-So was reaching three-score years and fifteen and might need a replacement. A rather more likely explanation is that if the bishop is still relatively hale and hearty, and has not too often departed from the party line, another year or so of active ministry might be extracted from him, never mind what the rules might say.

In accordance with the guidelines, Cardinal Cormac Murphy-O'Connor duly submitted his resignation on reaching the age of 75. At the time of writing he is still in post, but is thought to be about to depart, and a new Archbishop of Westminster will then inhabit the vast Victorian pile on Amrosden Avenue, just down beyond Bentley's splendid cathedral. Should the Cardinal survive until his retirement is accepted – and despite a health scare in April 2006 when he was forbidden to fly, he does indeed still look distinctly hale and hearty – he will be the first of the ten Archbishops of Westminster, the

1

subjects of this volume, who has not died in office. And if, as is likely, his successor is elevated in fairly short order to the rank of Cardinal, there will be two Englishmen holding that status. This has happened occasionally after the restoration of the hierarchy in 1850, though since the death of William Heard (Edinburgh born, but a long-term resident of the English College, of which he became Protector) in 1973, there has only been one.[1]

How England and Wales came to be given back its episcopacy[2] will be discussed below (cf. pp. 21ff). From the accession to the throne of Elizabeth I until 1685, the reign of the Catholic James II, except for a brief period from 1623 to 1631, there was no Catholic bishop in England. From then until 1850 the Church was under the guidance of what have been called by their historian 'emergency bishops'.[3] The country was divided into four 'districts', the Western District, including Wales and south-west England, the Northern, the Midland, and the London Districts, the last covering London and the south east. In charge of each of the districts was a Vicar Apostolic. A Vicar Apostolic may have the title of bishop, but does not have the full jurisdiction that a bishop usually exercises over his diocese. It is a form of jurisdiction commonly used in mission territories, and that is how, from Elizabeth's accession onwards, Rome regarded England – a mission territory. In 1850 that changed with the appointment of Nicholas Wiseman as Archbishop of Westminster, with the rank of Cardinal. There have been nine more Archbishops of Westminster, each holding the rank of Cardinal; Cormac Murphy-O'Connor being, at the time of writing, the tenth of them, and on the point of retiring.

---

1 Heard was a curial official, working on marriage annulments at the Rota in the morning and on canonizations at the Congregation of Rites (now Congregation for the Causes of Saints) in the afternoon. He did it that way round because he found the latter less depressing.
2 The restored hierarchy governed England and Wales. There was a separate structure for Scotland – and, of course, for Ireland.
3 Basil Hemphill, *The Early Vicars Apostolic of England* (London: Burns and Oates, 1954), p. vii.

What has occupied commentators more than how, and where, Cardinal Cormac will spend his retirement, is who will replace him. It is not a question which will be addressed here. In 1995 Peter Hebblethwaite wrote *The Next Pope: An Enquiry,*[4] but alas, Pope John Paul II being so long lived, Hebblethwaite himself had died long before his book became useful. His widow, Margaret, then revised it,[5] but even this new edition appeared five years before the conclave actually occurred to which it was intended as a guide. In any case, such are the workings of the Vatican that speculation, even the most scientifically based speculation, often turns out to be wrong. During the conclaves of 1978 the priest sociologist Andrew Greeley fed into his Chicago computers all the requisites for the next pope. In the list which the computer spewed out, based on the information which it had been given, the name of Karol Wojtyla did not figure.[6]

It might, nonetheless, be interesting to consider what qualities an archbishop should be expected to display. *The Tablet* asked a variety of people for their views. Mine was published, along with others, on 17 June 2008. I wrote:

> English Catholicism has suffered from divisiveness in the hierarchy, so the new Archbishop needs to be able to command the respect of his fellow bishops. It would be good, too, if he were a man of such perspicacity that his views were sought on a range of social issues, not simply when defending entrenched positions on bioethics. He needs the intelligence of Manning, the media-savvy of Heenan or Hume, the approachability of Murphy-O'Connor and the leadership skills of Hinsley. If that is asking too much, I would settle for another Hinsley, because he gave the laity their head and

---

4 London: Fount, 1995.
5 *The Next Pope: History in the Making* (London: Fount, 2000).
6 See Peter Hebblethwaite, *The Year of Three Popes* (London: Collins, 1978), p. 132.

had advanced views on ecumenism. Where to find such a paragon? Well, Hinsley's father was a village carpenter.

The editors took out the last two sentences.

In his fascinating book *Inside the Vatican*,[7] the best by far of a string of books with that, or a similar, title, Tom Reese, an American Jesuit, listed the qualities he thought the cardinals gathered in a conclave would be looking for in the ideal candidate to hold the office of pope. Some of them may seem not appropriate to the choice of an Archbishop of Westminster simply because he is not elected by ballot (it is odd that the Church is so often said not to be a democracy despite the fact that its top job is open to election). But nonetheless Fr Reese's criteria do indeed apply.

He insisted that a papal candidate needs to be fluent in Italian at least, and able to pick up other languages with some ease. Most of Westminster's Archbishops have spent a fair amount of time in Rome, and could certainly manage Italian. Even those who did not go to Rome for at least some part of their studies – Bourne and Hume – have been more than competent in languages other than English. Britain is part of the European Union. Though the Archbishops have appeared to be remarkably patriotic even while leading a Church in this country which is very largely immigrant in its membership, in recent decades they have played an important role in the counsels of European bishops, demonstrating that patriotism and being a good European can go hand in hand.

Another of the criteria is to be at ease with the media – not necessarily, says Reese, a media star but at least not a public embarrassment. This is even more important for the leader of the Church in England and Wales than it is for the pope. Popes can be shielded from the press. That is simply not possible for the Archbishop of Westminster. A pope who makes a controver-

---

7 Cambridge, MA and London: Harvard University Press, 1996. The section to which reference is made occurs on pp. 94–8.

sial statement is not required to face the press to defend it, but the man who is seen to be the public face of the papacy in Britain, as the Archbishop is, however mistakenly, taken to be, cannot escape the reporters' notebooks or the television cameras. When Cardinal Heenan, questioned by David Frost, appeared to give his, albeit reluctant, blessing to Catholics who practised contraception (cf. below, p.189f), the interview was flashed around the world in minutes. Heenan was a practised performer before the camera. Hume was just as good if not better – if only because he looked less smug. Murphy-O'Connor looks ill at ease, and his otherwise admirable habit of reflecting before he speaks gives the unfortunate impression that he does not know what he thinks.

Which brings me to a criterion Reese does not mention, perhaps because, in a modern pope he thinks it can be taken for granted: an Archbishop of Westminster needs to be something of an intellectual. No doubt a bishop can be an excellent pastor without a thorough grounding in theology: many are. It does not take a degree to be able to celebrate with liturgy in a manner which lifts the congregation's hearts and minds to God. But the leader of English Catholics, which the Archbishop of Westminster is taken to be, has to be at ease when dealing with the many major moral issues which modern society, and the government, throws at him. He will have his advisers. That is fine when writing a piece for a newspaper, but advisers do not have to give instant, public responses to the media's questions about why the Catholic Church has adopted such-and-such a stance on, say, the embryology debate, on 'assisted dying', or on the time limit on abortions. The Cardinal has to be able to think on his feet.

Age is also a factor, says Reese. Again, because the pope is still elected for life, this is perhaps more important in the choice of a pontiff than it is in the choice of a bishop who will retire at 75. One needs a relatively vigorous church leader, but not someone who will be in place for too long a period of time. Twenty years is too long (Cardinal Bourne was in post for very much longer than that), so it would probably be unwise to appoint an Archbishop of Westminster before he was 60 or so. A bishop can be moved; an Archbishop of Westminster has nowhere else to go – except in the event that an Englishman would be elected Bishop of Rome. Not that any cardinal of Westminster is a likely candidate for the papal throne. Never since Reginald Pole in the sixteenth century has any Englishman seemed a possible choice – though there have been English cardinals, quite a number of them, between Henry VIII's break with Rome and the restoration of the hierarchy in the middle of the nineteenth century. Britons still have too much baggage of an imperial past to make popular candidates.

Nationality, Reese points out, is an issue at conclaves. It is still something of an issue at Westminster. Apart from Manning, a convert; Vaughan, from an Old Catholic family; and Hume, whose mother was French, all the cardinals have had Irish ancestry. But, despite the number of Irish clergy in England and Wales, none have risen to the top. All of the archbishops have been born in England. People are touchy on the subject. Even Murphy-O'Connor's slight Irish accent was a matter for comment when he was appointed.

Popes are expected to have had some experience in the Roman curia as well as in a diocese. Diocesan bishops in England and Wales also commonly have had some administrative experience, if only as secretary to their own local ordinary. Having been bishop's secretary is almost a *sine qua non* for promotion. Some bishops have even served, as priests, in the Roman curia. Pope John Paul II appeared to think that appointment to a diocese was a way of rewarding long-serving prelates of the curia. It happened in the United States, it happened in Ireland. So far it has not occurred here, and ought not to. In the fourteenth century, English kings passed the Statutes of Provisors[8] to prevent this form of abuse of the local church.

---

8 To prevent clerics being 'provided' to a benefice by the pope.

Reese's 'final variable' is how far likely candidates for the office of pope compare with the deceased pontiff. One cannot help noticing that because Hume, once Abbot of Ampleforth, was regarded as an outstanding success at Westminster – even the Queen, it is said, referred to him as 'My Cardinal' – other abbots are earnestly presented as possible successors. There have been a number of members of religious orders, especially Benedictines, among the English and Welsh bishops. Since the restoration of the hierarchy there has never been a Jesuit, at least in Britain (but then there has never been a Jesuit pope either). There have, on the other hand, been several English Jesuit bishops in mission territories. One of these, Archbishop Thomas Roberts, one time of Bombay, resigned his see in favour of a local man and returned to this country to become the hero of radicals and a thorn in side of Cardinal Heenan (see below, p. 186f).

But Reese's chief criterion was that the candidate for the papacy was able to command consensus among the cardinal electors. He has, therefore, usually been a compromise candidate, acceptable to competing factions. This was in part a result of the two-thirds majority required for election, a rule which Pope John Paul unfortunately modified but which his successor has wisely restored. How Archbishops of Westminster are chosen remains much more of a mystery. The papal nuncio takes soundings. Bishops are asked for their opinions, so are 'leading' Catholic lay men and women, or so it is claimed. Hume was backed by the late Duke of Norfolk, though the rather maverick Duke had originally, it seems, wanted the parish priest of Bayswater, Michael Hollings. It is perhaps no accident that Hume's successor was from Arundel and Brighton. The Norfolk family home is Arundel Castle. In a country with as strong a democratic tradition as Britain – the survival of its hereditary aristocracy such as the Norfolks notwithstanding – it is time there was far more transparency about the choice.

England and Wales have been for the most part lucky in the more recent episcopal appointments – something often attributed to the influence at Rome of the late Cardinal Hume. Elsewhere the Vatican has clearly manipulated appointments to ensure that the conservative line coming out of Rome was foisted upon the Church at large. Nowhere is this conservatism more clearly demonstrated than the attempt to revive what is commonly, if somewhat inaccurately, known as the Tridentine Rite. Though bishops in this country made valiant efforts not to seem disloyal to Rome, it was clearly against what the majority, if not all, of them thought was in the best interests of the Church in England and Wales. A cardinal was despatched from Rome to celebrate it, with absurd pomp, in Westminster Cathedral – in the absence, it should be said, of Cardinal Murphy-O'Connor or of any of his assistant bishops (see below, p. xx). At one time it was possible to say that, no matter how much traditionalists and progressives within the Church differed on matters of doctrinal interpretation, at least they were united around the same altar as they celebrated the Eucharist. This, alas, is no longer necessarily true.

One wonders how a cardinal, 'swathed in yards of red silk' as one angry priest put it,[9] thinks he relates to the world in which the overwhelming majority of the faithful eke out their living. Adjacent to this priest's article in *The Tablet* was a survey which revealed that, of those Catholics questioned, an alarming 69 per cent either believed in, or were not sure about, reincarnation. One would think prelates, even Roman ones, had more important things to do for the faithful than flounce about in lace and silk.

The situation is set to become even more challenging for Catholics. Writing about the decline in church attendance, the Catholic commentator Peter Stanford remarked in his book on Cardinal Hume that the blame for it did not lie entirely at the Cardinal's door,[10] even though he may have felt himself some-

---

9 Fr Sean Middleton in *The Tablet*, 19 July 2008, p. 11.
10 Peter Stanford, *Cardinal Hume and the Changing Face of English Catholicism* (London: Geoffrey Chapman, 1993), p. 19.

thing of a failure because of this. I doubt whether there is a great deal which bishops and priests can do to stem the decline. It is, I suspect, the spirit of the age, and will in due course change, much of its own accord. Who could have expected the France of Voltaire to become, not a century later, the France of a multiplicity of new religious orders, or the laissez-faire broad churchmanship of eighteenth-century England turn into the earnest evangelicalism of the nineteenth?

But it does not help the Church's credibility as a guide to living when it is made to appear increasingly out of touch with modern society. Pope Pius IX anathematized anyone who believed that the pope could, or ought to, come to terms with modern civilization.[11] He had not apparently noticed that the Catholic Church has survived down the centuries by coming to terms with the culture in which it found itself. Pius IX's statement was mistaken then, and is mistaken now, even though there were Catholics then, as there are Catholics today, who would wish it to be true. If there is too much of a dissonance between what the Church teaches and what people believe to be right, then they will drop away from the Faith. Which is exactly what happened over birth control. To take another example, the Church's stance over the question of whether homosexual couples may adopt children has led one Catholic children's society to break its formal links with the Church.

That was not technically a question of homosexuality. It was a consequence of gender equality legislation, the law demanding of publicly funded bodies such as the Catholic children's societies, that people of whatever sexual orientation be treated alike. The suggestion in a document emanating from the Congregation for the Doctrine of the Faith when it was run by Cardinal Ratzinger that the law was right to discriminate against homosexuals, runs flatly contrary to the policy of the British government and, I suspect, contrary to the convictions of the greater part of the British people. Gender equality is not

---

11 Proposition 80 of the 1864 Syllabus of Errors.

something which church*men* can oppose without seeming foolish. Coming to terms with it, however, will present an enormous challenge both to the practice of Catholicism and to its doctrine. Cardinal Hume was not averse to the notion of women priests (see below, p. 212f), nor was the International Theological Commission. Rome, of course, will be utterly unmoved.

In the aftermath of the National Pastoral Congress of 1980 the Conference of Priests demanded to know why the representatives of the Conference of Bishops, Archbishops Hume and Worlock, had not been more forthright in their dealings with Rome (see below, p. 207f). More recently there are many, including bishops, who felt the same about the way in which Rome was imposing a new translation of the liturgy. But it is not easy. Bishops, and especially the Cardinal Archbishop of Westminster, have to balance the needs of the people of this country with the need to preserve the unity of the Church. In this they deserve our support. It was for the unity of the Church that the once Chancellor of England, Thomas More, laid down his life, even if he had no high regard for the popes of his day.

1

Nicholas Wiseman

By the time that the Congregation of Propaganda decided to advise Pope Pius IX that it was now opportune to restore the normal hierarchical structures to the Church in England and Wales, Nicholas Wiseman was the obvious choice to be the first Archbishop of Westminster. He was not, however, necessarily the most popular choice. For one thing, he was not really English.

Nicholas Patrick Stephen Wiseman had been born in Seville. His father James was an Irish merchant, living and trading in Seville as had his father before him. James was married twice. His first wife was said to have been the daughter of a Spanish general. Her first name was Mariana, but her surname was the very un-Spanish Dunphy. They had four daughters, one of whom died. Mariana Dunphy herself died in 1793 and James married again in April 1800. The wedding took place at the church of St Mary and St Michael on the Commercial Road in London's East End. His bride was Irish, though with a Spanish-sounding Christian name: Xaviera Strange.

James and Xaviera's first child, also baptized James, was born just over nine months later, while the couple were still in London. By the time Nicholas was born the family had moved back to Seville. He was born on 2 August 1802 and two days later was baptized in the church of the Holy Cross. A third child, Francesca, was born two years later. Not six months after that, in January 1805, Xaviera's husband died suddenly, and she with her three children returned to her father's house,

Aylwardstown Castle in County Kilkenny. The boys were at first sent to a boarding school in Ireland and then, in 1810, to St Cuthbert's College at Ushaw, four miles west of Durham.

Though originally founded at Douai in 1568 for the training of clergy for the English mission, the college had been forced to move to England, to Crook Hall, Durham, in 1793, only settling finally at Ushaw two years before the Wiseman boys arrived. Nicholas was not particularly happy, writing in later life of his 'desolate years' at Ushaw. He was quiet and studious, and attracted the attention of the vice-president, John Lingard, and became something of a protégé of the learned priest. Not that Lingard stayed long after the Wiseman boys' arrival. There was a new president appointed in 1811 and though he was offered a similar post at Maynooth, just outside Dublin, he preferred to retire to a parish at Hornby in Lancashire: he died there in July 1851. In his 40 years at Hornby he produced a much-admired history of England, and in 1821 he was promoted to the rank of doctor three times over by Pope Pius VII: doctor of theology, of civil law and of canon law. He had little time for things of Rome, however, and when in 1826 it became known that Pope Leo XII had created a number of cardinals *in petto* ('in secret'), he was afraid that he might be among their number. The suspected elevation never came, much to his relief. Lingard remained in England as perhaps the foremost exponent of the English tradition of Catholicism, forged in the penal years, which Wiseman and his successors at Westminster came to denominate as Gallicanism.[1]

---

1 Manning regarded Gallicanism to be a greater danger to English Catholics than Anglicanism: 'Gallicanism is within its [i.e., the Catholic Church's] unity, and is neither schism nor heresy. It is a very seductive form of national Catholicism, which, without breaking unity, or positively violating faith, soothes the pride to which all great nations are tempted, and encourages the civil power to patronize the local church by a tutelage fatal to its liberty. It is therefore certain than Gallicanism is more dangerous to Catholicism than Anglicanism. The latter is a plague of which we are not susceptible; the former is a disease which may easily be taken.' Mary Heimann, *Catholic Devotion in Victorian England* (Oxford: Clarendon, 1995), p. 20.

In October 1818 he left Liverpool with nine others destined for the English College in Rome. This was the first intake of new students since Rome had been captured by the French in 1798, Pope Pius VI taken prisoner and exiled to France. He died at Valence the following year. Pius VII was elected in March 1800 and he, too, suffered the indignity of being imprisoned by the French, but after the defeat of Napoleon in 1814 returned to Rome. One of his first acts was to bring back into existence the Society of Jesus which had, before the suppression of the Order in 1773, been in charge of the Roman College where Wiseman and his fellow students first studied. In 1824, however, the Jesuits were reinstated, and the traditional hostility of the English College to the Society meant that the English students then went elsewhere for their education in philosophy and theology.

By that time Wiseman was already in minor orders. He received the orders in 1820, rather to the displeasure of his mother, who considered him to be too young. He was still only eighteen and Xaviera thought she ought to have been consulted. She had never particularly wanted either of her sons to enter the priesthood (James had left Ushaw to return to Spain), but she was especially unhappy about the missionary oath which Nicholas was now obliged to take. This committed those who swore the oath to return to work in the English mission, should their superiors so decide, but Xaviera seems to have understood it to imply that her son might be sent to any place in the world that fell under the jurisdiction, as England then did, of the Congregation of Propaganda. Nicholas himself was also uneasy about the oath, thinking that it might tie him down too much, yet took it nonetheless.

But rather than return as a missionary to England, he stayed on in Rome. He was flourishing. It was not simply that Roman weather was a great relief after the cold and damp of Ushaw, so that his health improved: he was also entranced by the antiquities of the city. As the historian of the English College has remarked, Wiseman 'was in many ways but another romantic

Englishman visiting Italy and ready to be impressed by the classical sites. Macaulay was two years his senior and John Keats arrived in Rome only two years after Wiseman.'[2] He was likewise attracted by the scholarly opportunities that Rome appeared to provide. He became a Doctor of Divinity in July 1824, defending his thesis by 'Public Act', of which he left a vivid description:

> When the time comes, the respondent finds himself, he hardly knows how, seated behind a table at the end of an immense hall which it requires a sustained voice to fill, supported by his professors, who may edge in a word in his ear, in case of possible straits. A huge oval chain of chairs stretches down the room, on either side, and soon begins to be occupied by professors, doctors and learned men, of whom he has heard perhaps only in awe; each of whom receives a copy of the thesis, and cons it over, as if to find the weak points between the plates of mail, into which he will later try to thrust his spear.[3]

He was ordained priest on 10 March 1825 and had to consider his career. He hoped for a professorship at the (papal) university of Rome, but in order to gain that distinction he had

---

2 Michael E. Williams, *The Venerable English College, Rome* (London: Associated Catholic Publications, 1979), p. 95.

3 Nicholas Schofield and Gerard Skinner, *The English Cardinals* (Oxford: Family Publications, 2007), p. 145. The passage cited by Schofield and Skinner goes on: 'I remember well, in the particular instance before my eye, that a monk clothed in white glided in, and sat down in the inner circle, but though a special messenger was despatched to him by the professors, he shook his head, and declined becoming an assailant. He had been sent to listen and report. It was Fr Capellari, who in less than six years was Pope Gregory XVI. Not far from him was seated the Abbé de Lamenais, whose works he so justly and so witheringly condemned. Probably it was the only time they were ever seated together, listening to an English youth vindicating the Faith, of which one would become the oracle, and the other the bitter foe' (*ibid.*). The use of the word 'oracle' with reference to the pope is indicative of the attitude with which Rome-trained clergy regarded the papacy.

to publish some work of scholarship. Encouraged by Angelo Mai, a palaeographer and former Jesuit (he had left the Society in 1819 at the request of the pope to take charge of the Vatican Library), he made a study of a Syriac manuscript in the Vatican Library which he published in 1827 as *Horae Syriacae*. The book was an instant success, winning Wiseman the professorship of Syriac, and election to the Royal Asiatic Society. In 1831 he was also made an honorary member of the Royal Society of Literature. That same year as the publication of his book he became vice-rector of the English College.

He was still only 25 years of age. Nonetheless, when the College's rector was appointed coadjutor (assistant) to the Vicar Apostolic of the London District, he recommended that Wiseman succeed him. This was agreed, and in December 1828 he became rector of the English College. But not only was he rector, he was a professor in the University of Rome, a regular preacher, to admiring crowds, at a church on the Corso, and a frequent lecturer to English visitors to Rome. He needed an assistant. The man he chose was George Errington, a younger contemporary at Ushaw who had arrived at the English College in 1821 and proved himself a remarkable scholar, winning three theological prizes before becoming, in September 1827, a Doctor of Divinity. He was ordained in December of that year. When appointed vice-rector he was only 24. The strain of the role proved too much for him. He retired from the post in 1831 and spent the next dozen years travelling around Europe for the sake of his health.

While fostering scholarship in Rome, Wiseman was concerned to raise the level of theological awareness among clergy and laity alike in England. He was therefore delighted when a group of priests in the Midland District decided to start a journal, *The Catholic Magazine*. He undertook to be a contributor. He immediately wrote an article, but his association was short-lived. The problem arose in the person of his one-time patron at Ushaw, the learned Dr Lingard.

Lingard had contributed a piece to the magazine in which

he criticized the intention to include in an English prayer book the Litany of Loreto. This series of invocations in honour of the Virgin Mary had its remote origins in the later Middle Ages, and in its developed form had been in common use in Rome since the sixteenth century. Lingard's complaint was that many of the invocations ('Mystical rose, Tower of David, Tower of ivory, House of gold' and suchlike) were unintelligible. Wiseman could not countenance such criticism of Roman practice and apparent insult to the Virgin, and withdrew his collaboration.

He had been ready to commit himself, as has just been indicated, because he was concerned to see an improvement in the educational and cultural awareness of English Catholics. Britain had never had, at least since the Reformation, a Catholic university. Wiseman was delighted to learn that the Vicar Apostolic of the Western District, Bishop Peter Augustine Baines, was planning to start one, and even more excited by the news that Baines wanted him to become his coadjutor bishop, in charge of the enterprise, to be located at Prior Park. The 'ebullient'[4] Baines, before his elevation to the episcopacy, had been a monk of Ampleforth Abbey, near York, and he had attracted sundry monks – and pupils – from Ampleforth to his new school at Prior Park, a property he had acquired near Bath. But he had bigger plans, and wanted Wiseman to assist him. Wiseman was ready to do so, but Baines's organizational skills were not of the best, and the appointment kept being delayed. Wiseman's own bishop, the Vicar Apostolic of the Northern District, would not release him. And in any case, Pope Gregory XVI would not approve of Wiseman becoming a bishop, a reluctance that Baines put down for no obvious reason to the machinations of the Jesuits.

Bishop Baines was himself a Benedictine, a member of a religious order. Jesuits apart, he was fairly sympathetic to the

---

4 Dominic Aidan Bellenger and Stella Fletcher, *Princes of the Church* (Stroud: Sutton Publishing, 2001), p. 118. The school still exists.

regular clergy, though their influence had been on the wane in England for several generations. The secular priests (diocesan clergy as they might now be called, except that there were so far no dioceses) were in the ascendant, feeling themselves empowered by the Catholic Emancipation Act of 1829 which had laid considerable restrictions upon the re-emergent Jesuits – though these restrictions were not enforced in practice. But tensions remained between seculars and regulars. As agent in Rome for the vicars apostolic by virtue of his office as rector of the English College, Wiseman was expected to lobby the pope on behalf of the bishops in England in their conflict with the regulars. In particular, when they presented a petition and Wiseman simply forwarded it rather than hand it over in person, they felt aggrieved.

Nicholas Wiseman, however, had acted circumspectly. The regulars were prominent in Rome, not least because the intransigent Gregory XVI was himself a Camaldolese monk. That Wiseman was not unsympathetic to the regulars was confirmed for the vicars apostolic when he had Cardinal Thomas Weld declared Protector of the English College. Weld was an English aristocrat who had only become a priest after the death of his wife, and was unexpectedly made a cardinal by Pius VIII. His family was very close to the Jesuits, and it was Thomas's father, also Thomas, who made over the house he had inherited in the depths of Lancashire, Stonyhurst, to the (by then ex-) Jesuits after they had to abandon their college at Liège in 1794.

In 1835 Wiseman decided to make a lengthy visit to England. The ostensible reason was to prepare for publication the lectures he had been giving in Rome. He now lectured in England, and he was again well received, not least by John Henry Newman – not yet, of course, a Catholic. But after his experience with *The Catholic Magazine* he was eager to found something else of a similar kind. Together with the politician Daniel O'Connell, and the Irish barrister turned journalist Michael Quin whose idea it seems originally to have been, he produced *The Dublin Review*. The name of the quarterly was chosen with an obvious nod in the direction of *The Edinburgh Review*, and like the *Edinburgh* it set out to be a literary, historical and religious publication; but despite its title and its green cover it was always published in London. Quin was the first editor, but it was hardly a profitable undertaking and he withdrew. The editorship was then given to Mark Tierney, chaplain to the Duke of Norfolk and a historian and antiquarian. But he was of precisely the same school as Lingard, and he and Wiseman quickly fell out, leaving Wiseman in effective charge.[5]

Wiseman used his journal as a vehicle for debate with members of the Oxford Movement, a group within the Church of England who wished to revive the Catholic, or High Church, tradition in Anglicanism. The Movement's convictions were expressed in particular through *Tracts for the Times* (hence members of the Movement became known as Tractarians), a series of pamphlets, the first and the last of which (*Tract 90*) among others were written by Newman. It is probably fair to say that the majority of the English Catholic clergy, including the bishops, had little time for the Tractarians. Wiseman was unusual in that he took them seriously. It was an article by him in the August 1839 issue of *The Dublin Review*, in which he compared Anglicanism to the fourth-century Donatist schism, that so deeply affected Newman. He wrote to a friend, 'I have had the first real hit from Romanism which has happened to me.'[6] The phrase that had made the impact was a quotation Wiseman had made from St Augustine's writings on Donatism, '*securus iudicat orbis terrarum*', 'It is the whole world which judges safely.'

Not only did Wiseman debate with the Tractarians in the hope of bring them into the Catholic Church, he also prayed. He became involved with the Association of Universal Prayer for the Conversion of England, which had been started in 1838

---

5 It survived until 1969 when it was absorbed by the Jesuit publication *The Month*. In the 1960s it was briefly known as *The Wiseman Review*.
6 Ian Ker, *John Henry Newman: A Biography* (Oxford: Clarendon, 1988), p. 182.

by Ambrose Phillipps de Lisle. De Lisle was a convert, but not a member of the Oxford Movement,[7] having become a Catholic in 1825 when only sixteen. He fostered the hope of a corporate reunion with Rome of the Greek Orthodox as well as the Anglican Churches, and in 1857 started the Association for Promoting the Unity of Christendom (APUC). By this time Wiseman, a friend and a one-time supporter of what would now be called the ecumenical movement,[8] had become the Cardinal Archbishop. He was unhappy with APUC because he believed waiting for corporate reunion might discourage individual conversions, but did not object to Catholics being members; nor did he feel, as did other bishops, that APUC should be condemned by Rome. By the end of his life, however, he had changed his mind, not least because APUC was also campaigning for Catholics to be allowed to attend Oxford and Cambridge – something to which the bishops were firmly opposed (see below, pp. 47f and 75f). In September 1864 Rome's rescript addressed to the bishops of England[9] condemned APUC and instructed that no Catholics might be members.

Meanwhile, although Wiseman may have scored a 'hit' for 'Romanism' as Newman put it, several years were to pass before the latter's conversion. In the meantime the Vatican was receiving mixed messages from England. Wiseman sent a long memorandum proposing a band of missionaries to raise the fervour of Catholics, while two Italian Rosminian missionaries complained that 'the English clergy are infested with Gallicanism and are dominated by a spirit of ambition and national independence. The result is that the bishops, as vicars apostolic, do not show the respectful dependence on the Holy See that their duty requires'.[10] Whether a consequence of these

---

7 In fact he went to Cambridge, but by that time he was already a Catholic.

8 In 1841 he published *A Letter of Catholic Unity* which went so far as to suggest that, in the cause of unity, Catholics might have to reform their ways.

9 It was indeed simply called *Ad omnes episcopos Angliae.*

10 R. Schiefen, *Nicholas Wiseman and the Transformation of English Catholicism* (Shepherdstown: Patmos, 1984), p. 106.

interventions or not, Rome decided that the time was not yet ripe for the restoration of normal episcopal governance in England. But there was a further problem. The division of England and Wales into four districts, each with its vicar apostolic, meant that the area under his responsibility was too large to be governed adequately. It was therefore agreed that each should be divided into two, to create eight vicariates.

Naturally this entailed finding more bishops. Although rector of the English College in Rome, Wiseman had played a significant, if rather controversial part in Catholic life in England itself. Several of the vicars apostolic thought his enthusiasm for the Tractarians seriously misguided, that he had too great an expectation of conversions. The newly founded weekly *The Tablet* criticized him for devoting too much time to Anglicans and too little to the Catholic poor.[11] This complaint particularly must have hurt. In 1837 he had made a retreat under Jesuit guidance, and decided that henceforth he would commit himself to the poor – though it is true that there was not a great deal of evidence of any practical effect of this resolution.

Nevertheless, Wiseman had too high a profile in England to be discounted. Although not given a vicariate, he was made co-adjutor to Bishop Walsh of the Midland District, and given charge of the seminary at Oscott, just outside Birmingham. He was consecrated bishop, with the titular see of Melipotamus, in June 1840, and was formally installed at Oscott as its president early in September. It was not a happy time for him, not even when Errington, with whom he had worked at the English College, arrived at Oscott as prefect of studies. Errington thought he was too tied up with his converts from the Oxford Movement real or, as Errington suspected, imagined, and Wiseman later complained that he had no support among the staff of the college.

Not that he was without some triumphs. Though one of his converts reverted to Anglicanism,[12] causing Wiseman to take to

---

11 *Ibid.*, p. 123.
12 Richard Waldo Sibthorpe. At the end of 1864 he once more became a Catholic.

his bed in distress, Newman finally became a Catholic in October 1845 and subsequently received the sacrament of confirmation at Wiseman's hands. He then moved with his small community from Littlemore into a property at Oscott, made over to him by Wiseman, and renamed by him Mary Vale. It was Wiseman who suggested that Newman might become an Oratorian and establish a community in Birmingham, as of course subsequently occurred.

The new bishop was eager to encourage religious orders from abroad to set up houses in England. The traditionalist clergy, with their history of antipathy to the religious, objected. 'This is not the time or place for dirty or idle saints', said Lingard.[13] Nor did they like the new devotions, though the differences between the 'Garden-of-the-Soul' Catholics, so named after their favourite book of prayers, composed by Richard Challenor and first published in 1740, and those of a more Italianate or Roman mind, was perhaps not as great has been depicted. Though Wiseman 'found much of the spiritual legacy of the eighteenth century cold and over restrained, he explicitly distanced Challenor from such criticism'.[14] Wiseman's own style may perhaps be gauged from the prayers for the conversion of England – itself a notion of which the Lingardians were uneasy – to be said at Benediction: 'May [the Virgin Mary's] sweet name be lisped by little ones and linger on the lips of the aged and the dying.' This was a sentimentalism with which the traditionalists were unhappy, but it could be argued that it was more in keeping with the sensibilities of the nineteenth century than was their own, more rational version of Catholicism.

On the whole, however, a more pressing concern of the clergy was the restoration of the hierarchy which they believed would give them greater autonomy and security. The vicars apostolic were not too eager, but at their Low Week[15] meeting

---

13 *Ibid.*, p. 135.
14 Heimann, *op. cit.*, p. 85.
15 Low Week is the week after Easter week, and it was the occasion when all the bishops met in conference. They still do so.

in 1845 they decided to request Rome for it. They decided to send two bishops, one of whom was Wiseman, to the Vatican with their petition. They arrived in the summer of 1847 and Pope Pius IX seems to have agreed to the request in mid-August. But he also moved Wiseman from assistant to Bishop Walsh in Birmingham to acting (or 'pro') vicar apostolic in London. This was clearly a temporary arrangement. It soon became generally known that a new Diocese of Westminster was to be created[16] in place of the London District, and that Wiseman was to be its bishop.

The clergy were divided on his appointment. Some welcomed it, but all wanted some say in the future appointment of ordinaries when the hierarchy was eventually to be established. The changeover foreseen by Rome did not, however, happen immediately. Wiseman himself advised the Vatican that there could be legal difficulties in simply converting the eight districts into dioceses, so there was a delay while an attempt was made to sort out these issues – in the event, not wholly successfully. A further delay was incurred when, in 1848, because of political events in Rome, Pius IX had to flee the city. When Wiseman had returned from Rome the year before, it had been to lobby the Foreign Secretary, Lord Palmerston. He was proposing that the British government would guarantee the pope's safety. Because of the pope's brief flirtation with a more liberal regime in the papal states, the Foreign Office had agreed. Now the government undertook to protect church property in Rome.

Meanwhile he got on with running the London District. He made it known that he was available to be called on by the clergy of the District three days a week, from mid-morning to mid-afternoon, and every Tuesday evening he held a 'soirée',

---

16 It was a requirement of the Catholic Relief Act of 1829 that Catholic dioceses were not to take titles already in use in the Church of England, a provision that the Vatican was careful to observe. See Jeffrey von Arx, 'Catholics and Politics' in V. Alan McClelland and Michael Hodgetts (eds), *From Without the Flaminian Gate* (London: Darton, Longman and Todd, 1999), p. 250.

open to all who cared to come – a practice that Lingard promptly denounced as too Roman. Also too Roman for the Lingardians were a number of devotions he introduced into England, *Quarant'Ore*, the Three Hours devotion for Good Friday, and Marian devotions throughout May. He encouraged new religious orders to establish themselves, asking Newman to open a branch of his Oratory in London – which he did in 1849. The same year he opened the Jesuit church in Farm Street. When in 1840 the Society had first asked permission, it had been refused, but the vicar apostolic was overruled by Rome, though with the proviso that the church should not serve as a parish. He was also able, in 1848, to open St George's in Southwark which served as his cathedral, the London District encompassing both sides of the River Thames.

And at last he had an opportunity to help the poor, for his failure to do which *The Tablet* had criticized him. During the 1840s some 400,000 Irish emigrated to Britain, a quarter of whom came to live in London. There was a pressing need for Catholic schools. Wiseman had led a campaign against Sir James Graham's bill which would have required every child who was employed to provide a certificate of attendance at school. The bill effectively gave control over running schools to the Church of England, and Dissenters joined the Catholics in opposing the measure. That had been in 1843. Wiseman, with the assistance of Charles Langdale,[17] founded the Catholic Poor Schools Committee to campaign, as it did successfully and in short order, for the government to make grants to Catholic schools as well as to the state, or board schools. Catholic schools had in fact been eligible for government funding from

---

17 Langdale's family name was Stourton, but he adopted his wife's maiden name in order to inherit from her side of the family. He was perhaps the most active Catholic layman in the middle years of the nineteenth century, entering Parliament in 1832. He was active in a number of Catholic causes, especially education: on the Poor Schools Committee he was the only representative of the old Catholic families. He was succeeded as chairman by the convert Thomas Allies.

1839, and between 1848 and 1863 the Committee received almost a quarter of a million pounds.

The Congregation of Propaganda had been receiving lengthy, and far from favourable, reports written by the Rosminian priest Luigi Gentili. But it was Pius IX's exile in Gaeta, rather than these animadversions on the English bishops and their failings, that had delayed the re-establishment of the hierarchy. When in 1850 Wiseman learned that he was to be made a cardinal, he first took it to mean that he would have to return to Rome, where, in normal circumstances all cardinals who did not have charge of a diocese were required to reside. Much as he had loved Rome, he now did not want to leave England. He was moreover aware that the British government, and indeed the Queen herself, were uncomfortable with the idea of a cardinal based in London. He went off to Rome at the end of the summer of 1850. The brief *Universalis Ecclesiae*, re-establinsing the hierarchy and naming Wiseman as Archbishop of Westminster as well as administrator of Southwark (London south of the Thames being created a separate diocese from Westminster), were dated 29 September. On the following day he was named cardinal, with the title of Santa Pudentiana.[18]

He promptly sat down to compose a triumphal letter announcing the restoration of the hierarchy. 'Catholic England has been restored to its orbit in the ecclesiastical firmament, from which its light had long vanished, and begins now anew its course of regularly adjusted action round the centre of unity, the source of jurisdiction, of light and of vigour', he wrote. He meant, of course, the papacy. And in rather grandiloquent terms he delineated his own jurisdiction: 'Till such time as the Holy See shall think fit otherwise to provide, we govern and shall continue to govern, the counties of Middlesex, Hertford and Essex, as Ordinary thereof, and those of Surrey, Sussex, Kent,

---

18 There were twelve other cardinals created in the same consistory, all but one of them diocesan bishops.

Berkshire and Hampshire, with the islands annexed, as Administrator.'[19]

There was an enormous outcry, led by the Prime Minister Lord John Russell who introduced the Ecclesiastical Titles Act of 1851 forbidding Catholic bishops yet again to take titles already held by Church of England bishops. It was a pointless exercise, and was quietly repealed exactly twenty years later by Gladstone, who had spoken against it at the time of its passing. Wiseman wrote a pamphlet attempting to explain in more moderate language than had been employed in the Flaminian Gate letter just what he was about. In particular he stressed the Church's desire to assist the poor, mentioning especially those living in squalor – mainly Catholics, he claimed – around Westminster Abbey. He managed to suggest that the clergy attached to the Abbey had not bothered about them, leaving the Abbey's funds 'stagnant and not diffusive'. Odd though this approach may have been, it seemed to work. Protestant unrest abated. 'I now drive about everywhere with my cardinal's arms on the carriage . . . I meet with nothing but respect', he wrote at the end of December.[20] In fact Wiseman was worried that he did not have enough money to maintain the state to command the respect which he considered proper to a cardinal of the Roman Church.

The brief created thirteen sees in all, eight of them being occupied by the former vicars apostolic. In a sense they regarded their new status as something of a demotion. Hitherto they had been individually accountable to Propaganda, now they were subordinated to the Archbishop of Westminster. And it was not only the bishops who felt aggrieved. 'I should think that many may feel, as we do,' said the Duke of Norfolk,

---

19 'Am I Queen of England or am I not?', Queen Victoria is said to have asked, not unreasonably. Schiefen, *op. cit.*, p. 189. The letter was entitled, again grandiloquently, 'From without the Flaminian gate', the Flaminian gate being the start of the Via Flaminia, the road to be taken en route to Britain from Rome. The Flaminian gate is now the Porta del Popolo.

20 Schiefen, *op. cit.*, p. 191.

'that Ultramontane opinions are totally incompatible with allegiance to our Sovereign and with our Constitution.' His sentiments were echoed by Lord Beaumont: 'The late bold and clearly expressed edict of the court of Rome cannot be received or accepted by English Roman Catholics without a violation of their duties as citizens'.[21]

Now that the bishops composed a properly constituted hierarchy, they had to act as such. In the second two weeks of July they met at Oscott in their First Provincial Synod.[22] They were confronted with a petition by a good number of the clergy that in future bishops be elected by the priests of their dioceses. New norms for the conduct of priests were introduced: they were not to go to the theatre or to follow the hunt; they had to wear a clerical ('Roman') collar in public. The letter, composed by Wiseman, which the bishops addressed to the faithful at the end of the Synod, was concerned with the education of the poor. Their hope was that it should be as good in the voluntary (Catholic) schools as it was in the state ones.

---

21 V. A. McClelland, *Cardinal Manning* (Oxford: Oxford University Press, 1962), p. 5.

22 It was upon this occasion, on 13 July 1852, that Newman preached his famous sermon 'The Second Spring' on the text from the Song of Songs, 'Arise, make haste, my love, my dove, my beautiful one, and come. For the winter is now past, the rain is over and gone. The flowers have appeared in our land': 'O Mary, my hope, O Mother undefiled, fulfil to us the promise of this spring. A second temple rises on the ruins of the old. Canterbury has gone its way, and York is gone, and Durham is gone, and Winchester is gone. It was sore to part with them. We clung to the vision of past greatness, and would not believe it could come to nought; but the Church in England has died, and the Church lives again. Westminster and Nottingham, Beverley and Hexham, Northampton and Shrewsbury, if the world lasts, shall be names as musical to the ear, as stirring to the heart, as the glories we have lost; and Saints shall rise out of them if God so will, and Doctors once again shall give the law to Israel, and Preachers call to penance and to justice, as at the beginning.' But he also warned of problems to come: 'But still could we be surprised, my Fathers and my Brothers, if the winter even now should not yet be quite over? Have we any right to take it strange, if, in this English land, the spring-time of the Church should turn out to be an English spring, an uncertain, anxious time of hope and fear, of joy and suffering . . . of bright promise and budding hopes, yet withal, of keen blasts, and cold showers, and sudden storms?'

Wiseman had prepared for the Synod by producing a summary (*Epitomē*) of its likely decrees. The summary had included a proposal that Rome should be approached on the question of the validity of Anglican ordinations. The bishops were against this, on the grounds that to question the orders of the Established Church might annoy the government. In a way it was an odd decision, because they voted to insist on conditional baptism for converts to Catholicism. If they did not trust Anglican baptisms, then *a fortiori* they could not countenance Anglican ordinations. It was a matter of some importance because there was a renewed flow of converts after the Gorham judgement. The details of this will be recounted in the next chapter, because one of those to become a Catholic as a consequence was Henry Edward Manning, destined to succeed Wiseman and Westminster. The issue between the Revd George Cornelius Gorham and the Bishop of Exeter, Henry Phillpotts, was precisely the question of the efficacy of baptism.

Conversions were not of course all one way. After the announcement of the restoration of the hierarchy the Duke of Norfolk started patronizing the Church of England. Much more of a problem, however, was Giacinto Achilli. He was a former member of the Dominican Order who was dismissed for sexual misconduct several times over, and then proclaimed himself a Protestant and travelled to England under the auspices of the Evangelical Alliance to denounce the papacy in general and the Jesuits in particular. He produced a book listing his charges which Wiseman, not yet a cardinal, reviewed in *The Dublin Review*, detailing the ex-friar's licentious background. Relying on Wiseman's account, Newman referred to Achilli in a lecture, and was sued by Achilli. Newman eventually lost the case, and was fined £100 with costs, though a subscription was taken up among Catholics which raised much more than was needed – the surplus went to pay in part for the new university church in Dublin. The trial did little harm to Newman, whereas Achilli's reputation never recovered and he left the country.[23] Newman, however, became increasingly annoyed by the Cardinal, as Wiseman had now become, because of his failure to back up the allegations in *The Dublin Review* with the documentary evidence he claimed to have. Relations with Newman were further soured by his failure to urge the promotion of Newman to the office of bishop, and never properly explaining why, when Newman had been expecting it, it had not happened.

Newman of course was notoriously prickly where he thought his personal reputation was at stake. Nevertheless Wiseman was not the most diplomatic of men. He was not in favour of the London District being divided into two separate dioceses, but once it had happened he was relieved when the new Bishop of Southwark, appointed in 1851, was an old friend, Thomas Grant, who had been a student at the English College when Wiseman was rector, and in 1844 had himself been made rector with Wiseman's backing. Grant's specialization was church law, which was why the hierarchy wanted him back among them; but this made him a problematic individual to clash with, as Wiseman very promptly did. St George's was now Grant's cathedral, and Wiseman was left without one. He therefore tried to recover some of the money which the London District had invested in a building which was no longer in his diocese. Grant refused. After all, he pointed out, it was Wiseman who had incurred the debt. More difficult still was the issue of funds which had been bequeathed, or otherwise acquired, to run the bishoprics. These should have been divided out between the two dioceses in London. But it transpired that Wiseman's accounts for the expenditure from these funds were wholly inadequate. Other funds, Wiseman claimed, were simply too small to divide. When London had been split in two, Wiseman

---

23 In an entertaining account of Achilli in *The Oxford Dictionary of National Biography* Sheridan Gilley suggests in his defence that he may have embraced a form of antinomian Calvinism, according to which he could do no wrong.

had transferred a good many of the clergy who had opposed him to Southwark. Grant gave offence to the Cardinal when he appointed some of them to the Southwark chapter. He gave even more offence when he proposed that some of those antagonistic to Wiseman should be on the committee to be set up to adjudicate between Westminster and Southwark over the division of funds.

In the midst of all this controversy, Wiseman managed to produce a novel, *Fabiola: A Tale of the Catacombs*, which appeared in 1854. Written at least in part as a response to Charles Kingsley's anti-Catholic novel *Hypatia* which had appeared the year before, the book was an opportunity for the Cardinal to display some of the knowledge of Roman antiquities he had acquired in his early days as a student. It had certain resonance for the situation in which he found himself at the time of writing, for a chief theme is the solidarity of the early Christian community in Rome, and its sense of unity in the face of persecution. The book was published to favourable reviews.

Disunity among the bishops in England and Wales was abundantly evident during the mid-1850s, after the euphoria which had produced Newman's 'Second Spring' had dissipated. The major issue which set them one against another was control of the colleges for the training of clergy for the priesthood. All the colleges – Oscott, Ushaw, St Edmund's at Ware and Prior Park – were suffering financial problems in different degrees. The last had to be shut. In the case of Oscott part of the problem was Wiseman's financial incompetence when he had served as president. The Bishop of Birmingham, who had primary responsibility for Oscott, the Benedictine William Bernard Ullathorne, was constantly putting pressure on the Cardinal to sort the matter out, but to no avail. Ushaw in the north was on a relatively sound footing, but then the Bishop of Liverpool, George Brown, decided to withdraw his students and establish a seminary of his own. There was also a problem affecting them all, that bishops who sent their students to seminaries outside their dioceses wanted final say about the future careers of their priests, though technically the colleges themselves had first call on their brighter students who might become members of staff.

Wiseman had his own troubles over St Edmund's, which rather differed from the squabbles about the other colleges. This story, however, belongs rather to the next chapter and, to some extent that on Herbert Vaughan, and will be recounted there (cf. pp. 41f and 63ff). But part of his problem was George Errington, since early 1855 a Bishop and co-adjutor to the Cardinal, appointed after election by the Westminster chapter. He was at odds with Wiseman over the seminary, but that was only part of the problem. He had conducted a visitation of the diocese which had deeply upset the clergy. He also objected to Vaughan being appointed as vice-president of St Edmund's. He was, it is true, far too young for the post (only 23 at the time) and a priest for only a year. The Westminster chapter was equally unhappy, particularly so when in 1857 its provost resigned to become a Jesuit, Wiseman appointed Henry Edward Manning, passing over the obvious candidate John Maguire. The reason was not far to seek. Maguire was, according to the egregious Mr George Talbot, 'the greatest Gallican in London'.[24] He passed a similar judgement on Bishop Grant, accusing him of a 'lack of Roman spirit' because of his disputes with Wiseman.

Among those disputes was the matter of the colleges. This

---

24 Schiefen, *op. cit.*, p. 255. Talbot, born in 1816, had briefly been an Anglican priest before being received as a Catholic by Wiseman in 1843 at Oscott, and ordained by him there three years later. He served on the staff of St George's, Southwark, before being sent to Rome by Wiseman in 1850. This was while Wiseman was still a Vicar Apostolic, and it seems he wanted his own eyes and ears at the Vatican, quite apart from those of the agent of the Vicars Apostolic. Talbot at first protested against his posting but soon came to revel in the opportunities that Rome afforded him. He was appointed to a canonry of St Peter's, and a papal chamberlain. He became a confidant of Pius IX. He established the forerunner of the Beda College for training converts and older men who wished to become priests. In 1869 he was sent to an asylum for the insane just outside Paris, where he died in 1886.

was the chief topic for discussion at the 1859 Third Provincial Synod at Oscott, held, like the two before it, in mid-July. Errington was there, speaking against the man whom he served as co-adjutor – though, not being a diocesan bishop, he did not have a vote. There were a number of other 'Gallican' opponents of the Cardinal who felt snubbed when he went to his room expecting to receiving the synod members and no one turned up. The outcome of the discussions about the colleges was that the ordinary of the diocese in which each was situated should have charge of the spiritual formation of the ordinands. The financial affairs, however, were to be regulated by a board of all the bishops who had students in the institution, the board to meet annually, and the ordinary of the place was to have a casting vote. Errington interjected that where there were only two bishops, disputes should be referred to Rome – an obvious reference to St Edmund's. Wiseman formulated the decrees – and then added another one, that bishops should move towards founding seminaries on the model required by the Council of Trent.[25]

It was Wiseman's intention to go off to Rome to present the decrees immediately after the Synod, but his health would not permit it. He went instead in December, closely followed by Errington whom the Cardinal was hoping to dismiss as his co-adjutor. Apart from the decrees, on Wiseman's agenda were disputes with Grant and Ullathorne. He was told he had to pay half the debt on St George's, which he failed to do. Before the Synod opened, the Cardinal had produced a document which had proposed that the bishops move towards the Tridentine model of seminaries. This had been rejected by the bishops in favour of the form of governance of the colleges outlined above. Wiseman was therefore delighted when the Congregation of

---

25 Trent, which had met during the sixteenth century, determined that diocesan bishops should establish seminaries. These differed from the English 'colleges' in that the latter commonly served as schools for laymen as well as training colleges for priests.

Propaganda expressed a preference for Wiseman's version rather than that of the Synod, and instructed that more information be gathered before a final decision was made. Wiseman regarded this as an endorsement of himself and a rebuff for his fellow English bishops. However, when Propaganda came to a decision, they upheld the bishops' model rather than Wiseman's. It was some small consolation that the Congregation supported him in his dispute with the chapter.

As his novel *Fabiola* demonstrates, he had never lost interest in Rome or its antiquities. In 1858 he published *Recollections of the Four Last Popes* and went on a lecture tour of Ireland, with great success. In 1861 he founded in London the Academia of the Catholic Religion, modelled on the Roman Academia of which he had been a member. He himself gave the Academia its first lecture on the Church and contemporary culture, rather mocking Darwin's theories about the origins of the human race, then a matter of much public debate. In August 1869 he gave a lecture, in heavily accented French, at a congress held at Malines in Belgium, about Catholicism in Britain. He listed the communities' achievements, in many of which he had been the prime mover, such as separate schools for Catholic children, Catholic chaplains in prisons and in the armed forces, and Catholic reformatories. He put success down to the pressure which Catholics were able to exert on members of parliament, a good number of whom, especially those elected in Ireland, were themselves Catholic.

It was all the more strange, therefore, that he should have taken such exception to his old friend Charles de Montalembert's two lectures, one on freedom of conscience and the other on 'A Free Church in a Free State' during which he urged the virtues of democracy. Montalembert later reported that Wiseman was one of his main opponents, and it was rumoured, though the Cardinal denied it, that he had reported him to Rome.

The *Horae Syriacae* had marked him out as a rising star in the European academic world. He had become friendly not only with Montalembert but also with the distinguished historian Johann Joseph Ignaz von Döllinger. But the paths of Wiseman and these early friends had diverged. The liberal-minded English Catholics Sir John (later Lord) Acton and Richard Simpson had in 1848 founded as an alternative to *The Dublin Review* a weekly (within the year it became a monthly) called *The Rambler*, intended 'to unite an intelligent and hearty acceptance of Catholic dogma with free enquiry and discussion on questions which the Church left open to debate and while avoiding, as far as possible, the domain of technical theology, to provide a medium for the expression of independent opinion on subjects of the day, whether interesting to the general public or especially affecting Catholics', as they declared in 1862 in the final issue. It had – briefly – been edited by Newman, and it was opposed to the extreme Romanism of people such as Wiseman and W. G. Ward, of whom more in the next chapter. It was replaced in 1862 by *The Home and Foreign Review*, still under the aegis of Acton and Simpson, and espousing the same liberal principles. Wiseman felt obliged to write to his clergy warning them against it, though intimating that he was being pressured into doing so by Rome. In 1863, at a congress in Munich, Döllinger called upon the Church to embrace modern scholarship and update the arid scholasticism then the norm in the theology schools. Pope Pius IX wrote to the Archbishop of Munich, in whose diocese the historian, a priest, taught, condemning his lecture. In the light of the letter, Acton and Simpson believed they could not continue to propagate their liberal views, and closed their journal.

Liberalism had never been Wiseman's outlook, religiously or politically. He had supported the Whigs when Lord Palmerston was prepared to back Pope Pius and to safeguard church property in Rome, but turned against them when they supported the unification of Italy. In the election of 1859 Wiseman advised his co-religionists to vote Tory. 'Catholicism: A Conservative Principle' was the title of an article which W. G. Ward wrote for *The Dublin Review* in December 1850. Fifteen years later, Ward was prepared to vote in his Isle of Wight constituency for someone who was explicitly 'no popery' because the alternative candidate was a liberal Catholic.

That was 1865, the year in which Cardinal Wiseman died. He had grown quite portly,[26] he was often depressed and gave in to bouts of self-pity. In his later years he was frequently ill, and there was much speculation as to his successor – though it was clear it was almost bound to be his close friend Henry Edward Manning. He died in his home at York Place, Portman Square in London on 15 February 1865. In just under fifteen years as Cardinal Archbishop he had massively expanded the number of churches and schools. He had encouraged religious orders to move to London, especially those who worked with the poor. The poor of the Catholic Church, greatly increased by the influx of the Irish during his term of office, had a great deal for which to thank him, not least for the hospital for children at Great Ormond Street staffed by Sisters of Mercy. He left squabbles over money to be settled by his successor, but he also left the campaign which he had started to attract state funding for the voluntary schools. This was to become a major issue in the episcopates of his successors in the See of Westminster.

---

26 Calling on someone unexpectedly, the surprised host addressed him as 'Your Immense'.

2

Henry Edward Manning

If Nicholas Wiseman had been, at least on the face of it, an unlikely choice as the first Cardinal Archbishop of Westminster, the same could not be said of Henry Edward Manning. Manning was born to high office – though not to high office in the Roman Catholic Church. His father William had been a West Indies sugar merchant and Member of Parliament in the Tory interest who ended his days as governor of the Bank of England, while his mother Mary's brother was elected Lord Mayor of London when Henry was three years old. Henry had a former prime minister for a godfather, and Christopher Wordsworth, the poet William's youngest brother who eventually became Master of Trinity College Cambridge, was a close friend of his childhood.

That childhood was passed at Coombe Bank, near Sevenoaks in Kent, though he had been born on the other side of London at Copped Hall, Totteridge, on 15 July 1808. After a brief period of schooling in Streatham, he returned to Totteridge for his education before being sent to Harrow at the age of fourteen. There he distinguished himself neither by his scholarship nor his piety, but for two years played cricket as a member of the school's First Eleven. He had studied so little that he needed a year's private coaching before he was able to go up to Balliol College, Oxford in 1827. William Ewart Gladstone, the future Prime Minister four times over, was a contemporary, and became a friend. As an undergraduate, Manning applied himself to the study of Classics, and graduated at the end of 1830 with a first-class degree.

Bolstered by his success in the Oxford Union debating chamber, Manning considered a career in politics, but politicians were not paid so this became impossible when his father's business collapsed leaving him bankrupt. Manning found a job in the Colonial Office, but at about the same time seems to have found religion of an evangelical sort, and settled upon a future as a cleric in the Church of England. He therefore went back to Oxford as a fellow of Merton, and was ordained deacon in December 1832. He needed a living, and found a curacy in Lavington, Sussex, where the rector was the Reverend John Sargent.

To say that he found the benefice is not quite accurate. Manning was friendly with his slightly younger Oxford contemporary Henry Wilberforce, the youngest son of the great anti-slavery campaigner William Wilberforce. As a child, Henry had been sent to be schooled by John Sargent, and in January 1833 it was a curacy with Sargent which was allotted to Manning – on loan, as it were, until Wilberforce was ready to take it up. But this did not happen. Instead, Sargent died in May, and Manning and Sargent's daughter Caroline were married in November. Caroline's grandmother presented the living to Manning who had been ordained shortly after Sargent's death. The two Wilberforces, Henry and his elder brother Samuel who was afterwards to become successively Bishop of Oxford and of Winchester, also married daughters of John Sargent, thereby becoming Manning's brothers-in-law.

And then, after less than four years of marriage, Caroline died. Manning was stricken with grief. There were no children of the marriage, and all Manning had was a bundle of her letters to him, and a prayer book which had been hers. The letters were lost when a bag was stolen as, in 1851, Manning journeyed to Rome. The prayer book he kept by his bedside. One of his last acts was to give it to his successor, Herbert Vaughan, telling him that he had prayed using it every day of his life. The book disappeared. It has been presumed that Vaughan laid the volume in Manning's coffin.

While at Oxford, Manning had come to know Newman, but they were not close friends: Henry Wilberforce was, and remained, much closer to Newman. He was not unsympathetic to the growing High Church convictions of those who eventually became known as the Tractarians – that was his own family's tradition – but he also began to read the Anglican divines and especially those in the evangelical tradition. The latter influenced his rather austere spirituality,[1] but not his theology. He once wrote to Gladstone that the Church of England was Catholic 'objectively'; that is to say, in its dogma and ecclesiology, but not 'subjectively', in its devotional and spiritual practices.[2] When he arrived as a curate at Lavington he had no ecclesiology, no theory of the Church, but this began to develop as he read the Fathers of the Church. He came to think of the bishop as the Church's centre of unity and the source of authority, but he still rejected the notion of infallibility: 'Investing the pope with infallibility is the *Italianate* doctrine, the *Gallican* and *British* Romanists placing it in the Church assembled in Council' he said in a sermon preached in Chichester Cathedral in 1838 and published as *The Rule of Faith*.[3] The dogma of papal infallibility was still to be defined, and Manning (and Newman likewise) at this point invested it with a good deal greater scope than did the First Vatican Council.

Manning was clearly a good deal more sympathetic at this stage to what he took to be the 'Gallican' or British Catholic understanding, that infallibility lay in a General Council. This was a common view. In his *Controversial Catechism: or, Protestantism Refuted, and Catholicism Established* the Revd Stephen Keenan wrote: '*Q. Must not Catholics believe the Pope in himself to be infallible?* A. This is a Protestant invention; it is no article of

---

1 'Manning's legendary asceticism seems to have extended to the avoidance of a clutter even of devotional objects'. Heinmann, *op. cit.*, p. 25.

2 James Pereiro, *Cardinal Manning: An Intellectual Biography* (Oxford: Clarendon Press, 1998), pp. 50–1.

3 *Ibid.*, p. 29.

the Catholic faith; no decision of his can oblige, under pain of heresy, unless it be received and enforced by the teaching body; that is, by the bishops of the Church.'[4] At this point he was still convinced of the theory, which Newman himself was beginning to doubt, that the Church of England was part of the Catholic Church, the *via media* between Catholicism and Protestantism; it was a 'branch' of the Church Catholic, though because of its 'schismatic temper' Rome could not see it. By now he was now very much a Tractarian. With a friend, Charles Marriott, he produced one of the Tracts, no. 78, a string of quotations from the Fathers of the Church on the Catholic tradition.

Meanwhile his duties had increased. He had become a rural dean, and was instrumental in establishing in the Chichester Diocese a new theological college with Charles Marriott as its principal.[5] Manning's health suffered. He was advised by his bishop to take a holiday and decided to spend Christmas in Rome with his old friend William Gladstone. As rural dean, in practice he had also been Archdeacon of Chichester because the incumbent of that office was senile. In December 1840 this anomaly was rectified: Manning himself became Archdeacon and with the position a much more significant figure in the Church of England. What he had to say about the poor, about their exploitation by employers, and about the obligation to educate the poor was read nationwide.

At this time he was firmly an Anglican. Though he wrote to Newman to sympathize with his resignation as vicar of St Mary's, Oxford, he was not in sympathy with the tenor of *Tract 90* and in effect said so in a sermon he preached in Newman's former church in November 1843. There was, however, no rift

---

4 Quoted from the third edition, published in Edinburgh, London and Manchester in 1854.
5 This was the first residential college for training Church of England clergy. Marriott was forced by ill health to retire after only two years, and return to Oxford.

at this point between the two. After Newman became a Catholic in October 1845, Manning set about, at Gladstone's instigation, the task of responding to Newman's *Essay on the Development of Christian Doctrine* which had appeared that same year. In *Tract 90* Newman had argued that the Church of England's foundational document, Thirty-Nine Articles, was compatible with the Catholic faith. Now he was arguing that the Roman Catholic Church had not, despite appearances, departed from the faith of the early Church as depicted by the Fathers of the Church, but had simply grown into a deeper understanding of the primitive faith.

Early in 1847 he fell ill and decided to spend much of his convalescence abroad, including another visit to Rome where in May 1848 he had an audience with Pope Pius IX, not long elected. In between times Renn Dickson Hampden had been appointed Bishop of Hereford. In 1834 Hampden had been appointed Professor of Moral Philosophy at Oxford, a position which Newman coveted, and believed he might gain. Then two years later he was made Regius Professor of Divinity despite a pamphlet, *Elucidations of Dr Hampden's Theological Statements*, in which Newman exposed the professor's very liberal theological convictions. When Hampden was appointed to Hereford, the Tractarians returned to the attack, but to no avail. The problem was not simply – to Manning's mind – that Hampden did not share the Tractarians' Catholic principles; more than that, it was the fact that the Prime Minister, Lord John Russell, was able to insist upon the appointment despite the somewhat violent campaign against him by members of the High Church party.

It was a similar issue with the Gorham judgement of 1850. The Revd G. C. Gorham was presented to a living by the Lord Chancellor. The benefice lay within the Diocese of Exeter, and it fell to the bishop of Exeter to instal him on the grounds that Gorham, who adhered to Calvinist theology, did not believe in a central doctrine of the Church of England – namely baptismal regeneration. That was in 1847. A Church of England tribunal upheld the bishop's decision, but then Gorham appealed to the newly established judicial committee of the Privy Council which eventually, in 1850, found in his favour. Manning expressed his objections to this procedure in *The Appellate Jurisdiction of the Crown in Matters Spiritual.* The question for him, as for others among the Tractarians, was not so much the rights and wrongs of the case but that the Crown, in the guise of the Privy Council, could make decisions about the doctrine of the Church. The issue was the authority of the State in matters spiritual and doctrinal within the Church of England.

Of course, someone had to decide. John Keble, whose 1833 sermon 'National Apostasy' attacking the proposal to suppress ten Church of Ireland bishoprics is commonly taken to be the start of the Oxford Movement, thought that the attraction of Catholicism was its apparent offer of certainty in faith. He thought certainty was not possible: faith was a decision based on probabilities. Manning found this unacceptable. Truth has been revealed, and is certain, he believed. Faith is not an objective decision but a subjective one, the act of faith coming from God, not from the believer. The believer needs to know, however, that the Church's teaching is free from error. He was perfectly ready to accept the teaching that the Church is infallible long before he became a Catholic.

What finally decided him to be received into the Catholic Church was – perhaps oddly – the restoration of the hierarchy in 1850. In all the controversy which surrounded this act of 'papal aggression' he was called upon as Archdeacon to preach against the event at a meeting of clergy on 22 November 1850. He did so, but expressed his disapproval that this protest meeting was taking place at all, and almost immediately afterwards resigned his post. Alongside his friend James Hope he became a Catholic at the Jesuits' Farm Street church in London on 6 April 1851. He was ordained priest a little over two months later, on 25 June.

He then, with George Talbot as a travelling companion,

went off to Rome. From the autumn of 1851 to the summer of 1854 he was in Rome studying under mainly Jesuit professors at the Academia Ecclesiastica. He came home from time to time, and in 1852 lectured in Southwark cathedral on *The Grounds of Faith*, as the subsequent publication was named. In Rome he became a regular confidant of Pope Pius IX, who wanted him to remain at court as a papal chamberlain – as George Talbot did. Manning, however, had decided that his future lay in England. His ideal, he told Robert Wilberforce, was to live in a small community of priests, with a library, a chapel and a refectory. At one time Wiseman had wished for something similar, though he saw his community as a group of missionary clergy. Though Manning's proposal was rather different, the Cardinal gave it his backing, and the Oblates of St Charles came into being, living at the parish of St Mary of the Angels in Bayswater, then one of the poorer areas of London.

He remained there as superior of the community until he was appointed Archbishop of Westminster. He completed his parish church, and built three more churches. He established eight schools plus a choir school, opened four convents, and set up a reformatory for Catholic boys. He was, moreover, appointed provost of the Westminster chapter, a sudden promotion for a recent convert which many of the Westminster clergy resented. They resented, too, his close relationship with Wiseman and the involvement of the Oblates of St Charles in running the seminary, St Edmund's, at Ware in Hertfordshire; but as Herbert Vaughan was particularly associated with this last, an account of it will be held over until the next chapter. The resentment was aimed not so much at Manning himself as at Cardinal Wiseman, and this had an impact upon the choice of Wiseman's successor.

Upon Wiseman's death the most favoured choice of the Westminster chapter was George Errington, whom Pius IX had removed as Wiseman's co-adjutor with right of succession to the see, and who had since been living in retirement. The other choices were Bishops Thomas Grant of Southwark and

William Clifford of Clifton.[6] They, however, wrote to Rome asking not to be considered – requests which were said to have annoyed Pius IX. Both of them, and especially Clifford, despite their Roman education, were thought to be representative of the recusant tradition in English Catholicism, hostile to the 'Romanization' that had been embarked upon under Wiseman.

The choice of Manning, then, was made by Pope Pius personally; though surprisingly in the light of his personal friendship with the Pope, he was not, unlike Wiseman, elevated to the cardinalate immediately: he was made cardinal priest of St Andrew and St Gregory on the Coelian Hill on 29 March 1875, after he had been Archbishop for almost a decade. He was consecrated Bishop at the church of St Mary Moorfields, which was serving as the cathedral, on 8 June 1865. Almost immediately afterwards a Catholic layman, Sir Charles Clifford, offered to organize an appeal to build a cathedral for the diocese, and a meeting was held. Manning seemed lukewarm. 'Could I leave 20,000 children without education, and drain my friends and my flock to pile up stones and bricks', he is reported to have said. Nonetheless he went ahead, and with £16,500 he bought a site in Carlisle Place in Westminster in 1867, and over the years added to the acreage he had originally acquired. He even instructed an architect to plan a cathedral 'proportionate to the chief diocese of the Catholic Church in England, and to the chief city of the British Empire'.[7]

But the 20,000 children nonetheless remained his chief concern. He dedicated his first three pastoral letters – the first

---

6 Clifford was only 33 when made Bishop, a personal choice of Pius IX. He had the unusual distinction of having a Cardinal as his grandfather: his mother was the daughter of Thomas Weld who, after the death of his wife, became a priest and then a Cardinal, spending the rest of his life in Rome.

7 Peter Doyle, *Westminster Cathedral, 1895–1995* (London: Geoffrey Chapman, 1995), pp. 14–15.

produced within a couple of weeks of his consecration – to the plight of the poor, and specifically of the poor children, in his diocese. He was concerned not simply with those who needed education, but those who were in trouble with the law and those who were in workhouses. There was a special issue about this last group. Even children of Catholic parents were in practice being brought up as Protestants. Manning wanted to set up alternative provision for them, but even when he did so he found that those in charge of workhouses were reluctant to hand over their Catholic charges. However, the Archbishop recognized that Catholic children in workhouses were receiving some form of an education, and was not quite so concerned about them as were other bishops. He concentrated on schools.

In June 1866 he called a meeting in St James's Hall to establish the Westminster Diocese Education Fund. The theme of the address was education in general, but he gave greater prominence to the problem of Catholic children in workhouses:

> In the workhouses of London there are one thousand Catholic children educated exclusively and explicitly as Protestants. They attend schools which are Protestant in their teachers, and Protestant in doctrine, and Protestant in their attendance at worship. I will admit that that is not the letter of the statute law; but it is the practical maladministration of the law.[8]

He claimed that the diocese needed at least 35 schools as well as two reformatories and two industrial schools. These last had been the subject of legislation from the late 1850s. They were institutions to which girls and boys – but in practice especially boys – were sent who were in trouble with the law where their

---

8 John Bennett, 'The Care of the Poor' in G. A. Beck (ed.), *The English Catholics 1850–1950* (London: Burns and Oates, 1950), p. 567.

offence was minor (in this they differed from reformatories) or were simply declared by their parents to be beyond their control. The 1866 Reformatory and Industrial Schools Act allowed for the establishment of Catholic institutions which were to be aided by payment from the rates.

A year after the meeting to establish the Education Fund, twenty schools had already been opened. He had also persuaded the monks of Mount St Bernard's Abbey in Charnwood Forest, Leicestershire, founded by Ambrose Phillipps de Lisle, to open an industrial school for 100 boys. With this sudden educational expansion, Manning was in need of men and women to staff the various institutions. He turned to the religious orders, many members of which in the 1880s were fleeing France because of anticlerical legislation. With their help he opened houses for destitute children, though he was also an active supporter of the emigration of children to a new life in Canada: the first group left Liverpool in August 1870.

There remained problems with the workhouses. Also the Poor Law Amendment Act had laid down that children who were not born into the Church of England might be moved to institutions of their own faith where they existed and if their godparents requested it, though very few were actually transferred. This may have been bureaucracy, but it was also anti-Catholic prejudice. In 1887 Dr Thomas Barnardo admitted that a fifth of all children who entered his care were Catholics. Manning's relationship with the evangelical Dr Barnardo, who was strongly anti-Catholic, was problematic, though it improved as time went on and Barnardo became more accommodating, agreeing to refer to the Cardinal any Catholic children who came to his attention. But he was only prepared to allow the Cardinal a fortnight to sort out a residence for such children, and refused to hand over those who were already in his charge except on the order of the courts.[9] Barnardo's establishment of 'ragged schools' and of homes for orphans, even his encourage-

9 *Ibid.*, p. 573.

ment of emigration, was roughly contemporaneous with the work of Manning for Catholic children.

The national response to the dearth of schooling was the Education Act of 1870 prepared by William Edward Forster, and known thereafter by his name. In the wake of the extension of the franchise in 1867 and in the famous phrase of Robert Lowe, then Chancellor of the Exchequer, parliament perceived a need to 'educate our masters'.[10] Much of the debate about the bill concerned religious education. Forster had wanted there to be non-denominational religious instruction given, but at first Gladstone, as Prime Minister, had rejected this and only conceded when it was suggested that voluntary (i.e., in effect religious schools, mainly Church of England but including Roman Catholic and potentially other religions) should be aided by the rates. Nonconformists opposed this measure on the grounds that Catholic and Anglican schools would then be publicly funded. The compromise, proposed by Lowe, was that voluntary schools should be directly funded by the Treasury, the 'board schools', as they were known, by local rates, administered by local boards.[11]

Manning was unhappy with the Act. He was concerned that the local boards would be prejudiced against Catholics and would not give them a fair share of the rates collected for education. V. A. McClelland suggests that it was the backlash to the First Vatican Council with its enhancement of the standing of

---

10 It seems, however, that literacy rates, at least in England, were already as good as, if not better than, most European states with the exception of Prussia. Economic pressures, the need for a more numerate as well as more literate workforce in a highly industrailized society were at least as important as the political ones in bringing about the 1870 Act.

11 To which women might be elected – the first time such a provision entered English law. Ballots for the board members were to be secret, also a first, and Forster was then tasked to achieve secrecy in subsequent parliamentary elections.

the papacy that precluded Catholics from enjoying a more equitable share of government money for schools. As it was, Catholics paid twice. Government grants did not cover the total cost of primary education, and fees had still to be charged with the result that Catholics paid twice: once in fees and once in the rates. Board schools were in any case better funded. One way to counteract the perceived hostility of the local boards to denominational education was to organize Catholics to vote for sympathetic members in the secret ballots. This had some success, until those who opposed the funding of voluntary schools noticed what was going on and mounted a counter campaign in the elections.

Although he encouraged men's and women's religious orders to establish themselves in the Westminster Diocese, there was one with which relations were difficult. He had been received into the Catholic Church by a member of the Society of Jesus, and in Rome he had imbibed from Jesuit lecturers the high doctrine of the papacy, and the infallibility of the papacy, of which he later became so effective a protagonist. When he returned to England from Rome for several years he even occupied a confessional in the Jesuits' Farm Street church in central London, an arrangement which came to an end in rather mysterious circumstances. Yet between himself and the Society in England there developed considerable tension.

There are many possible explanations. He disliked the way Farm Street seemed to attract the wealthy. Certainly the Jesuits were aligned with the old Catholic families who were, as has been seen, supporters of Bishop Clifford as successor to Wiseman. Manning noted that although some individual Jesuits had written to congratulate him on his appointment to Westminster, the Farm Street community, where the Jesuit Provincial Superior had his residence, had been silent. He was also irritated by the rather obvious attachment of the recusant families to the religious orders in general, and especially to the Society, regarding the 'secular clergy' (a term he also resented, preferring 'diocesan clergy') as somehow second class. Furthermore he was afraid that, were the Jesuits to open a school in his diocese, they would attract to themselves the best candidates for the priesthood. It is possibly for that reason that he point-blank refused permission to the Jesuits to open a school in his diocese, even though they had bought land for the purpose, and despite the fact that their Provincial undertook to open their school at some distance from St Charles's College, started in Notting Hill by Manning's nephew. His antagonism stretched to the Religious of the Sacred Heart, an order of nuns whom he thought too close to the Society. They, too, were forbidden to open a school.

Manning saw the relationship between himself and the Society as open war. In March 1875 he said as much to Herbert Vaughan:

> I have long felt that the English province is altogether abnormal, dangerous to themselves, mischievous to the Church in England. I have seemed to see it and feel it with more than natural intellect and natural discernment. I am now convinced that I am right, and I propose to go through the whole work or warfare which has now been begun – for their sakes as much as for ours.[12]

The particular occasion for this letter was the Jesuits' attempt to establish a school in Vaughan's Diocese of Salford, and will be discussed in greater detail in the next chapter, but there were issues which affected Manning's own projects and none more so than his desire to establish in Wright's Lane, Kensington, a Catholic university college.

Up to 1854 it had been impossible for Catholics to take a degree at either Oxford or Cambridge. To do so would require subscribing to the Thirty-Nine Articles of the Church of England – at Oxford before a student even started, at Cambridge

---

12 Robert Gray, *Cardinal Manning: A Biography* (London: Weidenfeld and Nicolson, 1985), p. 262.

before graduating. In 1854 the Oxford University Act permitted non-Anglicans to proceed to a degree. Could Catholics take advantage of this partial relaxation? This was the question which faced Wiseman. Advised by Manning, he decided against. There were several reasons, but the fundamental one Manning expressed in an article for *The Dublin Review* in July 1863:

> What we most fear is that Catholics may cast themselves willingly, or be drawn unconsciously, into the stream which is evidently carrying English society every year more and more decidedly and perceptibly towards worldliness and Rationalism.[13]

While this was no doubt his main motive, Manning also thought the two ancient universities too socially exclusive and likely to attract students away from the Catholic university he was hoping would be established.

They would also be attracted by the presence of Newman. Newman understood the hesitations of the hierarchy, but thought that the problem could be solved by establishing a Catholic college within the university. He purchased five acres in Oxford on what was then the edge of the university district and proposed to open an Oratorian house. It was clear to Manning and the other bishops that Newman's real intention was to start a Catholic college. At their request, Propaganda Fide said that while Newman might open a parish (not a college) in the city, he himself had to stay in Birmingham. At that Newman lost interest.

After a meeting in December 1864 the hierarchy petitioned Rome for a ruling on the attendance of Catholics at Oxford

---

13 Walter Drumm, *The Old Palace* (Dublin: Veritas, 1991), p. 25. This history of the Oxford Catholic Chaplaincy (the Old Palace of the title) has a full account of the arrival of Catholics at the Universities of Oxford and Cambridge.

and Cambridge. Propaganda took its time, replying only in 1867. The answer was negative. There would be a considerable danger, the Congregation declared, to 'purity of morals as well as to faith' in attending a non-Catholic university. By now Manning was Archbishop, and was free to take steps to set up his Catholic university. The idea was approved by the bishops in 1873, who provided £25,000, and it opened its doors – to very few students – in 1875. Newman was invited to become involved, but refused. The Jesuits were not invited. In any case, they already provided at Stonyhurst university-level education.

Manning recruited some distinguished teachers, including St George Jackson Mivart, a friend of Newman's, a Fellow of the Royal Society, and a follower of Darwin. As Rector he chose Mgr Thomas Capel, who turned out to be a disaster. He was chosen at least in part because he was already running a public school in Kensington and was thought to have contact among upper-class Catholics whose support was essential if the university were to prosper. His influence on the Catholic gentry was real enough, but they were deterred from sending their sons to the new university by the absence of Jesuits. Capel turned out to be more interested in promoting his own college than the university, kept totally inadequate accounts, and eventually had to be asked to go. He threatened to sue Manning, and had to be bought off for the sum of £3,000. He ended his days in the United States, living very comfortably but suspended from priestly office.

The failed university (in 1878 it was incorporated into St Charles's College) was intended for the wealthy middle and upper classes, but almost all of Manning's efforts in education were aimed at the poorest in society. He was not only concerned, however, to use education as a means to raise people out of poverty, he attempted to tackle some of the causes of poverty. One of those undoubtedly was drunkenness. In Ireland, from which very many of Manning's flock had come, the temperance movement owed a great deal to a Capuchin friar, Theobald Matthew, but in England it was associated chiefly with evangelical Protestants, which hindered its spread among Catholics. In 1866 he told a group of Catholic teetotallers that his doctor had told him to drink half a glass of wine a day. 'Then change your doctor', someone shouted from the back of the hall.[14] He only began to make an impact on drunkenness when he attached an indulgence to abstaining from alcohol for the feast of St Patrick. In 1867 he was invited to attend the Annual General Meeting of the largely Nonconformist United Kingdom Alliance. Not that he was wholly enamoured of its tactics. He preferred a step-by-step approach to licensing laws, believing that more likely to succeed than the radical demands of the Alliance – as was proved when the 1871 Licensing Bill failed in Parliament. He himself took the pledge in 1872, and at the same time founded for Catholics the League of the Cross. Members of the League wore medals of office and carried banners. They often provided a guard of honour for the Cardinal as he went on his visitations. In return he kept a close watch on the League's development, in the early years meeting its top officials once a week. He remained true to his pledge all his life, even on his deathbed refusing a medicinal brandy. This was one of the issues upon which he failed to carry his brother bishops. One even criticized him (under a pseudonym) in *The Tablet*,[15] while Herbert Vaughan greatly annoyed him by attending a Licensed Victuallers' dinner in Manchester. This led to a fierce argument between them during Vaughan's next visit, at the end of which Manning stormed out and deleted Vaughan's name as executor of his will.

Of perhaps even more practical assistance to the working class was Manning's support for the trade union movement, a support which extended to the American Knights of Labour when there was a move to forbid Catholics from being mem-

---

14 Gray, *op. cit.*, p. 219.
15 The Jesuit journal *The Month* opined in February 1879, 'The alcohol drinking nations taken comprehensively, are superior in mind and body to the abstaining nations.'

bers. But he is best remembered for his intervention in the London dock strike in 1889. The strike, which began in West India Dock but which spread throughout the whole of the port of London, involving, it was claimed, 130,000 men at its height, was about the workers' conditions of employment as much as about their wages, but it was the demand for 6d an hour (just a penny more than they were already being paid) which caught the popular imagination: the 'Dockers' tanner'. Their demands were rejected by the employers, and the stoppage lasted a month, from 14 August to 16 September. It brought great hardship on the dockers and their families, relieved only early in September by a large donation from dockers in Australia.

Many of the strikers were Catholics, and Manning was from the start deeply concerned for their welfare. On 6 September he intervened to prevent the employers bringing in dockers from Holland to break the strike. Shortly afterwards a conciliation committee was set up at the Mansion House under the chairmanship of the Lord Mayor. The employers agreed to the increase in pay, but not the request for 8d per hour overtime pay, and demanded that the dockers agreed at once. They refused, at which Frederick Temple, the Bishop of London (and later Archbishop of Canterbury), who had reluctantly returned from his holiday to sit on the committee, withdrew from the proceedings. Manning, also a member, went to see the dockers' leader, Ben Tillett,[16] and persuaded him to negotiate. A deal was finally struck after a meeting with union leaders in Kirby Street Catholic School – it falling to Manning to win over the employers, which he did.

As a consequence of his intervention in the dock strike, Manning won great respect among the working classes of London, and was represented on at least one trade union

---

16 Tillett later recounted that he found Manning sitting in front of the fire when he returned to his lodgings, reading the latest Sherlock Holmes episode in *The Strand* magazine.

banner. In an article written for *The Nineteenth Century*, his friend and successor Herbert Vaughan put his devotion to the cause of the dockers down to senile decay.[17] More sympathetic commentators have seen him rather in the mould of the continental social reformers behind the Union of Fribourg and Pope Leo XIII's famous encyclical of 1891, *Rerum Novarum*, commonly and somewhat misleadingly described as the 'Workers' Charter'. But although Manning was in correspondence with some of them, they were as a group socially, and romantically, conservative.[18] That Manning certainly was not. In 1850 W. G. Ward had written an article for *The Dublin Review* entitled 'Catholicism: A Conservative Principle' in which, like the continental reformers, he presented the Church as a bastion of social harmony. After all, Liberalism was associated in the minds of Catholics with the anti-clerical Italian Revolution which was threatening (and of course eventually overthrew) the Papal states.

Manning, however, had been a friend of the Liberal leader William Gladstone. His commitment to the cause of the poor in society was possibly greater than that of Gladstone. In a lecture delivered at the Leeds Mechanics' Institute in 1874 he said, 'I claim for Labour, and the skill which is always acquired by Labour, the rights of Capital. It is Capital in its truest sense.'[19] His political sympathies depended not so much on the ideology of one party or the other, but on specific issues. Ireland ranked high among them, but on that Manning's sympathies were divided. He supported Gladstone when he proposed to disestab-

---

17 'During the last short period of the Cardinal's long life the process of senile decay set in'. Robert O'Neil, *Cardinal Herbert Vaughan* (London: Burns and Oates, 1995), p. 331.

18 As Emiel Lamberts has made clear in his remarkable article 'L'Internationale noire; Une organisation secrète au service du Saint-Siège' in Emiel Lamberts (ed.), *The Black International* (Louvain: Leuven University Press, 2002), pp. 15–101.

19 McClelland, *op. cit.*, p. 23. The lecture was later printed as *The Dignity and Rights of Labour*. Manning's assertion is remarkably similar to the approach taken a century later by Pope John Paul II in his encyclical *Laborem Exercens*.

lish the Irish Church, but when Disraeli proposed to reform higher education in Ireland, he supported the Tories. Indeed, he worked actively to win the Irish bishops to Disraeli's plan, but although he won over Cardinal Cullen, the remainder of the Irish hierarchy refused to go along with the plan and it failed. For this Disraeli blamed Manning, though unfairly. On disestablishment, on the other hand, Manning's pamphlet published in March 1868, *Ireland: A Letter to Earl Grey* was one of the major influences in formulating Gladstone's policy as to disestablishment. What Manning failed to recognize, at least until the closing years of his life, was that Home Rule, in the form of a parliament in Dublin, was the fundamental demand of Irish nationalists. And he failed to recognize it because he depended upon the presence of Irish Members of Parliament at Westminster to represent the Catholic interest. This was particularly true for education, where it was the Tory party, rather than the Liberals with their commitment to non-denominational schools, which attracted the Catholic vote. As Lord Bury wrote in *The Tablet* in 1880, 'The Conservatives have at least this in common with Catholics, that they dread the complete secularization of education'.[20] In the election of 1886 Manning instructed Catholics not to vote for 'free', nondenominational, schools, which was tantamount to telling them to vote Conservative. When in 1883 the Primrose League was founded to further the Conservative cause, English Catholics signed up 'in droves'[21] so as to distinguish themselves from their Irish co-religionists who would be voting for the Liberals and Home Rule. Bishop Bagshawe of Nottingham, a supporter of Home Rule, claimed that membership of the Primrose League was incompatible with being a Catholic. Manning publicly contradicted him.[22]

---

20 Dermot Quinn, *Patronage and Piety* (Stanford, CA: Stanford University Press, 1993), p. 134.

21 *Ibid.*, p. 161.

22 The structure of the Primrose League had many similarities to that of the Protestant Orange Lodges, but even down to its demise in 2004 prominent Catholics were numbered among its officers and trustees.

One prominent Home Ruler, who helped to shape the Liberal policy, was the Marquis of Ripon. Ripon's conversion to Catholicism in 1874 gave rise to a storm of protest. *The Times* lectured him that his conversion meant 'a complete abandonment to any claim to political or social influence in the nation at large', and put it down to 'an irreparable weakness of character'. Gladstone, on the other hand, blamed the Jesuits, and then went on, 'You are bound to obey whatever the Pope enjoins, under the name of moral duty, even if it be, according to your judgement and mine, in the domain of civil loyalty.'[23]

These extremely harsh judgements were made in the aftermath of the First Vatican Council of 1869–70 where, it was commonly perceived, the pope had been endowed with absolute and personal authority over the consciences of Catholics through the declaration of the dogma of papal infallibility. And Archbishop (as he still was before the Council) Manning was one of the chief architects of that dogma. Manning had long believed in the pope's infallibility. As has been seen, he had become a Catholic precisely seeking a guarantor of freedom from error in matters of faith. In this he was, of course, not alone among English converts: W. G. Ward thought similarly, though he was not prepared to go as far as Manning. It was Manning's view that all papal pronouncements, even if not infallible, required from Catholics interior consent. This extended, for example, to papal encyclicals and to canonization ceremonies.

When the Council was first announced, Manning had not yet been elevated to the episcopacy, and when letters were sent out seeking the views of bishops as to the agenda of the Council, no English bishop was approached. A couple of months later, however, after his appointment, his views were solicited,

---

23 Ripon had the unusual distinction of having been born in 10 Downing Street and, even more unusual for a Catholic, of having been Grand Master of the Masons – though that was before he converted. Both *The Times* and Gladstone were proved wrong. Ripon went on to be Viceroy of India, an experience which, on his return to Westminster politics, strengthened his commitment to Home Rule for the Irish.

and he was a member of the international committee formally responding to the pope's letter. He wanted papal infallibility to be included in the response, in which he met, but overcame, stiff resistance from the Bishop of Orleans, Félix Dupanloup. With the Bishop of Regensburg, whom he met on the steps of St Peter's where they had been celebrating Vespers for the Feast of Sts Peter and Paul, he made a vow to commit himself to achieving the declaration of papal infallibility.

The Council assembled for its first session of 8 December 1869. There were broadly three parties. First there were the 'infallibilists', among whom Manning was a powerful force. Then there were the 'inopportunists', those who believed in infallibility but thought that the time was not opportune for such a declaration. Most English bishops fell into this group, much to Manning's chagrin, as did John Henry Newman, though Newman, not a bishop, was not at the Council. Finally there were those opposed to the doctrine outright. Manning put it about after the Council that the majority of bishops who were not in the first group belonged to the second, but that is not entirely true. There was a considerable number who were hostile to the whole idea, and not just because it was not the right time to define it.

One of those opposed was Karl Joseph von Hefele, Bishop of Rottenburg, whose opposition was all the more significant because he was precisely a historian of Councils of the Church. When he ventured to propose some historical objections to the proposed dogma, he received short shrift from Manning: 'We are not at school but at an ecumenical council. We are not to bring our questions to historians and critics but to the living oracle of the Church.'[24] This was an illuminating remark. Subordinating theology to history was exactly what Acton and Simpson had been accused of doing in the pages of *The Rambler* and subsequently in *The Home and Foreign Review*. 'It is time for

---

24 A. B. Hasler, *How the Pope Became Infallible* (New York: Doubleday, 1981), p. 179.

"historical science" and "the scientific historians" with all their arrogance to be thrust back into their proper sphere, to be kept within their proper limits. And the Council will do just that, not with controversies and condemnations but with the words "it has pleased the Holy Spirit and us"', said Manning who, one cannot help thinking, was a little intoxicated, not with the alcohol he was shortly to foreswear, but with the very fact of being present at a Council of the Church. He was now part of the Tradition of the Church which he considered more significant than history: 'No one who wishes to keep the name of Catholic may descend from the unshakeable rock of Truth, the Church's Magisterium, into the swamp of human history when the truths of faith are at stake.'[25] Now he was part of that Magisterium.

There was still something of a battle to be undertaken. Archbishop Manning was actively engaged with a group of infallibilists to ensure that the right people – their people – were elected to major offices during the Council. He himself became a member of the Congregatio de Postulatis, organizing issues to be presented to the Council, and on the Deputatio de Fide which was engaged in detailed work on the documents to be presented to the Council on infallibility. Unfortunately from Manning's perspective, the document *De Ecclesia* ('On the Church') was concerned with the infallibility of the Church, not with that of the pope personally. Therefore Manning persuaded the Congregatio de Postulatis to present to the Pope a petition, on 15 February 1870, to include papal infallibility in the decree. Pius IX gave his approval for a new chapter to be added to *De Ecclesia*, but at the pace the debate was going it would be a long time before the Council reached the topic of infallibility. Manning tried to persuade the presidents of the Council to change the order of the discussion, but this they refused to do.

---

25 *Ibid.*, pp. 178–9. Gaspare Mermillod, the Bishop of Geneva and a friend of Manning, was quoted by Dupanloup as saying 'Infallibility sets the nations free from their history' (*ibid.*).

Manning held a series of crisis meetings of the infallibilists. They proposed that a whole new constitution, as the Council documents were called, should be drawn up simply to deal with papal infallibility. The idea was put to Pope Pius on 19 April. He did not react at once, so a formal petition was prepared. He agreed on 27 April and the Constitution *Pastor Aeternus* was ready by 8 May. It consisted of four chapters, all of them on the status of the papacy. The first three were on papal primacy, the fourth was on papal infallibility. This was then debated. Manning was aware of the theological problem which had arisen. The Council was now discussing the infallibility of the pope within the Church before it had been given opportunity to discuss the infallibility of the Church itself, as outlined in *De Ecclesia*. But with the increasing likelihood that Rome would fall to the troops of Victor Emmanuel and be absorbed into the kingdom of Italy, the matter was urgent. Back in England, Newman was hoping that the pope would be driven from Rome before a vote could be taken. It was not to be. The definitive vote was taken (during a violent thunderstorm which some interpreted as God expressing his displeasure).

As a young man, Manning had considered a political career. During the Vatican Council he had the opportunity to exploit his political talents. A Protestant observer, Emile Olivier, commented:

Do not mistake him for those emaciated monks whom he resembles. Underneath his seraphic air of content there lurks a politician as insinuating and energetic as any of the kind. He has known how to keep in with the English liberals even while siding with the party of absolute authority at Rome. His activity is prodigious; he is involved with everything; he speaks about everything and upon everything; he writes indefatigably, and he does not neglect the fashionable world in which he is so pampered and sought after.[26]

---

26 Gray, *op. cit.*, p. 231.

When he returned home he immediately set about broadcasting the new doctrine in a 200-page pastoral letter. He ignored the considerable limitations with which the Council Fathers had surrounded the declaration of papal infallibility, giving to it the widest possible remit to include such matters as canonizations and encyclicals, but in fact Manning's and the other infallibilists' victory had been a very prescribed one, though it took several decades, if not indeed several generations of theological commentators, before this fact sank in.

Ecumenical Councils are far rarer occurrences than even papal conclaves, and one can understand, perhaps, Manning's enthusiasm. But the First Vatican Council happened quite soon after his promotion to Westminster, and he had still many battles to fight, as has been recounted above. Towards the end of his life he became a friend of Mrs Virginia Crawford, whose admission of adultery with Sir Charles Dilke during her divorce case in 1886 ended Dilke's political career. After the divorce she became a professional writer and in March 1888 she interviewed Cardinal Manning for the *Pall Mall Gazette*, an event which led to a lasting friendship and her conversion to Catholicism less than a year later. Manning was also a friend of Dilke himself, under whose chairmanship he had in 1884 sat on a royal commission on the housing of the poor. There still remains a mystery about the Dilke case, the truth of which, it is sometimes claimed, was known only to Manning as a confidant of both parties.

Virginia Crawford saw him quite often, and understood something of his loneliness in old age: 'I think he feels very much the sort of hidden antagonism to all his views which exists among the Catholic Upper Ten Thousand. He knows quite well that they only just tolerate him because they must and because they hope for better things when he is gone.'[27] Mrs Crawford shared many of his social concerns, but the Upper Ten Thousand did not, at least in the same way. They

---

27 *Ibid.*, p. 319.

tried, but failed, to have a papal diplomatic representative appointed so there would be someone to mediate between themselves and the Vatican, rather than leave the Cardinal in charge of the field. In Manning's successor, Herbert Vaughan, they were to find an Archbishop of Westminster more to their taste.

For someone so different, Vaughan was nonetheless very close to Manning. He was, though perhaps more by chance than by design, present at Archbishop's House on the corner of Carlisle Place and Francis Street on the night of 13–14 January 1892 as the Cardinal lay dying. In the early morning he slipped out to say Mass for him. Manning died before he returned from the altar. The crowds that turned out for his funeral had not been seen on the streets of London since the death of the Duke of Wellington, just 40 years earlier.

3

Herbert Vaughan

Colonel Francis Vaughan and his wife Elizabeth had thirteen children, of whom Herbert was the eldest. While the career of Herbert will be the subject of this chapter, those of his siblings deserve mention. Roger, born two years after Herbert became a Benedictine monk at Downside Abbey, then went out to Australia as Assistant Bishop of Sydney, and eventually became Archbishop of that city. Another brother, John, also became a Bishop, as assistant to the bishop of Salford, though not until 1909, long after Herbert's death. Kenelm became a diocesan priest: he was ordained at 25 when thought to be on the point of death, but lived to be nearly 70. Two other brothers entered religious orders. Joseph became a Benedictine who in 1876 established the abbey of Fort Augustus, Bernard became a Jesuit and a much sought-after preacher at Farm Street. His sermons on 'the sins of society' had the Mayfair smart set agog. There were five sisters, four of whom became nuns, and all of whom predeceased him.

All of that suggests the Vaughans were a particularly devout Catholic family, which indeed they were. Although Herbert was born, on 15 April 1832, in Beaufort Buildings, Gloucester where his grandfather was staying at the time, the family home was Courtfield Manor in Herefordshire, on a bend of the River Wye near Ross on Wye. It was a remote spot, a fact which no doubt helped them to retain their Catholicism throughout the penal years. They were well connected. His mother was a sister of Cardinal Thomas Weld (see above, p. 42n); his great-grandfather had given Stonyhurst to the Jesuits when in 1794 they resettled in England their school at St Omer. Colonel Weld had been at Stonyhurst; Herbert went there in 1841, but was removed in 1845 when his father fell out with the rector and, after briefly attending Downside, he was placed in a Jesuit college in Belgium. At Stonyhurst he had gone riding and shooting, but had not fared well in his studies. In Belgium, on the other hand, where his cricket bat was confiscated on his arrival, he did a good deal better academically, perhaps because there was nothing else to do: sport was no part of the curriculum.

His father's plans for his eldest son were for him to embark upon a military career, for which he believed him well suited. At the age of 16, however, and to his father's great disappointment, Herbert determined upon becoming a priest. His first thought was to serve as a missioner in Wales, close to his family home. Perhaps for this reason he briefly entertained the idea of becoming a monk at Downside, where the community served a number of mission stations near the Welsh border. But he was dissuaded. A monk advised him that he would need 'more elbow room' than was to be found within the bounds of Benedictine religious life. Instead, in October 1851 he left for Rome, arriving there exactly a month later, on 13 November. He found lodgings in a house near the Piazza della Minerva. There he came into contact with several of the former Anglicans who had converted to Catholicism, and when he returned to Rome in 1852 after a summer break in England he did so in the company of – among others – Henry Edward Manning. The two became close, and remained so until Manning's death. While in Rome Vaughan every day served Manning's Mass before going off to lectures. He had enrolled in the Accademia dei Nobili Ecclesiastici, and attended classes at the Jesuit-run Roman College.

Early in 1854 he became unwell, and left Rome and his studies for the sea air. He was not so ill that his life was despaired of, but some believed, himself included, that he might not live long enough to reach ordination in the ordinary course of events. The Vatican was therefore approached to obtain permission for him to be ordained before the canonical age. Permission was granted. Herbert went off to Lucca, and spent some time making a retreat at a Passionist monastery. He was ordained in Lucca by the city's archbishop on 28 October, at the age of little more than 22. He then went on a tour of Italy until summoned back to Rome for the proclamation of the dogma of the Immaculate Conception, on 8 December.

Shortly after his ordination Vaughan had received a letter from Cardinal Wiseman inviting him to return to England as vice-president of the seminary at St Edmund's College, Ware, in Hertfordshire. He accepted the posting, and made his way back home by a circuitous route which allowed him to visit, and make notes on, many of the better continental seminaries. He also made the acquaintance of a good number of leading continental Catholic scholars, among whom was Döllinger. He arrived at St Edmund's when he was just 23 years of age, and hardly six months ordained. He immediately stepped into controversy.

To be fair, it was not wholly his doing. On his arrival he immediately took exception to the presence on the college staff of William George Ward.[1] He thought it improper that a layman, no matter how distinguished as a scholar, should be lecturing to seminarians on theology. He expressed his views, but then went to hear a Ward lecture, and promptly changed his mind. Not only did he believe that Ward should stay, but became a firm and enduring friend of the family. The problem was, there were others who resented Ward's membership of the staff of St Edmund's, and chief among them was Bishop George Errington. Errington had been proposed as Assistant

---

1 Ward described Vaughan at this period as a man of 'extraordinary beauty'. 'Slim of figure, his fearless blue eyes, aquiline nose, and firm set mouth, the expression of sweetness and courage combined, made him in appearance an ideal Sir Galahad'. Robert O'Neill, *Cardinal Herbert Vaughan* (London: Burns and Oates, 1995), p. 122. Ward, on the other hand, who was vastly overweight, said of himself, 'I have the mind of an archangel in the body of a rhinoceros' (*ibid.*, p. 94).

Bishop to Cardinal Wiseman by the Westminster chapter in February 1855, and confirmed by Propaganda Fide a month later. One of his first acts was to conduct a visitation of St Edmund's, where he sided with those on the staff who opposed Ward. He could hardly dismiss Ward because he had been appointed by Wiseman, but he placed such restrictions upon his teaching that Ward felt obliged to resign. Wiseman managed to persuade him to stay on, but Errington claimed that the Cardinal had undertaken not to interfere with his decisions and, having decided he could no longer work with Wiseman, asked to be relieved of his office. Propaganda appointed him temporarily to the Diocese of Clifton (Bristol) as apostolic visitor, though he later returned to carry out a visitation of the Diocese of Westminster which only succeeded in alienating the clergy. After this fiasco Wiseman determined to get rid of his assistant bishop, which he succeeded in doing, though after the Cardinal's death Errington was rather quixotically proposed by the Westminster chapter as his successor,[2] no doubt because, at least in the matter of St Edmund's, they had sided with him against Wiseman.

And not only St Edmund's. The Oblates of St Charles came into being at the end of 1856 with its church of St Mary and the Angels in Bayswater, and its community house nearby at 12 Sutherland Place. Manning was the superior, while Herbert Vaughan was a quasi novice master despite retaining his post at St Edmund's. Other members of the Oblates soon became attached to the seminary, and the Westminster chapter, as well as Errington, objected to the presence of a form of religious congregation having so much involvement in what should, they believed, have been solely a diocesan enterprise. That was certainly true had it been a seminary in the sense defined three

---

2 Manning, of course, was appointed. Errington after leaving Westminster had lived for a time in retirement before taking up a parish on the Isle of Man. He attended the Vatican Council, and after the Council, was invited by the Bishop of Clifton to teach theology at Prior Park, which he did for the rest of his life.

centuries earlier by the Council of Trent; but, as Manning
pointed out, because St Edmund's had lay students – school-
boys – as well as students for the priesthood, it was not strictly
speaking a seminary. The diocesan chapter took Wiseman to
task for having allowed the Oblates such a prominent role in
the seminary. Wiseman retaliated by demanding to see the
minutes of the meetings of the chapter, which they refused to
hand over and appealed to Rome against the Cardinal. There
was a further complication because the Bishop of Southwark,
Thomas Grant, with whom Wiseman was already at odds over
finances (see above, p. 28f), wanted to have a say in the running of the seminary to which he sent his own students – a
request which Wiseman rejected.

Vaughan was involved in this controversy both as vice-
president of St Edmund's and as an Oblate. But he was also at
odds with the president, who accused him of spying on the
students. This charge was investigated and found to be untrue,
though the president was not wholly straightforward when
reporting this to the students. In fact Vaughan, who was hardly
older than the seminarians, was popular among them, but
there was something of a conflict of interest in his role of vice-
president, and he was accused of recruiting the students for the
diocesan priesthood into the Oblates of St Charles. Rome
finally sided with the chapter over the seminary, ruling that as
then constituted it was inconsistent with the requirements of
Trent, and that it ought to be in the hands of diocesan clergy;
but by the time that decision had been handed down, Manning
had withdrawn all the Oblates from St Edmund's.[3]

Vaughan was far from dispirited by the failure of his first
appointment. The Oblates had come into being because Wiseman's desire to have a band of missioners had dovetailed neatly
with Manning's desire to live in a form of religious community.

---

3 The college never did become a seminary in the strict Tridentine sense. The
boys' school survives to this day, while the seminary later moved to London,
during the episcopacy of Basil Hume.

Vaughan, meanwhile, had conceived the idea of a band of missioners who would work both at home and also abroad – he had been much impressed by the work of Protestant missionary societies based in England, and by the Catholic ones based in continental Europe. There was no English Catholic equivalent, and for a time he wondered whether it might not be possible to develop St Edmund's into a seminary to train students for the foreign, as well as the home, missions. He went to All Hallows seminary in Dublin to investigate how they trained their students, but was not impressed. He also visited seminaries on the continent. He did all this without much encouragement from Manning, but with a good deal from Wiseman with whom he talked about his idea in the summer of 1861. The Cardinal, it transpired, had for some time been thinking along similar lines but had not won the backing of other members of the hierarchy.

Ever the enthusiast, after he had attended the canonization of the Japanese martyrs in Rome in July 1862, Vaughan began to think that his own vocation lay as a missionary in Japan. When he returned to England he discussed his ideas at a meeting of the Oblates, but they were cool towards the idea of a training college for missionary priests, though Manning himself had warmed a little towards the proposal. Not quite a year later, while Vaughan was making a retreat in a Jesuit house in Spain, he decided on his course of action. He would himself raise the funds for his proposed college, and he would do so by making a lengthy trip around the Americas, both North and South.

He left Southampton on a paddle steamer in mid-December 1863, and arrived in Panama in early January, where he managed to get himself arrested but then released in short order. He went on to California, arriving in San Francisco at the very beginning of February. He spent almost half a year in California, and became very attracted to the region, not least because his health improved under the Californian sun. He then embarked on a distinctly adventurous trip around South America, visiting Ecuador briefly and Peru for longer, including

Lima and Arequipa. He went on to Chile and left for Brazil in a British man-of-war. He learned of the death of Cardinal Wiseman as he arrived in Rio de Janeiro. He then left for Bordeaux and arrived back in England at the end of July 1865. He had been absent from the country for more than eighteen months, and in his travels had raised £11,000. To that was added a gift of £2,000 from the Ward family.[4] He set about finding a property.

The site he selected for his new college of missionary priests was Holcombe House in Mill Hill, north London. The freeholder was at first not willing to sell to Vaughan, but was persuaded by a cheque for £5,400 – or perhaps by the intercession of St Joseph, Vaughan having left a statue of the saint in a cupboard at Holcombe House during one of his visits. A convent of convert nuns moved into the house itself, while work began on the college. It was opened on the feast of St Joseph, 19 March 1866. The first missionaries, four Mill Hill Fathers, left in November 1871 for Baltimore to work among former slaves. Vaughan went with them. He saw them settled, then travelled in the south of the United States where he was horrified by the degree of racial discrimination which he encountered. He then went on to New York to raise money for his new enterprise. He was extraordinarily successful, raising a total of $12,000, and much encouraged he went to Boston, where in one church alone he collected a further £1,100. He moved on to Canada, returning home in June 1872.

Meanwhile, he had bought *The Tablet*. There are many suggestions as to why he should have done so, including the fact that under its previous two editors the weekly had been highly controversial, but the probable reason is that he had been impressed, during his visit to the USA on his fund-raising tour, by the power of the press. He engaged in the task of running the paper with his usual enthusiasm, working late into the

---

4 Pius IX had said he would raise no money, and ought not to go. 'Tell his Holiness that his blessing was worth more than his prophecy', said Vaughan. O'Neil, *op. cit.*, p. 154.

night and even sleeping in the office, curled up beneath a table.[5] After Vaughan became Bishop of Salford he could no longer devote time to editing the paper, and handed this task over to George Elliot Ranken and, after him, to a relative, John Snead Cox, who was editor from 1884 to 1920 and who later became his biographer. 'Herbert Vaughan's simple rule of conduct,' Snead Cox wrote in his biography, 'his easy test for Catholic loyalty was always, and under all circumstances to stand on the side of Rome.'[6] Nowhere was this more evident than in the paper's coverage of the Vatican Council. Vaughan reported the Council in detail, but refused to publish any hint that there might be any views other than his own on the matter of papal infallibility. To find arguments against the proposed dogma, Catholics had to turn to Henry Wilberforce's *The Weekly Register* where the letters column was filled with the debate Vaughan banned from his own publication – and Vaughan himself was perfectly ready to engage in this debate in the rival weekly.

When Wilberforce wanted to sell his paper, Vaughan wanted to buy it, but did not have the money. It was eventually purchased by Manning himself, who handed it over to Wilfrid Meynell.[7] This annoyed Vaughan, but in Manning's eyes Vaughan was unsound on the issue of Home Rule, a position to which the Cardinal belatedly adhered (cf. above, p. 53). *The Tablet* had long been hostile to Irish aspirations. Manning advised Vaughan to stay out of the Home Rule debate on the grounds that the vast majority of Catholics in England were Irish, and of those who were not, a good number were sympathetic to Ireland. Snead Cox rejected the Cardinal's plea on the reasonable grounds that the paper he edited could hardly stand aside from one of the major issues of the day, but in a

---

5 See Michael Walsh, *The Tablet* (London: The Tablet Publishing Company, 1990), p. 16. In 1878 Ward gave him *The Dublin Review* which remained the property of the Archbishop of Westminster for almost a century (*ibid.*)

6 *Ibid.*, p. 17.

7 *Ibid.*, pp. 20–1.

letter to *The Pall Mall Gazette* in April 1887 Manning wrote, 'I regard *The Tablet* as responsible for all the soreness of feeling that now exists to so large an extent between the Catholics of the two countries.'[8]

The purchase of *The Tablet* had taken place before he went on his fund-raising tour. It was shortly after his return that Manning told him he had been appointed Bishop of Salford. The Salford chapter informed him slightly later, on 2 October 1872, just a fortnight before the official documentation arrived from Rome. It was an odd choice. He had in his career thus far little or nothing to do with the north of England, and there was a degree of unease towards him on the part of the local clergy, but with the energy and enterprise he had so far displayed he was an obvious candidate for a bishopric. So he was duly consecrated Bishop, by Cardinal Manning, in St John's Cathedral, Salford, on 28 October. Ullathorne, the Bishop[9] of Birmingham, preached the sermon. The service of consecration was followed by a splendid lunch in the town hall, attended by local dignitaries, including the mayors of Salford and Manchester, and the Member of Parliament. Two days later he accompanied Manning to a temperance meeting at Manchester's Free Trade Hall. There were several thousand people present who gave him a rousing welcome for his first public appearance as bishop. However, he then rather upset the platform party by announcing that he was not himself a teetotaller.

He launched upon the administration of his diocese with his customary vigour,[10] bringing in priests to help staff his poorly

---

8 McClelland, *op. cit.*, p. 192.
9 Ullathorne is commonly referred to as Archbishop, but the title was a personal one, conferred on him only after he had retired from his see.
10 His appointment distracted him from at least some of his enterprises. In 1868, to provide cheap Catholic literature, he started the Catholic Truth Society. Without Vaughan's input it came to a halt, but was revived in 1884 thanks to James Britten, a convert, who contacted Vaughan and received his backing.

manned diocese from continental Europe, and rather imagina-
tively providing them with a year's enculturation into English
ways before letting them out full-time on the parishes. He was
still, however, superior of the Mill Hill Fathers, and it was while
he was away on missionary business that the Jesuits opened a
college in Manchester, his territory. He shared Manning's distrust of the Society, perhaps, again like Manning, because
through their schools they were able to attract recruits who
might otherwise have put themselves forward for the diocesan
priesthood. It has already been commented that Jesuits drew a
good deal of support from the 'old' Catholic families, of the
sort to which he himself belonged, but he felt that they undermined the authority of a bishop in his diocese. He was also
opposed to their classical form of education which he did not
believe responded to the real needs of the majority of his flock.
When, therefore, the provincial superior of the Society
approached him about starting a school, he refused permission. But Jesuits were 'exempt' religious, which meant that they
could claim to be free from the jurisdiction of the local bishop,
and answerable only to Rome. So while Vaughan was absent,
just after Easter 1875, a Jesuit school was opened in a flat in
Manchester.

Vaughan was understandably furious. He consulted with the
other bishops, and at a meeting of the hierarchy in 1887 they
decided to send him to Rome to make their case against the
Society and other exempt religious. Vaughan himself was determined that, if he did not win the argument, he would resign.
He left for Rome on 2 December 1879 and did not return for
more than a year and a half, on 13 July 1881. But in the meantime, on 14 May 1881, the Vatican issued the Constitution
Romanos Pontifices which, while recognizing religious exemp-
tion, required that, when members of religious orders were
working in a parish, they would be subject to the jurisdiction of
the bishop. Moreover, they were not to open schools, other
religious houses or convents for nuns without the express permission of the bishop in whose diocese the new institution was

to operate.[11] Vaughan came back to his diocese feeling himself completely vindicated – all the more so because he had persuaded the superior general of the Society of Jesus to order the provincial superior in England to close the school in Manchester.

This was all the more important to him because he had already, in 1875, opened his own school, St Bede's. It has been noted that one of his objections to the Jesuit system of education was that it was based on a classical model, catering especially for the sons of the middle and upper classes. This, he judged, was not what was needed in industrial Manchester. His school was to specialize in commercial and business education, and to be open to a wider range than the Jesuits' would have been. He even opened an annexe in Bonn, so that his pupils might learn German. St Bede's began life in a Baptist chapel, and later moved to what had been the Manchester Aquarium (Vaughan tried to run the Aquarium as a commercial enterprise, but failed). The majority of the teachers came from the diocesan clergy.[12]

Education was one of the areas of pastoral concern where Manning and Vaughan saw eye-to-eye. As Manning had set up the Voluntary Schools Association, Vaughan did likewise in Salford. He also had the same worry as Manning, although rather belatedly, about 'leakage', the loss of Catholic children to the Church because they were being brought up by non-Catholic charities or in workhouses. He addressed a pastoral letter to the subject, 'The Loss of Our Children' in 1886 in which he blamed Catholic parents for their neglect and the various charities for proselytizing. His response was to set up the Salford Catholic Protection and Rescue Society.

---

11 The Scottish hierarchy had associated themselves with the English and Welsh bishops' plea, and in subsequent years the terms of *Romanos Pontifices* were extended to the United States and elsewhere.

12 It seems to have been the first college to be called St Bede's – possibly after Vaughan's Benedictine brother, who had been given that name on entering the monastery. The school still exists as an independent, fee-paying school (c. £6,000 a year), but is now co-educational, and has an academic, rather than commercial emphasis – including, ironically, Classics.

But on other issues, he and Manning were at odds, and especially over Ireland after Manning had changed his mind (see above, p. 68). Vaughan warned his flock against secret societies, clearly meaning the Fenians whom very many Irish Catholics in England supported. The fact that the Church was largely Irish did not worry him. The bishops, he said, must be careful about 'merging our office and our Church in the political aspirations of the foreign section of our flock. We are bishops to represent the Church to the English people and ought to be on our guard against presenting it to them in a colour which will be prejudicial.'[13]

In the 1880s Manning supported the Irish Land League and the Irish National League, led by Parnell, which succeeded it. The League was campaigning for better rights for tenants, and withholding the rents from landowners who would not reduce them to a level the Land League deemed fair. A Tory through and through, Vaughan did not approve, and nor, obviously, did the landowners. It was this issue in particular which led the Duke of Norfolk to call for diplomatic relations to be established between Britain and the Vatican,[14] a call backed up by Vaughan in an article in *The Nineteenth Century*. Manning thought that the bishops had too narrow a view of their role in England, and told Vaughan so.

Yet despite their differences, it seemed inevitable that Vaughan should succeed Manning as Archbishop of Westminster. He was third on the list of names submitted to Rome by the Westminster chapter, but he was put in the last place only because the list was drawn up in alphabetical order. Vaughan wrote to Pope Leo XIII asking not to be considered for the post, but the decision was swiftly made. He was formally appointed to Westminster on 29 March 1892.

Herbert Vaughan was solemnly enthroned as the third

---

13 O'Neil, *op. cit.*, pp. 286–7.
14 When the Vatican sent a papal visitor to Ireland he backed up Manning's view.

Archbishop of Westminster on 8 May 1892. The ceremony took place in the relatively modest surrounds of the pro (i.e., acting) cathedral, the church of Our Lady of Victories, just off Kensington High Street in west London. As a metropolitan, Vaughan was entitled to the pallium, the white stole bestowed by the pope to symbolize the union between himself and the archbishops. Wiseman and Manning had gone to Rome to receive theirs, but Vaughan asked that his be sent to London, where he was invested with the pallium in Brompton Oratory. It was the first time that such an investiture had been conducted in England since Reginald Pole received his pallium in 1556, and Vaughan ensured that the ceremony was conducted with great splendour. In December of that year he heard he was to be made a Cardinal: he was raised to that rank, alongside, among others, Michael Logue, the Archbishop of Armagh, in a consistory held in Rome on 16 January 1893. Perhaps as a sign of his devotion to the Holy See, Vaughan then petitioned that St Peter, the first Pope according to Vatican calculations, be declared a co-patron of England, a gesture which annoyed many non-Catholics.

As a great lover of pomp, Vaughan was disappointed that all the ceremonial surrounding his new office could not be conducted in a worthy cathedral. As has been seen (see above, p. 28) across the Thames the Diocese of Southwark had St George's Cathedral; Westminster had to make do with one or another of its churches for such grand occasions. It was one of Vaughan's first decisions that a worthy cathedral should be erected in the heart of London to serve his diocese. Manning had bought a property just off Victoria Street, Tothill Fields, the site of the former Middlesex County Prison,[15] but had not progressed much further. Vaughan was in far more of a hurry. He wanted his cathedral up and running in time for the celebrations to mark the half-century since the restoration of the hierarchy. This was almost an impossible task, but it dictated

---

15 See above, p. 42. There is a helpful plan of the site in Doyle, *op. cit.*, p. 16.

the style of the building. A Gothic structure would have been far too expensive and, perhaps more to the point, taken far too long – and in any case might have looked a poor relation compared to Westminster Abbey at the other end of Victoria Street.

The architect who was chosen was, however, a Gothic specialist. John Francis Bentley had been received into the Church by Cardinal Wiseman – at which point he had added Francis to his name. He had set himself up in business as a young man, and had for the most part prospered. It was he who had built the church in Bayswater for the Oblates, so he was known to Vaughan. At first the Cardinal had thought of having a competition, but Bentley had let it be known that he would not enter – so he was awarded the contract without the inconvenience of competing.

The foundation stone was laid, again with splendid ceremony, on 29 June 1895, the feast of SS Peter and Paul. There was a procession from Archbishop's House, then at the bottom of Carlisle Place, to the cathedral site to the sound of Mendelssohn's *War March of the Priests*. There followed a Mass celebrated by the cardinal of Armagh. There was an offertory collection which raised the extraordinary amount of all but £75,500. There was, finally, a lunch, at which Cardinal Vaughan proposed the health of both Pope Leo and Queen Victoria.

By the time the stone was laid, Vaughan had already received promises of half the estimated cost for a building in the 'early Christian Byzantine style', as Bentley described it in a guide to the cathedral which was produced in 1902, the year of his death.[16] He had travelled around Italy in particular looking at exemplars of Christian architecture. The first criterion which Vaughan had laid down was that the nave was to be big enough to hold a large congregation and that all should be able to see the ceremonies. The Cardinal had originally talked of a 'basilica' form, which in effect is what he got.

A further issue was how to provide for the services in the

---

16 Doyle, *op. cit.*, p. 17.

cathedral when it was completed. Vaughan's first thought was to bring in Benedictine monks to sing the divine office, and approached Downside Abbey. A site was purchased for a new priory in Ealing, the proposal being that the monks would travel in daily to perform the services. Negotiations dragged on for many months, one of the sticking points being the Cardinal's refusal to let the monks open a secondary school. A further complication was the presence in Ealing of a Fr Richard O'Halloran, a former priest of Mill Hill, who was antagonistic to the arrival of the monks. He and Vaughan had crossed swords several times, and the Cardinal failed to remove him from the Ealing mission, where he had indeed done remarkably good work, despite handing it over to the monks. Eventually they had to exist side by side with the recalcitrant cleric who remained until his death in 1925 ministering to a rump of his former congregation, despite having been formally excommunicated by Rome in 1914.[17] In the end the monks, whom Vaughan had further alienated by talking to the monastery of Solesme, renowned for its interpretation of Gregorian chant, when negotiations with Downside were in difficulties, did not supply the services, and in 1901 a choir school was decided upon in place of the monks. A final problem for the Cardinal was his wish to establish a shrine of St Edmund, King and Martyr, in the cathedral. His bones were reputed to rest at Toulouse, and negotiations began to translate them to Westminster. They eventually arrived at Arundel via Rome, but questions began to be asked about their authenticity and they never made it to the cathedral itself.

The construction of the cathedral was one bit of unfinished business which Vaughan inherited from Manning. Another was the university question: should Catholics be allowed to attend the universities of Oxford and Cambridge? Manning, as has

---

17 Vaughan's plans for the monks, and the battle with O'Halloran, are recounted in Rene Kollar, *The Return of the Benedictines to London* (Tunbridge Wells: Burns and Oates, 1989), pp. 1–50.

been seen (above, p. 48) was wholly opposed, but pressure continued to build. There were a number of Catholics at both institutions, with or without episcopal approval, and in 1893 Anatole von Hügel, brother of the more famous Baron Friedrich, and in charge of the Cambridge archaeological museum, appeared at an audience with Pope Leo XIII in full academic dress, and presented him with an address on behalf of Catholics at the university. He was one of the prime movers in the campaign for the situation to be regularized. Vaughan gave the appearance of bowing to the inevitable, but decided that if a change were to be made, it would be better if the bishops were seen to be taking a lead rather than following on behind. Over 400 laymen and clergy presented a 'memorandum of the universities question as affecting Catholics' to the bishops in 1894. Only one member of the hierarchy disagreed with the decision to send a petition to Rome in January 1895 asking for the ban to be lifted; it was, in a document dated 17 April. The rescript expressed the hope that a Catholic university be established in England, in the meantime gave permission for young men to study at Oxford or Cambridge, provided that they heard suitable lectures on philosophical, historical and religious topics from Catholic lecturers – which provision, in a modified form, became the task of the Catholic chaplaincies.

But if laymen, why not clergy? The Cardinal was concerned lest the laity become better educated than their priests, so when Edmond Nolan, the vice president of St Edmund's Ware, approached von Hügel about acquiring a property to house clergy who might attend the University of Cambridge, he had Vaughan's backing. A house belonging to an evangelical clergyman, the Revd William Ayerst, in Mount Pleasant on the outskirts of the city, became available. Vaughan was worried that Ayerst might not sell were he to realize the purpose to which his house would be put, so he arranged to be driven past it in a carriage to assess its suitability, and then brought in the Duke of Norfolk to handle the transaction, rather than an ecclesiastic. The purchase was completed on 25 September 1896, and St Edmund's House (now St Edmund's College) opened for business almost immediately.[18] Vaughan's perception of hostility seems to have been misplaced. When he eventually made a formal visit to St Edmund's House, Cambridge laid on a civic reception.

There were matters, then, on which Vaughan's policies departed from those of his predecessor, but in the relationship between the Church of England and the Church of Rome they followed the same path. In Vaughan's case, however, the situation between the two Churches was brought into sharper focus because of a chance meeting of two men, holidaying on the island of Madeira in the winter of 1889–90 – Charles Lindley Wood, the Second Viscount Halifax,[19] and Etienne Fernand Portal, a French Vincentian priest. Lord Halifax had been attracted to the Tractarian movement while he was a student at Oxford. The Church of England Protection Society had been established in May 1859 to defend the Catholic tradition in Anglicanism, and in May 1860 the Society changed its name to the Church Union: Halifax became its president in 1868 and, except for the period 1919 to 1927, he remained its president until his death at the age of 94 in 1935. He and Portal had much in common, and spent a good deal of time on Madeira in long walks, discussing the prospect for the reunion of the two Churches.[20]

It was Portal who suggested that the way forward was for a thorough examination of the question of the validity of

---

18 See Michael Walsh, *St Edmund's College Cambridge* (Cambridge: St Edmund's, 1996), pp. 26–33. It was given the status of a 'public hostel' by a vote in the Senate on 12 May 1898. One commentator noted that those who had voted 'non placet' had also voted against allowing women to take degrees.

19 He succeeded to the title on the death of his father in 1885.

20 There are many accounts of what happened during the debate about Anglican Orders. The classic treatment is that of John Jay Hughes, *Absolutely Null and Utterly Void: The Papal Condemnation of Anglican Orders 1896* (London: Sheed and Ward, 1968), but see also J. A. Dick, *The Malines Conversations Revisited* (Louvain: Leuven University Press, 1989), pp. 39–49, the section on Vaughan.

Anglican Orders, a matter on which, of course, Halifax had no doubt. The point, as far as Portal was concerned, was that without a mutual recognition of Orders, there was no possibility of corporate reunion, which was what both men were striving for. Halifax approached Vaughan about access to the Vatican archives, and the Cardinal at this point was supporting, though suggesting that a more important issue was papal authority. Portal, meanwhile, wrote an article in which he concluded in favour of the validity of Anglican Orders. This conclusion, not surprisingly, gave rise to much debate, but that was what Portal was hoping for – to raise the topic in public consciousness. Vaughan invited both the Abbé Portal and Lord Halifax to lunch to talk over the issues. Halifax arrived, but Portal did not. Whatever the reason for his absence, the Cardinal took it amiss.

In Rome, however, Pope Leo XIII was intrigued. Encouraged by his Secretary of State, Mariano Rampolla,[21] Rapolla invited Portal to meet the Pope, and Leo undertook to write to the archbishops of Canterbury and York calling for conferences to be held on reunion. He then, however, changed his mind, and decided instead to write to Portal a letter to be shown by the Abbé to Halifax and the two archbishops. If there were to be a positive response, then Leo would write directly to the two.

Vaughan was alarmed, believing that Rome was misinterpreting the situation in England, and he resolved to set the record straight. In a speech delivered in Preston to the Catholic Truth Society, he launched an outspoken attack on the Church of England, and especially on the Catholic party within the Church, and insisted that corporate reunion was impossible – only the conversion of individual members would bring about Church unity. The language of his polemic indicated just how alarmed he was. He went to Rome, arriving there on 19 January

---

21 Rampolla had the distinction of being the last cardinal likely to be elected pope, to be vetoed by a monarch, the Austrian Emperor Franz Josef, in the conclave following Leo XIII's death.

1895 and seeing the pope the following day. He assured Leo that there was no hope of corporate reunion because the Church of England would never accept papal primacy – a fact on which he was almost certainly correct. Halifax, who had been pressing the case, was hardly typical of members of his Communion.

For matters concerning England, Leo was relying on Rafael Merry del Val, a young monsignor in the papal court, who had been born in London, where his father was secretary to the Spanish embassy, part educated in England, and who had originally become a seminarian at Ushaw, near Durham. Merry del Val was close to Vaughan and kept him informed. He was influential in forming the text of the apostolic letter *Amantissimae Voluntatis*, better known as 'Ad Anglos', 'to the English', but which was largely drafted by Vaughan. It was moderate in tone, calling on all to pray to know the truth, and promising an indulgence to Catholics who prayed for the conversion of England. The letter was not addressed specifically to the Church of England, at which the archbishop of Canterbury took mild umbrage. Gladstone, on the other hand, was encouraged by its tone, though he wrote to Halifax saying that Vaughan 'and his band' would defeat the pope 'in his present purpose'.[22] Gladstone proved correct. A commission was set up in Rome to review the question of Anglican Orders. Vaughan insisted that it be made up only of Catholics; but Rampolla, who was sympathetic to the Anglicans, also insisted that both sides of the debate be represented. The president of the commission, however, was an ultra-conservative Italian cardinal, Camillo Mazzella.

The commission met a dozen times, between 24 March and 7 May 1896. At the end of its deliberations it was still evenly split, and the matter was put to the Holy Office on 16 July. But the matter had in a sense been predetermined. On 29 June Pope Leo had issued an encyclical, *Satis Cognitum*, which said

---

22 Dick, *op. cit.*, p. 46.

that reunion could come about only by recognition of papal authority – as Vaughan had argued from the first. The Holy Office did indeed decide against the validity of Anglican Orders, as having been, it was argued, the constant belief of Catholics. The bull *Apostolicae Curae*, laying out the reasons, was published on 13 September. After the Lambeth Conference of February 1897 the bishops of the Anglican Communion replied with their own letter, to which in turn the English Catholic bishops responded. In an article in his diocesan magazine, the Archbishop of York accused Vaughan of simply ignoring the Anglican arguments, and basing his rejection of the validity of Anglican Orders on the grounds that Anglicans would not accept the doctrine of transubstantiation which was, he pointed out, purely a medieval construction.[23]

The Machiavellian way the whole affair had been handled did not reflect well on Vaughan and his supporters. But he was undoubtedly correct: corporate reunion was a chimera. As he wrote in *Leo XIII and the Reunion of Christendom*, 'Tarry not for Corporate Reunion; it is a dream, and a snare of the evil one . . . The individual may no more wait for Corporate Reunion with the True Church than he may wait for Corporate Conversion from a grievous sin.'[24] His mouthpiece, *The Tablet*, was jubilant, describing the Church of England as 'a sect in manifest heresy and schism and as such as hateful as the contradictions of Korah, Dathan, and Abiran'.[25]

The adjective 'Machiavellian' could also be used to describe the writing of the joint pastoral letter of the bishops of the Province of Westminster, dated 29 December 1900, which appeared in *The Tablet* on 5 and 12 January following. The letter, a condemnation of Catholic theological liberalism, was occasioned by the writings of St George Jackson Mivart, the eminent biologist who had once been employed by Manning in

---

23 O'Neil, *op. cit.*, p. 403.
24 Dick, *op. cit.*, pp. 48–9.
25 *Ibid.*, p. 49.

his short-lived university college in Kensington. He was a firm believer in evolution (though not in the evolution of the mind), but it was not for these scientific views in themselves that he ran into trouble. In the 1880s and 1890s he wrote a series of articles for *The Nineteenth Century*, and in October 1899 he published a piece in *The Times* which was a scathing attack on the French hierarchy, and on the pope, for not having come to the defence of Captain Alfred Dreyfus, a rich young French army officer, who had been arrested in October 1894 and charged with, and found guilty of, passing on French military secrets to the Germans. He was sent to Devil's Island, but new evidence in 1899 occasioned a retrial. Though clearly innocent, he was again found guilty by a court martial in what was a flagrant act of anti-Semitism.

Many in the Church, the French bishops, the French Jesuits, the editorial staff of the Roman Jesuit journal *Civiltà Cattolica*, even the Jesuit Superior General, the Spaniard Luis Martín, among them, were prepared to believe Dreyfus guilty despite the evidence. The English Jesuits complained about the stance of their continental brethren, saying it brought dishonour to their Order. This did not improve their standing with Martín, especially as one of their number, George Tyrrell, was suspected by Martín of theological liberalism. A further problem for the English Jesuits was that they had rented out the hall attached to their central London church for a conference by Archbishop John Ireland, of St Paul, Minnesota.

Ireland was the leading figure in the attempt to adapt Catholicism to American culture – which in effect meant accepting democracy and the separation of Church and State. As a movement it was condemned as 'Americanism' by an encyclical on 1899, *Testem Benevolentiae*. When Martín discovered that Ireland had spoken at Farm Street he wrote to the rector of the church, complaining. The rector replied that, first, when the hall was booked he did not know who the speaker was to be; second, the hall had been booked by a very respectable organization, the Catholic Union; third, Cardinal Vaughan had given Ireland permission to speak in his diocese;[26] and fourth, the meeting was being held under the auspices of the Duke of Norfolk, an eminent Catholic whom it would be improper to alienate.

Martín had no great opinion of Vaughan. 'Catholics, who until now had been contained by the iron hand of Card. Manning . . . now no longer respecting the ecclesiastical authority represented by Card. Vaughan.' Though a 'sincere Catholic', thought Martín, he had shown himself 'a little weak' over the Dreyfus affair.[27] When, therefore, the Cardinal found himself in difficulties, the Jesuit Superior General was ready to help. The problem was a general one, of liberal Catholicism, but the immediate cause was the case of St George Mivart. In the summer of 1899 Mivart learned that some of his articles had been put on the 'Index of Forbidden Books'. He immediately protested to the Prefect of the Congregation of Index, who happened to be a Jesuit, but got nowhere. He therefore wrote an intemperate article for *The Times*, an article which in its tone alarmed even his supporters. Then there appeared an unsigned piece in *The Tablet* describing him as 'an opponent of the Catholic faith'. Mivart demanded an apology from Vaughan, who had not read Mivart's offending articles – which annoyed Mivart even more.

Vaughan tried to win Mivart over. He presented him with a profession of faith, and advised him to consult various people, including Mivart's supporter, the Jesuit George Tyrrell who was himself already on Martín's blacklist. Mivart refused to sign, and a formal sentence of excommunication was issued by Rome on 18 January 1900 – then Mivart died somewhat unexpectedly on the following 1 April. Behind all this was the person of Merry del Val, whom Vaughan constantly consulted. When Merry del Val heard that Mivart had refused the profession of faith, he

---

26 Vaughan did not himself attend the lecture, though – unusually – he went to the reception held afterwards by the Duke of Norfolk.

27 From Martín's *Memorias*, quoted by David Schultenover in *The View From Rome* (New York: Fordham University Press, 1993), p. 134. Schultenover's astonishing account has been followed here.

informed Vaughan that the pope wanted a general doctrinal statement from all the English Catholic bishops, or failing that from Vaughan himself, condemning liberalism. The issue was, who was best suited to write it? Del Val told Vaughan that the Cardinal could not trust any English advisers to do a thorough job, so he would, if Vaughan so wished, find Roman theologians to draft the pastoral for him. Vaughan gratefully accepted, and del Val approached Martín who assigned to the task the American (though Liverpool-born) Thomas Hughes, and the editor of *Civiltà Cattolica*, Salvatore Brandi. Del Val himself put the final touches to it, with help from Martín. It was a foretaste of the onslaught against modernism which was to come in a few years, with Merry del Val still one of the major influences.

However one may judge the affair of the joint pastoral, there were a number of successes to be credited to Vaughan towards the end of his life. A study of what happened to Catholic children who were brought up before magistrates revealed that they were handed over to the care of non-Catholics. Manning had attempted to address the problem years before. In 1899 Vaughan established the Crusade of Rescue in Westminster – now the Catholic Children's Society – to look after them, and Vaughan won an agreement that Catholic children applying to Dr Barnardo's would be offered to Catholic agencies.

Another important success, even a minor triumph, was the passing of the 1902 Education Act. Like Manning, he had constantly campaigned for a more equitable treatment for voluntary schools. They were funded by subscription, while the board schools were funded by a charge on the rates. In 1897 voluntary schools were freed from paying rates, which was something of a relief, if only a minor one. In 1902, however, all schools were put on an equal basis. The Church of England had at one time objected to this because, it was argued, their schools would lose their independence if publicly funded – but the Anglicans changed their mind in 1896. Nonconformists, on the other hand, continued to object even after the 1902 Act, claiming that this put 'Rome on the rates'.

By this time Vaughan's health was deteriorating. At the end of 1897 he had a heart attack, and in the following January went off to the French Riviera for three months to recuperate. He returned still depressed. In 1902 he spent two months of the summer in Germany, and then went to the house of Lord Edmund Talbot, Derwent Hall,[28] near Sheffield, for a long stay. But early the following year he believed that death was approaching. He decided to spend his last days at Mill Hill. He moved there on 25 March 1903, and died in his room on 19 June. The cathedral opened for his requiem, the first major religious event (there had earlier been a concert) to take place in the building. He was, however, not interred inside it. He wanted to be buried at Mill Hill, and he was laid to rest there on 26 June, after the funeral. His remains were taken back to the cathedral, for reburial, on 14 March 2005 after the members of the missionary society he had founded decided to sell their property in north London.

'Has there within the last hundred years been a single priest or bishop in England who could have contemplated such an enterprise, and not turned from it in dismay?' asked Vaughan's successor, Cardinal Bourne, of the building of Westminster Cathedral.[29] Herbert Vaughan left money to pay off the debt on Archbishop's House. And he left *The Tablet* to his successors. Its profits, at that time a very respectable £2,000 a year, were to be divided between the Mill Hill missionaries and the provision of a noble liturgy in the cathedral.

---

28 It was later to disappear under a reservoir, upon which King George V gave Talbot, Viscount Fitzalan Howard as he had become, Cumberland Lodge in Windsor Great Park as a grace-and-favour residence.

29 Doyle, *op. cit.*, p. 47.

4

Francis Alphonsus Bourne

Wiseman, Manning and Vaughan had all been interconnected. All were more or less Establishment figures. Vaughan's family had been gentry, Wiseman's and Manning's respective fathers significant businessmen. Francis Alphonsus Bourne was different. When Lady Kenmare said of him disparagingly that he was 'an effective postman', her description was close to the mark. His father Henry had worked as a clerk for the Post Office. At the time of Francis's birth, 23 March 1861, the family was living at Larkhall Rise, Clapham, in south London, though half a dozen years later they moved to Greenhithe, near Dartford. Henry and his brother were in 1845 both converts to Roman Catholicism. Henry married an Irish Catholic, Ellen Byrne, who was two years older than her husband, the daughter of a Dublin merchant, and there were two sons of the marriage: Francis had an elder brother, Joseph, who died in 1874.

Ellen seems to have been a powerful woman. After her husband's death from typhoid in 1870 she took a job as a governess in France – she had been educated in that country. By this time the two boys were already at boarding school – St Cuthbert's College at Ushaw, near Durham, which Francis did not like. A year after Joseph's death, Francis was moved to St Edmund's College, Ware, which, as has been seen, was a school as well as a seminary for the Westminster Diocese, though it was expected that some of the pupils would moved seamlessly from school to seminary, which is what Francis did, starting his priestly studies there in 1877, and moving on to St Thomas's seminary in

Hammersmith, London, three years later to begin theological studies. Apparently he was not considered bright enough to be sent to the English College in Rome, and for the rest of his life he harboured some hostility towards that prestigious institution. Soon after he became Archbishop of Westminster he declared that it ought to be closed because it was no longer the centre of English Catholic life in Rome, the bishops did not control the funds, and the course that students embarked upon was too long.[1] He was prepared to send his seminarians to Rome, but only for further degrees after they had completed their theology at St Edmund's. In 1923, however, he announced that England needed an institute of Catholic higher study, and that he was about to acquire a property in Cambridge for that purpose. This might have meant the end of the English College, but the Cardinal's plan came to nothing because, as was rather his wont, he had neglected to consult the other English and Welsh bishops, and, when they learnt of the scheme, they were opposed to it.

Though he retained a great affection for St Edmund's, he appears to have been less settled at the Hammersmith seminary. He considered becoming a religious, and went off to enter the noviceship of the Dominicans at Woodchester in Gloucestershire. He soon decided that the Dominican way of life was not for him, and left, but instead of returning to Hammersmith he went to Paris, to the seminary of Saint Sulpice. There he was open to more liberal influences than prevailed in English – or Roman – seminaries, which perhaps accounts for his disappointment at Cardinal Vaughan's treatment of St George Mivart (see above, p. 80f). He was ordained to the subdeaconate and deaconate in Paris in 1883 before going on to the University of Louvain for further studies. Ill health forced him to leave Louvain and return home without completing his course. In 1884, therefore, he was ordained in London by the bishop of

---

1 Williams, *op. cit.*, p. 146.

Southwark at St Mary's in Clapham, the Redemptorist church where he had been baptized.[2]

His first post as a 23-year-old curate was to Blackheath, where he did not get on well with the parish priest – a not uncommon experience for the newly ordained. Still as a curate he went on to serve at Sheerness, Mortlake and West Grinstead. There was an orphanage attached to the last, and he so enjoyed his work with the boys there that he wondered about joining the Salesians. He therefore went off in 1887 to Turin to meet the Salesians' founder, (St) John Bosco, but in the end he remained on the parish at West Grinstead. He was there for a dozen years before in 1899 being unexpectedly put in charge of Henfield Place, a nascent seminary for the Diocese of Southwark. Two years later a seminary proper was started at Wonersh, near Guildford, and the bishop appointed Bourne as its first rector. For his work in the seminary in 1895 he was named a domestic prelate, a rank which carries the title of Monsignor, and the following year he was consecrated a Bishop as assistant to the Bishop Butt of Southwark, with the right of succession to the see. Butt resigned two years later, and Bourne succeeded at the comparatively young age of 36.

Southwark, of course, represented the 'other half' of London, which meant that, as Cardinal Vaughan's health declined, its bishop was required to play something of a national role in, for instance, the debate about the 1902 Education Act (see above, p. 83), and acting on behalf of all the bishops in negotiating with the War Office over military chaplains during the Boer War. In the light of what was to happen later, it is worth recording that Bourne asked Cardinal Vaughan to transfer one of his diocesan priests, Peter Amigo, whom he had known at St Edmund's, from the parish of Commercial Road to the Diocese of Southwark – it seems that Bourne was considering starting

---

2 The founder of the Redemptorists was St Alphonsus Liguori – hence the future Cardinal's middle name.

some kind of association of diocesan clergy similar, perhaps, to the Oblates of St Charles in Westminster (see above, pp. 64–6). The request was refused, but he renewed it in 1901, and this time Vaughan gave way. Amigo moved on loan to Southwark and effectively became the vicar general of Southwark when Bourne's responsibility for military chaplains took him to Rome for a prolonged stay in the first months of 1903. Amigo was to succeed Bourne at Southwark, and the two London bishops promptly fell out.

At the death of Cardinal Vaughan the Westminster chapter prepared a 'terna'. Vaughan was known to have favoured Archbishop Rafael Merry del Val, who in 1902 had represented the pope at the coronation of Edward VII, and he was therefore on the list sent to Rome, along with the names of Abbot Aidan Gasquet of Downside and another Benedictine, the Bishop of Newport, John Cuthbert Hedley. The list was sent to Propaganda. The Duke of Norfolk was unhappy about the choices. Merry del Val, though English born, he did not think English enough; Gasquet he regarded as too young, and Hedley as too old – and, moreover, too scholarly for the Duke's taste. Propaganda tended to sympathize with Norfolk, all the more so because Cardinal Moran of Sydney, who sat on the committee selecting bishops, had a strong dislike of Benedictines. Bourne, though the youngest member of the English hierarchy, was selected because of his organizational ability: after Vaughan, it was decided, the Diocese of Westminster needed a bureaucratic hand. The appointment was announced at the end of August, Bourne took possession of his see at the end of September, and he was enthroned in Westminster Cathedral, in the first major ceremony there apart from Vaughan's funeral, in December 1903.

Immediately after the appointment was announced, the Southwark chapter moved to elect a Vicar Capitular, fearing that otherwise Bourne would have himself appointed administrator of the diocese in the absence of a bishop, and that this would be the first step to an amalgamation of the two Dioceses of Westminster and Southwark. Bourne was furious, and took steps to excommunicate the whole chapter, which would have been a major scandal. Both sides were persuaded to back down. Peter Amigo was swiftly appointed to Southwark, which he ruled for over 45 years, and was consecrated Bishop by Archbishop Bourne. As has been seen, the two had been friends, but the friendship swiftly deteriorated. The issue was, as so often, money. Both Bourne and Amigo were trustees of a large fund which assisted Southwark, but soon after Bourne moved to Westminster it emerged that some of those administering the fund had been acting fraudulently. The Charity Commissioners examined the workings of the fund, and advised the Attorney General that there were grounds for prosecution against the trustees. If this had gone ahead there would have been yet another major scandal, but the Attorney was persuaded not to take action. Amigo, however, decided that the diocese's financial administrator, Canon Edward St John, should be removed from his post. He was offered alternative employment, but refused to accept it and after his sacking in 1909 went to live for a time with Bourne at Archbishop's House. Bourne took St John's side, and refused, as a trustee, to sign any of the documents which Amigo sent him. The Bishop of Southwark then appealed to Rome (sending Arthur Hinsley to represent him, the man destined to succeed Bourne as Cardinal Archbishop). In retaliation, Bourne requested that Amigo be moved. Amigo refused to budge, and Bourne was then instructed to resign from the trust.

All this was happening against the background of a suspicion on the part of the Southwark clergy that Bourne was plotting to take over their diocese, and create a single Diocese of London. He hinted at this in 1911, when he went to Rome to receive his cardinalate. A meeting of protest was immediately organized in the hall attached to St George's Cathedral, attended by some 2,000 people. The priests drew up their own letter of protest which was signed by all but six of the diocesan clergy: Amigo wrote to the six who had refused, accusing them of a lack of loyalty. A committee of bishops and laymen was established to look into the question of redrawing diocesan boundaries: all but one of its members sided with Southwark. Clearly, Bourne had not been expecting this rebuff: the 1913 *Catholic Directory* had a map of the dioceses showing one see for the whole of London. The debate continued throughout the First World War. It was complicated as far as the majority of the bishops were concerned because from 1916 Bourne became a member of the Vatican's Consistorial Congregation which regulated such matters. While he was in Rome in March 1917 the bishops met at Oscott and passed a resolution against division of the dioceses. Bourne was furious that they had come together without him. At the Low Week meeting in April the topic was again on the agenda. 'The Low Week meeting should be of interest, and may give occasion for the police to be summoned'[3] commented Gasquet, who was by this time himself a cardinal.

On the issue of the division of dioceses, Bourne was at odds with the other bishops, and finally had to apologize. Although created cardinal in 1911, he suffered some diminution of his authority when the Apostolic Constitution *Si qua est* of the same year created two more provinces,[4] those of Liverpool and Birmingham. Bourne, therefore, was no longer the only archbishop in the country. He was not declared Primate of England, but the Constitution gave him pre-eminence over the other two, and laid down that he was to chair the meetings of the bishops. He was, moreover, to represent the whole of the country's hierarchy in their relations with the government. This was bound to cause difficulties. In 1906, when a newly elected Liberal government attempted to restrict the Churches' involvement with

---

3 Michael Clifton, *Amigo: Friend of the Poor* (Leominster: Fowler Wright, 1987), p. 48. Much of the above account of problems between Bourne and Amigo is drawn from chapter 5 of Clifton's book.

4 The Apostolic Constitution *Sapienti Consilio* of 1908 had already removed England from the oversight of the Congregation of Propaganda. It was, in other words, no longer being regarded as missionary territory but as a country with a Church fully established and operational.

education, the bishops were united in opposition to the government. Nonetheless, opposition to the bill split the Catholic Church, because the Liberals were in favour of Home Rule for Ireland, a measure obviously strongly supported by the very large Irish contingent in the Church. The Catholic peers in the Lords, led by the Duke of Norfolk, wanted to wreck the bill entirely; the Irish MPs in the Commons, on the other hand, wanted to reach an accommodation with the government. Much to the fury of Norfolk, Bourne backed the Irish MPs. But the Irish did not regard Bourne as generally sympathetic. Bourne, the Irish Nationalist leader T. P. O'Connor told Lloyd George, 'has declared war against us'.[5]

He was not alone in his hostility to Home Rule. The Catholic Union was also strongly opposed – not least, of course, because of the diminution of Catholic influence in the House of Commons which would be the inevitable consequence of a Dublin government. When in 1918 the Westminster government attempted to bring in conscription in Ireland, the Irish bishops vigorously opposed the measure. The Catholic Union was incensed, but the English and Welsh bishops, Bourne apart, were sympathetic. They wanted formally and publicly to repudiate the Catholic Union's stand, but the Cardinal would not let them do so. Instead they produced a letter of protest. All signed except for Bourne. In his position as representative of the Catholic Church before the government, he did not want to seem disloyal – he had even distanced English Catholics from Pope Benedict XV's Peace Note of 1917.

The great opponent of conscription was Cardinal Daniel Mannix, the Irish-born Archbishop of Melbourne. He had been chosen as a co-adjutor bishop in Australia as a strong figure who would fight hard and intelligently for Catholic schools there, and for the rights of the Australian Catholic community in general. He accepted perhaps because – and perhaps paradoxically – he was not originally thought of as enough of an Irish

---

5 Kester Aspden, *Fortress Church* (Leominster: Gracewing, 2002), p. 28.

nationalist to be given an Irish bishopric. This was a mistaken judgement. He was very much a nationalist, and regarded by the British government as dangerous, especially because he had been in the United States, while on his way to Rome, rallying support for the Irish cause. He had intended, after leaving America, to visit his mother in Ireland, but his liner the *Baltic* was intercepted by a British destroyer and the Cardinal was landed at Penzance. While in England he was, however, to do as he pleased apart from addressing large gatherings of Irishmen. This prohibition did not prevent a reception being held for him at the Cannon Street Hotel, which Bourne rather conspicuously failed to attend. He was widely believed by his fellow Catholics to be implicated in the arrest of Mannix and, though he denied it, the suspicion remained.

Mannix also administered the Last Rights of the Church to Terence MacSwiney, the Sinn Fein Lord Mayor of Cork who was arrested on charges of sedition, and imprisoned in Brixton gaol, within Peter Amigo's diocese. MacSwiney announced he would go on hunger strike until released, a tactic which had worked for him before, and for other IRA prisoners, but this time the government, which tried and failed to get the Vatican to condemn hunger striking as a tactic, stood firm. MacSwiney died on 25 October 1920, and Amigo gave him a funeral in Southwark Cathedral, an occasion which turned into a Sinn Fein celebration. There was nothing equivalent at Westminster Cathedral, though in mid-November there was a Requiem Mass for three British army officers who had been shot dead in their beds, while there was a service at Westminster Abbey for the nine non-Catholic officers killed at the same time.

After this, Bourne slightly modified his stance on Home Rule. He published a letter in *The Times* on 12 November arguing for self-government in Ireland, but as a country within the Empire.[6] He continued to blame the violence in Ireland on the

---

6 'The protection of the Empire is as important for Ireland as for us: and it is important for civilisation, I think, as for us both. Given *that*, I am for Irish

IRA, and the following February re-issued Manning's letter condemning Fenianism. Catholics, declared Bourne, could not be members of any secret society, but there was no mention of the reprisals by the British forces searching for the IRA. Much to the embarrassment of the English Catholic bishops, it was left to the Archbishop of Canterbury to condemn the reprisals in a speech before the House of Lords. Even the Belgian bishops issued a joint pastoral letter about the situation in Ireland. When at the Low Week meeting of 1921 the English bishops finally prevailed upon Bourne to write in protest to the Prime Minister, he did so in the third person, as if to distance himself. The Catholic Union protested against the interference, as they saw it, of the Belgians, which led the English bishops to turn against the Union – all of them, that is, except Bourne.

This subservience of the Cardinal to the government was far removed from his early years at Westminster, when the Liberal government under Herbert Asquith tried to ban a procession in London during the Eucharistic Congress of 1908, despite the fact that the Commissioner of the Metropolitan Police, himself a Catholic as it happened, had given permission. That in London was the nineteenth in the sequence of these gatherings of religious services and conferences dedicated to devotion to the Blessed Sacrament. The high point was commonly a final procession, carrying the Sacrament. A great deal of interest was aroused, and not just among Catholics, by the Conference, which was held from 9 to 13 September. For one thing, it was the first time a papal legate had arrived in London since the sixteenth century. It was also the largest collection of ecclesiastics, with episcopal representatives from Italy, France,[7] Spain,

---

self-government as far as the Irish people themselves desire it. I want England to trust Ireland and Ireland to trust England, for I love them both as I love justice and peace.' Gordon Wheeler, 'The Archdiocese of Westminster' in George Andrew Beck (ed.), *The English Catholics,* p. 177.

7 The Cardinal Archbishop of Toulouse was taken ill soon after arriving, and died in London after an operation.

Belgium and elsewhere, as well as from many countries of the Empire. But the government was edgy. There was a strong Nonconformist element in the Liberal Party, and the Protestant Alliance was also active in opposition. The Prime Minister wrote to Bourne on behalf of the government asking that the Eucharistic procession be abandoned. It went ahead, but without the Sacrament, the legate being accompanied by a dozen members of the House of Lords, led by the Duke of Norfolk, and by two French noblemen. Members of religious orders carried, rather than wore, their distinctive habits as a protest at the government's interference. There was a large, sympathetic and peaceful[8] crowd lining the street, and at the end of the procession the papal legate delivered a blessing from the balcony in front of Westminster Cathedral. It was something of a triumph for Bourne, and Pope Pius X was appreciative.

Triumphs were few. The cathedral choir won plaudits, but it was Vaughan, not Bourne, who had hired (Sir) Richard Terry as director of music, and when he retired he was replaced by two priests. Bourne took his responsibility for the enhancement of the cathedral seriously. After criticism of some of the mosaic work, he travelled to Italy to inspect mosaics in Monreale and elsewhere, but his own choice of artists often proved unsatisfactory, even to Bourne himself. He was, for instance, unhappy with the mosaic over the main door to the cathedral despite having himself chosen the artist. He eventually abolished his committee of artistic advisers on the grounds that when consulted they would only disagree among themselves. There was much talk of what Bentley, the cathedral's architect, had in mind, but Bourne removed his great crucifix hanging over the sanctuary (his successor replaced it). The one undoubted success during Bourne's period as Archbishop – undoubted now, but disputed at the time – was the commission

---

8 There was some talk of there having been scuffles, but if so they were not significant enough to make the pages of the papers.

to Eric Gill to produce the Stations of the Cross. However, the only part the Cardinal played in this was to express irritation at the delay of the artistic committee, then still in existence, in finding someone to do the work, and threatening to select someone himself. Gill was surprised to be chosen, having at the time only recently become a Catholic, and put the commission down to the fact that he was inexpensive. He himself hinted that Bourne was far from happy with the finished work.[9]

As had all the other bishops in England and Wales, Bourne had to contend with the challenge of a rising Catholic professional middle class. The Cardinal handled this with rather more success than did many of the other members of the hierarchy. His attitude was typified by his response to the publisher Frank Sheed: 'Don't ask my advice. Just tell me what you are doing. I'll stop you if I think it necessary.' He never did. Another time he put it more concisely: 'I never start anything. But I never stop anything.'[10] When Herbert Fisher introduced his Education Bill in 1917 (it became law in 1918), many Catholic bishops saw it as the end of the dual system which had served the Church well since 1902, and they wanted Bourne to lead a campaign against it. He refused to do so. He thought the bishops were over-reacting, and that the Fisher Act was, on the whole, beneficial. In this he was supported by the Catholic Teachers Federation which had been founded a dozen years earlier. Bishop Casartelli of Salford saw the intervention of the teachers in favour of the Act as an example of the laity trying to determine church policy – which perhaps they were, but in Bourne's view they were correct. Casartelli also founded the Catholic Federation to campaign specifically against the 1906 Education Act, but also to defend Catholic interests wherever they were under threat. This was in a sense a mobilization of the Catholic laity in the form of Catholic Action as envisaged by

---

9 Doyle, *op. cit.*, pp. 77–8, and 78–9 for Bourne's attitude to the mosaics.
10 Aspden, *op. cit.*, p. 43.

Pius X's 1905 encyclical *Il Fermo Proposito*: 'You clearly see, Venerable Brethren', the Pope wrote in paragraph 7, addressing the bishops of the world,

> the services rendered to the Church by those chosen bands of Catholics who aim to unite all their forces in combating anti-Christian civilization by every just and lawful means. They use every means in repairing the serious disorders caused by it. They seek to restore Jesus Christ to the family, the school and society by re-establishing the principle that human authority represents the authority of God. They take to heart the interests of the people, especially those of the working and agricultural classes, not only by inculcating in the hearts of everybody a true religious spirit (the only true fount of consolation among the troubles of this life) but also by endeavouring to dry their tears, to alleviate their sufferings, and to improve their economic condition by wise measures. They strive, in a word, to make public laws conformable to justice and amend or suppress those which are not so. Finally, they defend and support in a true Catholic spirit the rights of God in all things and the no less sacred rights of the Church.
>
> 8. All these works, sustained and promoted chiefly by lay Catholics and whose form varies according to the needs of each country, constitute what is generally known by a distinctive and surely a very noble name: 'Catholic Action', or the 'Action of Catholics'. At all times it came to the aid of the Church, and the Church has always cherished and blessed such help, using it in many ways according to the exigencies of the age.

And he went on in paragraph 11:

> Catholic Action, inasmuch as it proposes to restore all things in Christ, constitutes a real apostolate for the honour and glory of Christ Himself. To carry it out right one must have divine grace, and the apostle receives it only if he is united to

Christ. Only when he has formed Jesus Christ in himself shall he more easily be able to restore Him to the family and society. Therefore, all who are called upon to direct or dedicate themselves to the Catholic cause, must be sound Catholics, firm in faith, solidly instructed in religious matters, truly submissive to the Church and especially to this supreme Apostolic See and the Vicar of Jesus Christ.

The lay apostles were to be firmly under the control of the bishops. As an introduction to an English translation of the encyclical published in 1910 remarked, 'Christian Democracy is strictly bound to dependence on ecclesiastical authority by complete submission and obedience to the Bishops and their representatives.'[11]

The Catholic Federation spawned a short-lived Catholic political party which Bourne found an embarrassment for its anti-Liberal views – echoing those of Casartelli. He had to point out to the Westminster branch of the Federation that the members constituted a purely advisory body: they did not make policy. In Bourne's view they were not, at least en masse, even advisers. At the end of 1928 a large group of Catholic laymen, most of them prominent in public life, proposed that there should be parish councils as a forum for them to air their expertise on issues where the clergy might not be expected to be particularly skilled – money matters, for example, or property. Bourne ignored their approach, but when one of them returned to the issue some years later he was slapped down. Although both laity and bishops were firmly behind the campaign over education, on other matters their interests diverged. As Kester Aspden has shown,[12] while the laity, undoubtedly inspired by Pope Leo XIII's 1891 encyclical *Rerum Novarum*, often rather romantically and inaccurately described

---

11 *Ibid.*, p. 46.
12 *Ibid.*, pp. 45–6.

as 'The Workers' Charter', were discussing major social issues of the day, at their Low Week meetings the bishops were discussing more traditional moral issues. When the Catholic Social Guild held a meeting, chaired by the archbishop of Birmingham, during the 1910 National Catholic Congress in Leeds, Bourne and Amigo were presiding at a rival and much better attended meeting on temperance.

The bishops likewise were affected by *Rerum Novarum*. Some were hostile to trade unions, but this was a difficult stance to maintain when the papal encyclical had commended, not trade unions exactly, but 'guilds' rather in the medieval pattern, whose main purpose, according to Leo, was to see to the spiritual needs of their members. Bourne was, however, more sympathetic than most to the unions, reflecting what Aspden describes as his 'concern for the vulnerable'.[13] He had, however, clear and often expressed views on strikes. In a speech at Norwich in 1912 he insisted that before a strike could be called, the consequences had to be carefully considered to decide whether it was justified. The following year in Leicester he repeated the point, adding that he was opposed to general strikes, and to sympathy strikes by workers not directly affected by a dispute. It should not therefore have come as a surprise when, on 9 May 1926 and from the pulpit of his cathedral, he condemned the strike as without moral justification:

The time through which we are passing is of exceptional character, and the present strike is of a nature quite unlike the many others which have preceded it. It is necessary that Catholics should have clearly before their minds the moral principles which are involved:

1. There is no moral justification for a general strike of this character. It is a direct challenge to a lawfully constituted

---

13 *Ibid.*, p. 42. This concern was across the board: Aspden illustrates it by Bourne's decision to ban caning at the junior seminary.

authority and inflicts, without adequate reason, immense discomfort on millions of our fellow countrymen. It is therefore a sin against the obedience which we owe to God, who is the source of that authority; and against the charity and brotherly love which are due to our brethren.

2. All are bound to uphold and assist the Government, which is the lawfully constituted authority of the country, and represents, therefore, in its own appointed sphere, the authority of God himself.

3. As God alone can guide both rulers and ruled to a wise and successful understanding, it is the duty of all to pray earnestly and constantly for His guidance, that the day may be hastened when these unhappy conflicts shall terminate in a just and lasting peace.[14]

The message was indisputable: Catholics should not take part in the general strike. This was of course the message which Stanley Baldwin's government wanted to hear, and it was given considerable prominence in the newspapers and on radio. Baldwin afterwards wrote to thank the Cardinal: 'Your clear and strong pronouncement will be of the greatest value to the Government in the present crisis.'[15]

Aspden suggests[16] that Bourne's intervention has to be seen against the background not just of the strike but of the Roman Catholic Relief Bill then going through Parliament, which was to remove a number of the disabilities from which Catholics still suffered despite the Emancipation Act of 1829. But it is also true that he could argue that his position was entirely in keeping with the tenor of Catholic social doctrine. Naturally, although obedience to authority among Catholics was then far more readily accepted then than it has become, not all Catholics agreed with him, especially not the socially aware

14 Gordon Wheeler in Beck, *op. cit.*, pp. 178–9.
15 Aspden, *op. cit.*, p. 166.
16 *Ibid.*, pp. 164–7.

Catholics who were members of the Catholic Social Guild, founded by the Jesuit Charles Dominic Plater and others in 1909 to spread knowledge of the teachings of *Rerum Novarum.*

He also upset Randall Davidson, the Archbishop of Canterbury, who was attempting to mediate in the dispute. Davidson had tried to associate the Cardinal with his plea to the strikers and the employers to settle their differences, and thought that he had succeeded in doing so, but Bourne's position, unlike Davidson's, was that the strikers had to return to work before any negotiations could begin. There may have been a misunderstanding, but Davidson, who in 1920 had sponsored Bourne's membership of the Athenaeum Club, felt aggrieved, especially when the more militant opponents of the strike among his own clergy berated him for letting the Cardinal take the lead.

Although, as has been indicated, he had much earlier expressed reservations about a general strike and sympathy strikes, the fierceness of his support for the government against the strikers in 1926 was surprising. At the end of the First World War, and with the advice of members of the Catholic Social Guild – Plater in particular – he had written a highly regarded pastoral letter entitled *The Nation's Crisis* in which he appeared to sympathize with the discontent of the working class. In their unrest, he wrote, one could discern 'the true lineament of the Christian spirit'.[17] And although himself politically somewhat conservative, he came to the defence of the Labour Party which, in February 1918 had added to its constitution clause 4, calling for the 'common ownership of means of production'. This was evidently a socialist provision, and socialism had just as evidently been declared anathema in Leo XIII's *Rerum Novarum.* The leaders of the Catholic Social Guild had read widely about socialism, but managed to avoid having its own

---

17 Sheridan Gilley, 'The Years of Equipoise' in V. Alan McClelland and M. Hodgetts, *From Without the Flaminian Gate* (London: Darton, Longman and Todd, 1999), p. 44.

attitude towards it discussed at any of their conferences, lest, in the light of the encyclical, it scandalize their membership. Bishop Casartelli of Salford was strongly opposed to the Labour Party, and so, not surprisingly, was the Catholic Union. Bourne was more circumspect. The Labour Party's progamme, he wrote in 1924, 'contains nothing which threatens religion. No doubt there are extremists among them, but the Party as such has nothing in common with the Socialists of the Continent.' He had to repeat this endorsement after Pius XI's encyclical *Quadragesimo Anno* of 1931, with its renewed condemnation of socialism: 'I think it will be generally admitted that very few members of the Labour Party would base their desire for social reform on the principles which His Holiness has so rightly and so strongly condemned.'[18]

Given this general attitude on the part of Bourne, it is not surprising that he backed the initiative of the Catholic Social Guild to take part in the Conference on Christian Politics, Economics and Citizenship, which was to take place in 1924. The conference was the brainchild of William Temple, who late in 1920 became Bishop of Manchester – he was to move to York in 1929 and succeeded Cosmo Gordon Lang as Archbishop of Canterbury in 1942.[19] It was Temple's hope that the Conference would contribute a Christian dimension to the post-war reconstruction, and also that it would be attended by Christians from all the major denominations. Catholics being Catholics, they felt it necessary to ask permission of their bishops, without whose approval, of course, there could be no formal Catholic involvement. The bishops agreed to establish a 12-person delegation. It was a mixed bunch, but certainly on the whole competent, but when they reported back to the bishops the experiment in ecumenical co-operation came to a swift halt. Not all of the bishops had been sympathetic, both because of the leftward-leaning tenor of the conference preparations, and

---

18 *Ibid.*
19 He died in October 1944.

precisely because of the ecumenical aspect – Pope Pius XI was shortly after expressly to forbid Catholics to engage in conferences with non-Catholics.[20] The reasons for the disenchantment of many, though not all, of the delegates were various. Some discovered a strong element of pacifism among the Anglicans and others; there were those who thought it too socialist. But one has the impression that the underlying issue was the belief of the Catholic delegates that the Church's social teaching had the answer, only to find that members of other Churches were not immediately convinced. One has the impression that there was an element of arrogance on the part of some at least of the Catholics.

At the same time as this failure of an ecumenical initiative, another was grinding slowly forward. After their rebuff over Anglican Orders (see above, pp. 77ff), the Abbé Portal and the indefatigable Lord Halifax, now well into his eighties, had not given up. Under the presidency of Cardinal Mercier, the Archbishop of Malines in Belgium, they had launched the 'Malines conversations' between 1923 and 1925, discussions between Anglican theologians and Catholic ones, though the latter were continental rather than English. When the idea was first mooted, Halifax went to see Cardinal Bourne and found him, he informed Portal, 'completely sympathetic'.[21] That is not the common understanding of Bourne, who is often presented as firmly opposed to the talks. The cause of this misunderstanding is Bourne's biographer, Ernest Oldmeadow,[22] who was also in charge of *The Tablet*, chosen from a dozen candidates (G. K. Chesterton was considered) by the Cardinal himself in 1923. As editor Oldmeadow went to see the Cardinal every Thursday at 4.30 to receive his instructions, and he ran the paper, in the view of one writer on the English Catholic press 'in the closest

---

20 In the encyclical *Mortalium Animos* of 1928.
21 Dick, *op. cit.*, p. 71. The meeting of Bourne and Halifax took place on 28 November 1921.
22 On Oldmeadow, see Michael Walsh, *The Tablet*, pp. 33–45.

conformity with the views of the Cardinal. The curious thing about this partnership was that . . . there was hardly any discernible similarity of outlook between Cardinal Bourne and Ernest Oldmeadow.'[23]

The second part of that quotation is undoubtedly true, the first part less so, as was demonstrated by *The Tablet*'s treatment of the Malines conversations. At the very beginning of 1924 Cardinal Mercier wrote a pastoral letter on the meetings. The letter was very positive. It stressed that, though these were conversations and not negotiations, they were taking place with the approval of 'the supreme authority', that is to say, the approval of Pope Pius XI. Oldmeadow, who was a convert to Catholicism, though from Nonconformity rather than from Anglicanism, treated the letter with disdain. 'It is a futile and prolix document', he wrote to Canon Moyes, Bourne's theologian, who had, over a quarter of a century before, been involved with the issue of Anglican Orders. Bourne, on the other hand, was delighted with the pastoral. 'Give it the most sympathetic and cordial treatment', he wrote to Oldmeadow, 'and quote largely from it.'[24] He himself then wrote a pastoral, *The Union of Christendom* for Lent 1924.

The conversations progressed well. A number of central issues were discussed and agreed upon. Those opposed to talk of reunion, particularly a group of three Jesuits of whom Francis Woodlock was the chief, became alarmed. In the issue of *The Tablet* for October 1925 he published a long letter criticizing the tenor of the discussions. Ultramontanism and Catholicism, he said, are one and the same thing. The views of the continental Catholic theologians diverge very sharply from English Catholic theologians precisely on the authority of the pope. Bourne was disturbed by what he read in Woodlock's

---

23 J. J. Dwyer, 'The Catholic Press, 1850–1950' in Beck, *op. cit.*, p. 487.
24 Quotations from Dick, *op. cit.*, pp. 122 and 123. When the Vatican newspaper, *L'Osservatore Romano*, published Mercier's pastoral, the editor omitted the reference to 'the supreme Authority', though at this point Pius XI was sympathetic.

piece, and wrote a rather peevish letter to Mercier complaining 'I have been treated as if I did not exist.'[25] In Dick's view he saw himself as the counterpart to Randall Davidson, and should have been treated as such, whereas those engaged in the debates regarded Rome as the equivalent of Davidson. That in itself was a bad mistake for those in Rome – Gasquet, Merry del Val, were far more opposed to the conversations than was Bourne. But there was also an underlying theological issue: there was a suggestion that Canterbury should be seen as a patriarchate, relating to Rome. The corporate reunion left the existing English Catholic hierarchy on the sidelines.

This realization turned Bourne against the conversations (though not against reunion talks as such), and he in turn spoke to Pius XI, and turned the Pope also against them. When in April 1927 he went to York to celebrate the 1,300th anniversary of the Minster's foundation, he preached a surprisingly hostile sermon in St Wilfrid's church. The Church of England, he said, 'is in no way connected in faith or in ecclesiastical law or authority with the Catholic Church which, from the days of Paulinus until the religious upheaval of the sixteenth century was the sole spiritual teacher and guide of the people of this city and of this country'.[26]

The rest of the bishops in the English and Welsh Catholic hierarchy, or most of them, would have echoed such sentiments, but generally Bourne ploughed his own furrow, especially after the row over the division of dioceses. He was a loner, and appears to have preferred it that way. Evelyn Waugh said of him that he was a man 'singularly disqualified from normal social intercourse'.[27] His predecessor had been an advocate of

---

25 Dick, *op. cit.*, p. 157.
26 *Ibid.*, p. 172. Bourne was even less sympathetic towards the Jews. When, after persecution of the Jews began in Germany, his response was that he condemned persecution of whatever kind, but Catholics had been persecuted too, in Mexico, in Spain and in Russia, and he had not heard Jews raise cries of protest.
27 *Ibid.*, p. 52.

a central seminary at Oscott near Birmingham, and this had worked. Of the original nine diocesan seminaries under Manning (those of Westminster, Birmingham, Liverpool, Leeds, Nottingham, Northampton, Clifton and Southwark, and that of the Northern bishops at Ushaw), only Liverpool and Southwark retained their own – over the latter, of course, Bourne had presided. A single major seminary might have provided the nucleus for a Catholic institute of higher study in Britain, as in theory Bourne himself wanted, but it was not to be. A central seminary would at least have provided a better standard of education for the clergy. Instead, as soon as he was appointed, he started his own seminary at St Edmund's, Ware. In 1904 he built Allen Hall as a house for the 'divines', as students for the priesthood were called, and when it burned down a decade later he rebuilt it again in even more splendid fashion. He also added the Galilee Chapel for the divines, in which he was to be interred.

Whatever Bourne's own particular reasons for withdrawing his students from Oscott (and also from the English college in Valladolid in Spain), they reflected the constant failing of the English bishops to act together for the good of the Church in England as a whole. Each was conscious of his own authority within his own diocese. But Bourne, although himself no scholar, was unlike the other bishops in having been educated in France (as a consequence he spoke the language fluently) under a much more theologically liberal regime than that prevailing in England. He was always suspect in Rome for not having been educated at the English College and for his reluctance to send his seminarians to Rome for theological studies. But there was also an issue over Modernism.

Modernism is difficult to define. It was a movement among Catholic intellectuals from the late nineteenth century until the early twentieth century to bring the Church's traditional teachings into line with contemporary scholarship, both historical scholarship and the natural sciences: St George Mivart was a casualty of the latter. There was also a strong philosophical element beneath it, and impatience with scholastic theology.

As 'the synthesis of all heresies' it was formally condemned by the decree *Lamentabili* and the encyclical *Pascendi* as well as, insofar as biblical interpretation was concerned, by decrees of the Vatican's Biblical Commission. These decrees, Pope Pius X instructed, both those already issued and those still to be issued, were to be treated as if they were the decrees of the Pope himself.[28]

Mivart apart, the chief and perhaps the only significant person to be condemned for holding Modernist views, was the Jesuit George Tyrrell, but his biographer Maude Petre was refused Catholic burial in Southwark, though Bourne's successor granted her a requiem in Westminster.[29] From Tyrell's death in 1909 until her own in 1942 she was, at least in theory, banned from receiving Communion in Amigo's diocese but was in practice free to do so in the Diocese of Westminster. In 1907 Bourne wrote to Merry del Val, the Cardinal Secretary of State under Pius X, that Modernism was insignificant in England, but Amigo appears to have suspected him of sympathizing with the Modernists, and told Rome so – though he denied it. As a consequence of the Modernist crisis, Rome demanded a 'vigilance committee' in every diocese to discover and censure anyone thought to be harbouring Modernist convictions. The required vigilance committee was especially active in Amigo's diocese, but not in Bourne's, or, for that matter, elsewhere in England and Wales.

Sheridan Gilley suggests that 'some of the most brilliant of its [i.e. the Catholic Church's] converts were primarily attracted to Rome by its resolute resistance to Modernism, in contrast to the Church of England'. Gilley goes on to quote Ronald Knox: 'I came into the Church, it seems to me, in a white heat of orthodoxy, Manning's disciple rather than Newman's; and

---

28 The decrees have since been rescinded.
29 The requiem took place at the Convent of the Assumption, Kensington Square, London. She was buried alongside Tyrrell in the Church of England graveyard at Storrington in Sussex.

when I took the anti-Modernist oath it was something of a disappointment that the Vicar General was not there to witness
the fervour I put into it – he had gone out to order tea.'[30] But
the peak of the conversions occurred in 1920, long after the
'white heat', such as it was in England, had gone out of the
controversy, and an end had effectively been put to the witch-
hunt by the death of Pius X and the accession of Pope Benedict
XV. In any case, the notable conversions under Bourne's
presidency of the Church in England were for the most part of
literary and artistic figures rather than those whose concern
was theological. In that, his episcopacy differed sharply from
those of Wiseman and Manning.[31]

Apart from his visits to Rome on official business, he travelled
abroad fairly frequently. He went to Canada in 1910 and to
Poland in 1927. He was twice in France for celebrations concerned with Joan of Arc, in 1929 and 1931: on the second occasion he was acting as papal legate. He went to the Eucharistic
Congress in Dublin in 1932. But his most significant journey was
that to the Near East, undertaken soon after the First World War.
The ostensible reason for his trip was to visit Catholics serving in
the British Navy: the real reason was the desire by the British
government that some senior Catholic should travel there to
calm fears that in its mandated territories it would promote
Protestantism in the region to the detriment of Catholicism and
Orthodoxy. He referred obliquely to this concern in a speech he
delivered in French in Cairo: 'There is one word in your address
of welcome which is not acceptable. You have spoken of my
country as a Protestant State . . . I would rather say that our
Government is a Christian Government . . . From my own
experience I can declare there is nothing to fear. One may
openly be a Catholic, a practising and even militant Catholic.'[32]

---

30 Gilley, *art. cit.*, pp. 37–8.
31 On conversions, see Michael Walsh, 'Catholics, Society and Popular
   Culture' in McClelland, *op. cit.*, pp. 356–60.
32 Wheeler, *art. cit.*, pp. 179–80.

This visit, and the sermon on the general strike just over half a dozen years later, were Bourne's most public interventions in the life of the nation. Aspden suggests that Bourne, and the rest of the hierarchy in England, withdrew from what has come to be called 'the public square': he entitles chapter 4 in *Fortress Church* 'The Eclipse of Social Catholicism 1924–1935', and instances the cancellation of a Catholic Social Guild conference on housing in 1934 on the instructions of the Cardinal. Bourne did not want criticism to be voiced of the housing policy of the Municipal Reform Party, led by a Catholic, at the time of the London County Council elections which would have coincided with the conference. He feared that the conference might influence Catholics against the Municipal Reform Party and in favour of Labour, which would, he believed, be detrimental to the Church's policy on schools. During the depression in the 1930s the bishops did not speak out about housing, possibly fearing that slum clearance might disrupt parish life. But nor did they raise the issue of unemployment.

Gordon Wheeler, an Anglican clergyman who converted to Catholicism the year after Bourne's death and eventually became a bishop, wrote of the Cardinal:

> Throughout his life Archbishop Bourne developed a singularly harmonious relationship with the Government. The 'silent Cardinal' was always dignified, never irresponsible. He could speak when need be; never without necessity, and this was increasingly appreciated and stood the Church in this country in the greatest good stead. His happy relations with the first Lord Baden-Powell and his encouragement of scouting for Catholics reflect his realisation of civic values and ideals of service in the Commonwealth of nations.[33]

---

33 Wheeler, *art. cit.*, p. 175.

This is a very positive assessment of Bourne, but in the eyes and of many the 'silent Cardinal' was shy and remote. Even those who admired him found him cold and reserved – but efficient, and it was for his organizational skills that he had been chosen.

There is a curious reflection on his episcopacy from the Archbishop of Canterbury, Cosmo Lang. Lang had been asked his advice as to whether, in the event of the Cardinal's death (this was a year before), King George V should send a representative to the funeral. Lang advised against. It cannot be said, he wrote in January 1934 to the King's Private Secretary,

> . . . that Cardinal Bourne with all his merits has occupied a place of very distinguished leadership in the national life compared with Cardinal Manning, or in the sphere of learning compared with Cardinal Gasquet, or in the sphere of international life like Cardinal Mercier. He is more in the position of Cardinal Vaughan though not even as prominent as he was in general social life.[34]

He died at Archbishop's House, Westminster, on the first day of 1935.

---

34 Thomas Moloney, *Westminster, Whitehall and the Vatican* (Tunbridge Wells: Burns and Oates, 1985), p. 83.

5

Arthur Hinsley

It is surely rare that one cardinal writes the biography of another; nonetheless, the first life of Arthur Hinsley was produced by the future Cardinal Heenan just a year after the former's death.[1] Heenan's book begins with the funeral which marked Hinsley's passing, 'an event of unique significance . . . one of the most important events in the Cardinal's life', wrote Heenan,[2] a claim which he illustrated with a lengthy series of quotations from the British national press. 'The greatest English Cardinal since Wolsey', wrote the *Daily Mail*, 'and probably the best loved Cardinal England has ever had.'[3]

He was a Yorkshireman, born on 25 August 1865 at Carlton, a small village near Selby where his father Thomas was a joiner: his mother Bridget Ryan was from County Galway. When he reached the age of eleven he was sent to Ushaw College as a possible candidate for the priesthood, and in 1890 went on to the English College in Rome after completing, the previous year, an external BA at London University. In Rome he was awarded the degree of Doctor of Divinity, and in 1894 returned to Ushaw to lecture in moral theology and to catalogue the college's library which was, and remains, a vast collection of historic importance.

---

1 John C. Heenan, *Cardinal Hinsley* (London: Burns, Oates and Washbourne, 1944).
2 *Ibid.*, p. 6.
3 *Ibid.*, p. 8.

His stay at Ushaw as a teacher in the seminary was short: his methods of instruction were not approved of. In 1897 he was sent to Keighley as a curate, and two years later founded St Bede's Grammar School in Bradford, serving as its headmaster. But again his methods met with disapproval, and he fell out not just with the school's governors but with his bishop as well. In 1904, therefore, he sought, and was granted, permission to move dioceses: he was incardinated in Southwark where he became close to Bishop Amigo who used him as an emissary to Rome during his dispute with Cardinal Bourne (see above, p. 89). He served first as a chaplain to a convent near Brighton, and afterwards administered the parish at Sutton Park while lecturing in Church History at the seminary at Wonersh. In 1911 he became parish priest at Sydenham.

And then, unexpectedly to most people, though Hinsley himself had an inkling of it, in 1917 he was appointed to be Rector of the English College in Rome. At the time of his appointment the Venerabile was described by one member of staff as 'a down-at-heel college, with a great past, an unworthy present and a problematic future'.[4] There had been, shortly before he arrived, a formal visitation of the College which had highlighted a number of issues – lack of administrative structures, poor discipline among the students, no proper spiritual direction, the entanglement with the Beda, a college for older students founded in Wiseman's day partly for convert clergy, which shared the same premises. The Cardinal Protector[5] of the College was Aidan Gasquet, and it appears to have been Gasquet who wanted Hinsley as Rector. Several of the English bishops had their doubts: his career hitherto, or so it seemed to them, had been beset by problems and, although his talents were recognized, he had been originally recommended for the

---

4 Schofield and Skinner, *op. cit.*, p. 195.
5 According to the college constitution, the Cardinal Protector stood in the same relation to the Venerabile as a bishop did to his diocesan seminary.

Beda rather than the Venerabile. His name had not appeared on the list of the possible Rectors of the English College.

Nonetheless, he was appointed and got down to work with the speed, and the energy, which were typical of him. He did so despite continued opposition from the Roman Association, a group in England which raised money for the College, and now refused to release the funds until ordered to do so by a Cardinal from the Congregation of Seminaries. Hinsley brought in nuns to look after the domestic arrangements, sold the former villa (summer residence)[6] house and bought another, the (still) much admired Palazzola in the Alban hills not far from the papal summer residence at Castel Gandolfo. A spiritual adviser for the students was brought in, a college magazine was started, the practice of putting on an annual Gilbert and Sullivan operetta was begun. Hinsley even succeeded in fighting off Mussolini, when his plans for the development of Rome entailed a destruction of part of the college property: here Hinsley was aided by a campaign in the British national press. More importantly for the future of the English Catholic Church, a considerable number of whose bishops were students during his regime, Hinsley considerably improved the academic standard of those in his charge, some of whom went on to higher, or more specialized, degrees in the various Roman institutes. In the first volume of his autobiography, Heenan provides a picture of life at the Venerabile:

> Mgr Hinsley, while treating his students as men, maintained firm discipline. He trusted them so long as he regarded them as trustworthy. A man of moods, he was liable to become unduly depressed by occasional transgressors. He was, on the other hand, excessively elated if an English student scored an outstanding success at the university. Because he was the most humane of disciplinarians, the students

---

6 The students did not usually return to England in the summer vacation.

loved him and made allowance for his occasional moodiness.[7]

Given the success of his rectorship, it is not surprising that he was thought of as a bishop, in charge of an English diocese. He was, however, also thought to be doing too good a job to remove from the Venerabile, and was left in post, even after being raised to the episcopacy in the college chapel by Cardinal Merry del Val, who had been a fellow student at Ushaw, in August 1926. But the bishopric presaged a change of post, intended at first to be temporary. In 1927 he was made Apostolic Visitor to British Africa, based in Mombasa. He enjoyed the job greatly, and got on well not only with the Africans but with the colonial administration, whose officials appreciated what the Church was doing for education as much as Hinsley appreciated the support the church schools were receiving from the Colonial Office. He had expected to return to his office at the Venerabile, but it was not to be. In 1930 he was raised in rank to the status of Archbishop, which meant resigning the Rectorship, and given the post of Apostolic Delegate[8] to British Africa. He retained the post until 1934 and a bout of typhoid, which meant his returning to Rome. There he contracted eczema, and it was decided that he should retire from his post and be granted a canonry in St Peter's. He was, after all, in his late sixties.

And then, on 25 March 1935, it was announced that he had been named Archbishop of Westminster in succession to Cardinal Bourne. It was a surprise appointment, not least to Hinsley himself, and he attempted to dissuade Pope Pius XI. Pius, who

---

7 John C. Heenan, *Not the Whole Truth* (London: Hodder and Stoughton, 1971), pp. 52–3.

8 An Apostolic Delegate is not formally a diplomatic position, though it is fairly parallel. A Delegate represents the papacy to a country's Catholic Church, whereas a Nuncio, the term the Vatican uses for ambassador, represents the Vatican to a country's government.

admired Hinsley, was not to be moved. It proved to be an inspired choice. In place of the imperious Bourne, Westminster had a prelate who was 'warm-hearted and avuncular',[9] though not averse to standing on his privileges, as a clash with Downey of Liverpool over the prerogatives of Westminster swiftly demonstrated. As Evelyn Waugh wrote of him, 'though he was an old and ailing man, [he] was a grateful refreshment to English Catholics inside and outside the Archdiocese. There was now at the head of the hierarchy a man amenable to suggestions, of deep human sympathies, who was also a shrewd judge of men, able and willing to recognize diversities of character and talent in his subordinates.'[10] He had retained a good deal of his early energy, and he needed it. A whole series of events almost immediately crowded in upon him.

One of them was the future of *The Tablet*. The paper had been bequeathed to the Archbishop of Westminster by its then owner, Cardinal Vaughan, at a time when its profits were considerable. This was no longer the case: it had become a financial liability, and with his penchant to sort out the accounts, Hinsley decided to get rid of it. His solicitor advised him of a young Catholic publisher, Tom Burns, who might be persuaded to take it on, and it was handed over for a modest sum to Burns and to his friend Douglas Woodruff who became the paper's editor from 1936.[11]

There was almost immediately a problem. Woodruff decided to serialize in the paper Alfred Noyes's study of Voltaire,

---

9 Aspden, *op. cit.*, p. 196.
10 Evelyn Waugh, *Ronald Knox* (London: Chapman and Hall, 1959), pp. 243–4.
11 This account differs somewhat from that told in Tom Burns' own memoir, *The Use of Memory* (London: Sheed and Ward, 1993), pp. 144–5, and follows that given my myself in *The Tablet: A Commemorative History*, pp. 42–3, where the evidence can be found. The divergence is of some importance because Hinsley is often credited with great foresight in handing the weekly back to lay ownership. The decision was, however, clearly taken not on any anachronistic conception on the part of Hinsley about the role of the laity, but simply because the paper was losing money.

published by the Catholic firm of Sheed and Ward. Then Rome informed Hinsley that the book had to be withdrawn from circulation or it would be put on the 'Index of Forbidden Books'. Noyes at first seemed ready to comply, but then wrote a letter to *The Times* criticizing Rome's decision: he later reissued the volume with a non-religious publisher. Noyes was one of the high-profile literary converts to the Church, and when he hired lawyers who worked for the Archbishop of Canterbury, Hinsley was afraid he was about to revert to his earlier faith. The Archbishop of Westminster was embarrassed by the whole affair, and wrote a private letter of support to Noyes, but also wrote to Amigo complaining about Sheed and Ward: 'I have given Sheed an ultimatum. It is neither fair to us or publishers to act in such an independent way. Sheed answers me that my predecessor told him not to trouble about the matter.'[12]

Some of the problems were perennial ones. There was to be a new Education Act, one which would raise the school leaving age to fifteen and enable local councils to make grants of up to three-quarters of the cost of building new schools. The catch was that the denominations would have to surrender their right to appoint teachers. Some of the bishops wanted to reject the proposals out of hand; Hinsley was for negotiating, and tried to take his episcopal colleagues with him. One immediate sign of the difference between himself and his predecessor was his manner of tackling the issue. He consulted widely and formed advisory committees rather than attempt to decide the matter himself. But even that was resented. At their autumn meeting in 1935 the bishops had agreed on a strategy: parliamentary candidates were to be questioned about their stance on the Catholic schools issue. As a newcomer to the English political scene, Hinsley thought he ought to consult the Catholic Education Council about how to go about this – or, indeed, if it was even advisable. The Archbishop of Cardiff got to hear of this, and berated Hinsley on the grounds that had

---

12 Aspden, *op. cit.*, p. 198. See also Michael Walsh, *op. cit.*, pp 52–3.

the bishops wished to consult with others they would have already done so. But they did not, so they had not.

Hinsley was aware that he did not have the same degree of expertise, gained over many years of negotiations, as did some of his fellow bishops. A preliminary scheme for what became (after the Cardinal's death) the 1944 Education Act was drawn up in 1941 under R. A. Butler as president of the Board of Education. Hinsley met Butler, but told him to consult others better informed than himself. Amigo was the chairman of the negotiating team, but the members kept changing, much to Butler's irritation and bewilderment.

Another problem inherited from his predecessor was what to do about Catholic Action. It had never got properly under way in most parts of England and Wales, and the bishops as a body were too tied up with the education debate to be able to give it much attention. At their October meeting in 1935 the bishops belatedly decided to establish a National Board of Catholic Action, of which Hinsley was to be president. The first thing he did was to commission a survey of all Catholic organizations and societies operating in parishes. Hinsley appeared to envisage a rather complex bureaucracy to run Catholic Action; his colleagues on the bench of bishops appeared to be uneasy about the whole thing – not the fact of Catholic Action itself, but the notion that people would be elected to parish councils, though the priests were to vet candidates and to appoint two-thirds of the members. Much more stress seemed to be laid, in the planning stages, on the spiritual formation of the laity, and little on what they were actually going to do – other than that which they were already engaged in through existing parish organizations. The task was vast, and, like the other bishops, Hinsley had already quite enough to do. His solution was to have David Mathew, a historian and chaplain to the Catholic students at London University, made a bishop, and hand the problem over to him. Then the war came along, and the structure envisaged for Catholic Action fell apart.

Hinsley, although himself no bureaucrat, had a firm belief in structures. Soon after his arrival in Westminster he established a much-needed Schools Commission, and he also set up a powerful Board of Finance. As his hiving off *The Tablet* demonstrated, he was determined to get the diocese's finances under control. To that end he set up a separate trust to administer all the funds and legacies with which the diocese, over the years, had been endowed. He was concerned that no more money should be raised for the further ornamentation of the cathedral when there were so many other calls on the diocesan finances, but he was perfectly ready to allow money already raised to be spent. He was determined that it should be spent well: another issue for which he thought it best to consult a committee.

A further immediate issue, though in this instance one much to the Archbishop's liking, was the canonization of John Fisher and Thomas More. Naturally proud of the lives – and deaths – of these two English martyrs of the Reformation, Hinsley wondered whether King George V might not be represented at the ceremony in St Peter's. He made the request through the British Minister to the Holy See, but Lord Fitzalan made a similar suggestion to the King himself. The Foreign Office was alarmed. In the simplest terms, Fisher and More had been executed for rejecting royal authority. It would be paradoxical if the royal house now chose to be represented. There was a further consideration. There were Catholic territories – Malta and Ireland – which were discontented with their links to the British Crown: would this event further fuel their unrest? In the end the Crown was not represented, though the British Minister attended, as did the wife of the British Ambassador in Rome.

The concern over Malta arose at least in part from fear of Italian expansionism under Mussolini's Fascist regime. Mussolini's sights, however, were set on Africa rather than on the Mediterranean: on 30 October 1935 Italy invaded Abyssinia. The League of Nations voted in favour of sanctions against Italy. The Vatican had never been greatly enamoured of the

League, and the perception, at least in England, was that although Pius XI had formally condemned Fascism, as an Italian he was sympathetic to Mussolini's imperial aspirations.[13] In an effort to defend the Pope, Hinsley described Pius in a sermon delivered at the church in Golders Green as 'a helpless old man', which hardly endeared him to the Vatican.[14] Nor did he improve relations when in a note to Eugenio Pacelli, the Cardinal Secretary of State (and future Pope) he said it was imperative for the Holy See to separate itself from the government of Italy and to support the League of Nations as the means of settling Italian claims on Africa. In practice the Holy See was having difficulty in communicating with the British government, a fact which led to the establishment of an Apostolic Delegation in London, but this story can be more conveniently told in the chapter on Cardinal Godfrey (see below, p. 158f).

Hinsley left few in doubt about his personal attitude to Fascism. When a Catholic wrote to him about his standing as a British Union of Fascists candidate in a parliamentary election in February 1938, he responded that he had nothing against any political party as such, but any party must 'avoid anything

---

13 The British Foreign Secretary, Sir Samuel Hoare, advised British representatives abroad that 'the voice of the Vatican has come to be scarcely distinguishable from that of the Italian government'. Moloney, *op. cit.*, p. 53.

14 As Heenan in *Not the Whole Truth*, pp. 98–9, records it, what Hinsley said was 'What can the Pope do to prevent this [i.e. the Italian invasion of Abyssinia] or any other war? He is a helpless old man with a small police force to guard himself, to guard the priceless treasures of the Vatican, to protect his diminutive State . . . He could excommunicate [Mussolini] and place [Italy] under an interdict. Thus he would make war with his dictator neighbour inevitable besides upsetting the peace and consciences of the great majority of Italians . . . The Pope is not an arbitrator. He was expressly excluded by the secret Pact of London in 1915 from future deliberations in the Councils of Peace.' It was after this no doubt correct but unfortunately phrased remark that Hinsley attempted to get Heenan, then a curate in Barking, which lies in the Diocese of Brentwood, seconded to his own staff. The Bishop of Brentwood refused to release his priest, but from then on Hinsley made increasing use of Heenan to write his speeches or broadcasts, and then to write and speak on behalf of the Church in England.

that makes the State or government or party supreme master of the personal dignity of man'.[15] Less than a year later, in a speech in Birmingham, he was taking a harder line, associating Fascism with Nazism and Communism. There were many among English Catholics, however, who were far more sympathetic to Oswald Mosley's party than Hinsley. In his *Fascism and Providence*, published by Sheed and Ward, J. K. Heydon wrote: 'Fascism, in fact, is of Catholic origin and no English Catholic has a scintilla of right to condemn the Nazis. Catholics who do, and there are some few who are busying themselves considerably, may be found to be fighting against God.' Kester Aspden, who quotes this passage, points out that Heydon's book did not carry Hinsley's imprimatur.[16]

The Spanish version of Fascism, however, was, as far as the English episcopacy was concerned, quite another matter. In theory, and despite the Joint Pastoral Letter of 1936 which attacked the 'anti-God forces' (i.e. the Republicans), the bishops adopted a position of neutrality during the Spanish Civil War. But inevitably, perhaps, they were sympathetic to Franco's 'crusade', as was the Vatican – though the Vatican refused formally to recognize Franco's government as the legitimate government of Spain until May 1938 despite the Generalissimo's promptings. There were a number of English Catholics who were opposed to the bishops' attitude. Francis Drinkwater, a parish priest in Birmingham and editor of the catechetical magazine *The Sower*, wrote to the virulently pro-Franco weekly the *Catholic Herald* under its editor Michael de la Bedoyère, to question support for Franco. Hinsley wrote back, 'Your utterances are beyond explanation. I regret your imprudence, your own inaccuracy and ill-timed, ill-placed outburst.' Similarly, when a group of Catholics wrote directly to the bishops, Hinsley condemned their letter's 'lack of discrimination and judgement'.[17]

---

15 *Ibid.*, p. 59.
16 Aspden, *op. cit.*, pp. 216–17.
17 *Ibid.*, pp. 220 and 222.

The bishops set up a fund for the Relief of Spanish Distress. It was intended to help all suffering from the ravages of the Civil War, but in practice much of the money went to providing mobile ambulances for Franco's troops. When a large number of Basque children were sent by the Basque government out of the war zone for their safety, and arrived in England, Hinsley was extremely suspicious, regarding them as Communist sympathizers, and their evacuation as a political ploy – which it quite possibly was.

There was a further complication in the attitude of the League of Nations Union, a support organization for the League of Nations, of which 'the secular saint' Gilbert Murray, Regius Professor of Greek at Oxford, was a foundation member and enthusiastic supporter. There was a good deal of support for the LNU from Catholics, including by Rosalind Murray, Gilbert Murray's daughter and wife of Arnold Toynbee, a convert to Catholicism whose book *The Good Pagan's Failure* reflected on the lives of her father and mother. The secretary of the LNU was a Catholic, John Eppstein, and the Cardinal was among the Union's honorary vice-presidents. The Vatican itself never whole-heartedly committed itself to the League of Nations, especially after the League brought sanctions against Italy after the invasion of Abyssinia.

The problem for Hinsley was that the LNU increasingly aligned itself with the Republican cause in Spain. A further difficulty was the attempt by Lord Robert Cecil to associate the LNU with his International Peace Campaign. The IPC was regarded by many Catholics as a Communist front organization, and something altogether distinct from the LNU, but when Eppstein made fun of the IPC he nearly lost his job.[18] The bishops as a body decided to disassociate themselves from the LNU at their April 1938 meeting: the Cardinal himself eventually resigned from the LNU, after several times threatening to do so, in December 1938. 'Your Eminence's action will be

---

18 Eppstein had been private secretary to Cecil.

received with great pleasure by the governments of Berlin and Rome', wrote Cecil.[19]

Hinsley's support for Franco was not wholly uncritical. He kept a signed photograph of him on his desk which had to be removed, as the actor Robert Speaight records, when a BBC team went to interview him,[20] but in 1942 the Cardinal – he became a Cardinal on 13 December 1937 – wrote to Anthony Eden, the Foreign Secretary, asking him to investigate reports that the Generalissimo was persecuting Protestants.

Nor was he similarly uncritical of the actions of the British government in Northern Ireland. He tried to build bridges with the Irish hierarchy, especially with regard to the vast number of Irish immigrants in Britain. And, almost immediately on his appointment, he approached Cosmo Lang, the Archbishop of Canterbury, as someone whom, he thought, would have more influence than he with the government, to protest at discrimination against Catholics. Lang said he would do so, but confessed he did not think the government would pay heed,[21] which they didn't. When three IRA bombs went off in London in June 1939, however, Hinsley spoke out strongly against such acts of terrorism. He also attacked the IRA itself, declaring that members of any organization which plotted against Church or State were subject to excommunication, and would be refused the sacraments – a statement for which he was roundly condemned by the IRA's Army Council. When a number of IRA prisoners in English gaols began a hunger strike he tried to get the bishops with such prisoners in their dioceses to adopt a common strategy, stating that such action was morally wrong. There were three bishops involved, and Hinsley received three different answers, but in the end the prisoners gave up their strike, and the mettle of the bishops was never tested.

---

19 Aspden, *op. cit.*, p. 208.
20 Robert Speaight, *The Property Basket* (London: Collins and Harvill Press, 1970), p. 220.
21 Lang took to Hinsley, and in February 1938 proposed him for membership of the Athenaeum.

Even though he was so vigorously opposed to the IRA, he pleaded for the lives of two IRA prisoners condemned to death, writing directly to the Prime Minister Neville Chamberlain, but to no avail. Two years later he wrote again to the Prime Minister, by this time Winston Churchill, asking him to spare the lives of six men condemned to death: five were reprieved. He also wrote to Churchill, though this time without success, asking him not to make the Ulster Defence Volunteers, the Northern Irish equivalent of the Home Guard, part of the hated B Specials.

It was the Second World War which thrust Hinsley into the forefront of national life, and occasioned the alleged remark of Winston Churchill when Cosmo Lang announced his retirement as Archbishop of Canterbury in January 1942, 'It is a pity we can't have that old man at Westminster.'[22] But he was kept busy even in the run-up to the outbreak of hostilities. There was the question of whether the British Prime Minister and the Foreign Secretary should call on the pope when they went to Rome for talks with Mussolini. Neither wanted to do so, but the advice from the Foreign Office was that they should pay a courtesy call, if only to distance themselves from Hitler who had refused to call on the pope when in Rome in May 1938.[23] Pacelli, apparently, had no high opinion of either.[24] After the death of Pius XI, Eugenio Pacelli was elected on 2 March 1939 as his successor. Hinsley attended the conclave. The Foreign Office wanted Pacelli to be chosen (which rather contradicts the view that he was perceived as pro-German), and wondered whether to attempt to put pressure on the English Cardinal Elector. In the event they did not do so.

Another preoccupation in the immediate pre-war years was what to do, were there to be an accommodation with Hitler which would hand over to him some African territories. As

---

22 Aspden, *op. cit.*, p. 235.
23 Pius XI withdrew to Castel Gandolfo during Hitler's visit.
24 John Cornwell, *Hitler's Pope* (London: Viking, 1999), p. 203. The visit to Mussolini attracted much criticism, as, from Protestant groups, did that to the pope.

Apostolic Visitor to Africa in the 1920s, Hinsley had experience of clergy from the former German colonies coming under British rule. When war finally broke out, German clergy in these territories were interned and their property confiscated, but thanks to Hinsley's intervention they were soon released and their property returned to them.

There was also the problem of what might happen were Britain to enter into an alliance with the USSR against Hitler's Germany. This greatly troubled the Cardinal, and he wrote to Lord Halifax, the Foreign Secretary, about it. After Germany invaded Russia in June 1941, and there arose the spectre of Franco siding with Hitler against Stalin, the Foreign Office wanted Hinsley to speak in favour of Russia. He was reluctant. The Ministry of Information was understanding, pointing out to the Foreign Office that such an abrupt reversal of policy on the part of English Catholics, and, indeed, of Catholics world-wide, would simply not be credible and might be counter-productive. Hinsley eventually agreed, in a broadcast to South America, to say something about the invasion of the USSR by Germany. 'The Russian people still have their rights', he said, 'which have been outraged by Nazi aggression.'[25] Despite this, he was against any treaty with the USSR which would legitimate its seizure of the Baltic states and of part of Poland. In a sermon in December 1942 he called for a full restoration of Polish sovereignty once the war was over.

When war broke out he immediately sent a message of loyalty to the Prime Minister. He followed this with a BBC broadcast on 10 December, which he entitled 'The Sword of the Spirit'. In it he condemned Russian persecution of the Orthodoxy and of Catholics – the USSR had just invaded Poland – as much as he did Nazi persecution of the Protestant Church in Germany. He defended the start of hostilities:

---

25 Moloney, *op. cit.*, p. 232. Hinsley was also asked by the Foreign Office to assure the French bishops that Britain was engaged in the war until there was victory – which he did.

A cynical and systematic disregard for the truth, a reckless breaking of the plighted word, the brutality of force and ruthless persecution, these are the immediate causes of the present war. Of these I hold my country guiltless.[26]

He went on:

Now the values of the Spirit are truth, justice and charity – charity, the love of our fellow men in God. These values received their full meaning and final power from the Christmas message: 'Glory be to God in the highest, and on earth peace, peace to men of good will'. I am convinced that Britain has engaged in this war in the main for the defence of the things of the Spirit. She has taken up arms in the cause of justice and freedom. They who take up the sword from lust for power or racial or party aims shall perish. Against such, armed force may justly defend and protect our country and rights of nations. Yet in the end the 'sword of the Spirit' will alone convert unjust assailants and recreate peace and good will.[27]

The movement which came to be known as 'The Sword of the Spirit', or simply 'Sword' to its membership, took its inspiration from this address. As Kester Aspden remarks,

Considerable academic attention has been given to the Sword.[28] Its features were social concern, commitment to democracy and disavowal of fascism, lay direction and cooperation with other Christians. As such it has appeared as the 'authentic expression of English political Catholicism', in

---

26 *Ibid.*, p. 135.
27 Michael Walsh, *From Sword to Ploughshare* (London: Catholic Institute for International Relations, 1980), p. 5.
28 Including, it should be said, by the present writer – see the previous footnote and 'Ecumenism in War-Time Britain' in the *Heythrop Journal* XXIII (1982), pp. 243–58 and 377–94.

contrast to the exclusivist, clerically led, nature of Catholic Action.[29]

Certainly, on the face of it the initiators of the Sword were lay people, members for the most part of the Plater Society, named after a Jesuit, Charles Dominic Plater, who had been active in the first two decades of the century in spreading Catholic social teaching. They were alarmed after the fall of France in June 1940 and the subsequent establishment of the Vichy regime by the talk of a 'Latin bloc' – Spain, Italy and Vichy – with whom Britain might be able to do business. For 'Latin' one must read 'Catholic', and a good many English Catholics displayed considerable sympathy for Vichy, led perhaps by the publisher Douglas Jerrold, chairman of Eyre and Spottiswoode, 'all of a right-wing piece' as his friend Tom Burns later described him,[30] who had been involved in flying General Franco from the Canaries to Africa in 1936 to start the Spanish Civil War. He told Barbara Ward, then on the staff of *The Economist*, that Churchill had been unfair to Marshal Pétain, the leader of Vichy France. But perhaps more significant than Jerrold was Michael de la Bedoyère, editor of the weekly *Catholic Herald* from 1934 to 1962, who was also an active propagandist for the notion of a Latin bloc, and whose paper in the late 1930s was enjoying a massive increase in circulation.

Barbara Ward went with the historian Christopher Dawson to see Hinsley on 10 July 1940 to say that there should be a propaganda campaign to unite Christians in Britain behind the war effort. Two days later a letter arrived from the Cardinal endorsing any efforts that members of the Plater Society might make, and offering to serve as president of any movement which they started. The Cardinal was determined that Catholics must be seen as loyal, Bishop David Mathew told

---

29 Aspden, *op. cit.*, p. 237. The quotation included in the citation from Aspden is J. von Arx, 'Catholics and Politics' in McClelland and Hodgetts (eds), *From Without the Flaminian Gate*, pp. 245–71, at p. 266.
30 Burns, *op. cit.*, p. 58.

Barbara Ward over lunch, and there must be no grounds given by Catholics which might revive anti-popery in the country. Dawson wrote formally to Hinsley requesting him to do something practical: he summoned a meeting for 1 August in the Throne Room of Archbishop's House. 'We are met together', he told those assembled,

> . . . to start a movement for a more united and intense effort for a true, just and lasting peace. Our aim is Catholic. We mean by prayer, self-sacrifice and work to do our part in the reconstruction of Europe. We are convinced that a better world can be built only on the foundations of faith, hope and charity. Our purpose is large and deep. We are not inspired by a narrow patriotism, which limits our Christian charity to the red patches on the world's maps where waves the British flag. We have no hatred for any nation or race. On the contrary, we will never lose sight of that kinship and love which ought to bind human beings to one another.[31]

This was a remarkable vision for the time, one that looked beyond the war to the inevitable reconstruction of Europe. Perhaps even more remarkable was the fact that the Sword came so swiftly into being. It may very well be that Hinsley was looking for something of the sort, prompted by the Ministry of Information. The head of its religious section was Richard Hope of a well-known, and influential, Catholic family. There was a meeting with the heads of the main Christian Churches which discussed, before war was a reality, how to bring them behind the war effort. But of the Churches, the Catholic Church was the most significant because of its ties with France and Italy, and with Catholic co-religionists throughout the Empire. But the Ministry also believed that the British policies coincided to a large degree with those of the Vatican, and wanted to turn this apparent link to British advantage. They

---

31 Walsh, *op. cit.*, p. 6.

wanted to disseminate Catholic attitudes through some propaganda machine, but felt they had to tread carefully. Anything too complex would need money, and the Ministry was eager that anything flowing out of Catholic sources in Britain should come from the Church directly and not seem to be sponsored by the British government. Although money came from official sources to pay some, if not all, the printing bills for Sword, and although RAF planes dropped Sword leaflets over occupied France and Belgium, as well as Germany, Sword appeared to be just the kind of entity for which the Ministry of Information had been hoping.

The second meeting of the Sword executive took place just a week after the gathering at Archbishop's House, and it was decided that Sword meetings should be open to all, of whatever Christian belief.. But therein lay a difficulty of which Sword members were not sufficiently aware: the issue of praying with non-Catholics. Hinsley himself gave rise to the problem. In May 1941 there were two meetings, attended by vast numbers, at the Stoll Theatre in Kingsway:[32] Hinsley presided at the first, Cosmo Lang at the second. The most impressive speech at the first meeting was, by common consent, that of George Bell, the Bishop of Chichester. He appealed to all the belligerent nations to accept Pope Pius XII's Five Peace Points, proposed by the Pope in his Christmas broadcast the previous year.

Clearly much moved by Bell's words, Hinsley closed the meeting. He said:

> Our unity must not be in sentiment or word only: it must be carried into practical measures. Let us have a regular system of consultation and collaboration from now onwards, such as his Lordship the Bishop of Chichester has suggested, to

---

32 In between the two meetings, held on successive days, London suffered one of the most severe bombing raids of the war. The Stoll Theatre was untouched, but those attending on the second day had to make their way through the rubble to do so.

agree on a plan of action which shall win the peace when the din of battle is ended.[33]

Nobody had thought how to bring the gathering to a close. Barbara Ward whispered to the Cardinal to say the 'Our Father', which he did, and the audience joined in, alongside the Anglican bishop on the platform. No one, least of all Hinsley, averted to the prohibition then in force on Catholics against joining in prayers with members of other religions.

Strange as it now seems, this issue presented Sword with its biggest problem, and undermined possibly the most successful collaboration in Britain across Christian boundaries, certainly up to that point, and for many decades to come. It almost destroyed Sword, and undoubtedly limited its effectiveness. But not only were Sword members forbidden from praying with Anglicans and members of the Free Churches, it became obvious that in effect only Catholics could be members of Sword, if it were to spread outside the Diocese of Westminster.

In September the Sword executive sent out a letter to all the clergy soliciting their support:

> The purpose of the organisation is briefly to try to bring home to our fellow-Catholics and to as many non-Catholics as we can reach the important Christian issues at stake in the present war, and also to insist that no post-war settlement or reconstruction, whether social or international, can hope to last unless it be founded upon a truly Christian basis.[34]

The Archbishop of Southwark would not allow the letter to be circulated in his diocese, though he did not prevent the formation of Sword of the Spirit groups.

The Cardinal had hoped for more. On 7 August 1941 he wrote to all the bishops to win their support for the new

---

33 Walsh, *op. cit.*, p. 9.
34 Clifton, *op. cit.*, p. 167.

movement. He did not get it. Some thought the aims of the movement too political for a Catholic organization, especially because there was no evidence that any member of its executive had ever been thoroughly pro-Franco.[35] There was a hesitation about opposing Fascism, even, on the part of some, of opposing Nazism – though recognizing what they saw as 'abuses'. Others objected that, unlike Catholic Action and despite the involvement of a number of clergy including Bishop David Mathew, it was being wholly run by the laity without much reference to the episcopate. What is more, said one, half the executive are women.

But the real problem was the notion that a Catholic organization should cross denominational lines. As Amigo of Southwark wrote in response to Hinsley's letter

> We welcome the reception which has been given to it [Sword] by non-Catholics but there is always the fear and danger that we should appear to recognise any other than the one True Church. Let us keep the Sword of the Spirit as a Catholic campaign under your guidance. Let non-Catholics make any use of it for the future restoration when the war is over. Avoid joint meetings if possible but in any case let there be no prayer in common.[36]

The 'no prayer together' rule greatly distressed many of the Sword executive, who thought of their movements as one of spiritual renewal as much as of social reconstruction. Largely as a consequence of the enthusiasm of Bishop Bell of Chichester, a solution was found which enabled Sword, as a Catholic organization, to co-operate with Religion and Life, a Church of England/Free Church body, through the holding of joint meetings, though without joint prayer. The effective division of

---

35 The Jesuit priest John Murray was a member of the executive, and was thought by one other member, Barbara Ward, to be a crypto-Fascist.
36 Clifton, *op. cit.*, p. 168.

the movement into two distinct parts was not what the Sword executive, nor what Hinsley, had wanted. Indeed, the Cardinal was no little put out to discover that in this arrangement the Archbishop of Canterbury took precedence over the Archbishop of Westminster. He even considered resigning, though in the end he did not do so.

A statement on co-operation was produced in January 1942 emphasizing the responsibility of all Christians to work together during and after the war to influence decision-making on social and economic issues. But there was a further paragraph on religious liberty, 'freedom to worship according to conscience, freedom to preach, teach, educate and persuade (all in the spirit of Christian charity) and freedom to bring up children in the faith of their parents'.[37] Hinsley backed this statement, though expressing reservations about some of the wording. Other bishops and their theologians were far more critical. Indeed, Hinsley himself had originally held rather more conservative views, as William Paton, the Presbyterian minister who was secretary of the International Missionary Council, and of the provisional committee of the World Council of Churches, recorded in a letter. It was, wrote Paton, the Cardinal's view:

> In countries where there is, so to speak, an established Protestantism strong enough and sufficiently rooted in national life, the Church of Rome would not take a hostile attitude towards it. That is to say, it would proceed on a basis of live and let live. Where, however, Protestants are so few and struggling that they must still be regarded without a place in the national life, as I [i.e. Paton] presume in Spain or Italy, then the Roman Catholic Church could not divest itself of the right to recommend to the State to repress such groups.[38]

---

37 Michael Walsh, 'Ecumenism', p. 256.
38 *Ibid.*, p. 254. It may be worth remarking that Paton's wife Grace was a convert from Presbyterianism to Roman Catholicism, by way of High Church Anglicanism, a conversion in which he supported her, though without experiencing any desire to follow suit.

Hinsley appears to have modified this view. He said of religious freedom in a letter to Bishop Bell that 'in principle individuals and groups and states must favour the *truth* if and when they know it, and should give practical tolerance to those who profess *falsehood* which they hold as *truth*'.[39] However, as a statement of where the Catholic Church stood until the Second Vatican Council, the words of Paton quoted above cannot be faulted.[40] The Sword executive realized that the issue of religious freedom was going to be a stumbling block to co-operation among the Churches (the Cardinal's theologians even objected to the use of the word 'Church' as referring to anything other than the Catholic Church), and tried to persuade Paton not to press the issue, but failed.

But the real problems were internal to the Catholic Church, not external. As Thomas Moloney remarks, 'Without doubt the 'Sword of the Spirit' foundered primarily in its own Catholic community on the rock of intransigence represented by the majority of the diocesan bishops.'[41] Bishop Bell, who seems in some respects to have shared the common view of the Catholic Church as a monolith, was taken aback by the independence displayed by local ordinaries.

Hinsley's own relations with leading churchmen of other denominations were warm and collaborative, as his remarks at the Stoll meeting, quoted above, suggest. The most remarkable example of this was the letter that appeared in *The Times* of 21 December 1940, signed by William Temple, as Archbishop of York, Cosmo Lang, Hinsley, and the Moderator of the Free Church Federal Council, George Armstrong. The church leaders began by listing Pope Pius XII's Five Peace Points, and then went on to add five of their own about the nature of British

---

39 Aspden, *op. cit.*, p. 252.
40 See Michael Walsh, 'Religious Freedom: The Limits of Progress' in Austen Ivereigh (ed.), *Unfinished Journey* (London: Continuum, 2003), pp. 134–48.
41 *Ibid.*, p. 203. 'Foundered' is perhaps too strong a term because the Sword survived the war, eventually changing its name to the Catholic Institute for International Relations. It currently operates under the name Progressio.

society. They called for the abolition of extremes of wealth and poverty, for equal educational opportunities for all, for the safeguarding of the family as a social unit, for the restoration of the sense of a divine vocation in work, and, most presciently, that 'the resources of the earth should be used as God's gift to the whole human race, and used with due consideration for the needs of the present and future generations'. Sword adopted these five points as part of its own manifesto.

There was much else to occupy the Cardinal. At their Low Week meeting in 1938 the bishops decided to establish a Catholic Committee for Refugees from Germany and Austria. This was intended originally to handle only Catholic refugees, but Hinsley soon expanded it to all refugees, and especially to Jews. At a time when anti-Semitism was rife among English Catholics, he was remarkably free of it. In 1936 the *Catholic Gazette*, the journal of the Catholic Missionary Society, printed what the Board of Deputies of British Jews regarded as a slander, and appealed to the Cardinal. He agreed with them. Two years later, on 1 December 1938, he appeared on a platform at the Albert Hall alongside William Temple and the Chief Rabbi to protest at the treatment of Jews in Germany, especially in the aftermath of Kristallnacht, which had occurred some three weeks before. It was, he declared, 'a violation of the fundamental principles of human society',[42] a speech for which he was mocked in a German newspaper which described him as a former missionary to Negroes. With the Chief Rabbi and Temple in March 1942 he founded the Council of Christians and Jews. After his death the *Jewish Chronicle* wrote of him that Jews 'have known him as an ardent champion of Jewish rights, a great reconciler of communities and creeds, a shining and unfaltering light in a world astray in darkness, a teacher in the best line of Catholic tradition'.[43]

---

42 Moloney, *op. cit.*, p. 210.
43 *Ibid.*, p. 221.

There was a special problem about Polish Jews. A Catholic Committee for Poland was established in 1940 with David Mathew as its president. Hinsley was a frequent speaker on the fate of Poland, and his speeches were sometimes broadcast back to Poland. But there was a degree of anti-Semitism among the Polish exiles in England. When one Polish-language journal was praised in a leading article in Michael de la Bedoyère's *Catholic Herald*, and the *Herald* even printed an article by a Polish officer calling for British help in purging Poland of Jews, the Cardinal took to the pulpit to condemn the treatment of Jews in Poland – and not just by the Nazis.

The Cardinal's private secretary was Mgr Valentine (Val) Elwes, and he left an account of Hinsley's last days. According to Elwes his health began to fail at the fall of France. He suffered from a number of illnesses, but most particularly from angina, attacks of which came on with increasing frequency. In the last few months of his life he took refuge at Hare Street House at Buntingford in Hertfordshire, the country residence of the archbishops of Westminster. There he suffered a heart attack and died on 17 March 1943. In his will he had instructed 'As to my funeral I desire as little pomp as possible. Let there be a Low Mass of requiem and the least possible expense. No profusion of candles. Bury my body wherever is most convenient. My brother and sister are buried at Kensal Green.'

But his instructions were impossible to carry out. The funeral was on 23 May, and most members of the government turned up. So did Bishop Bell. Archbishop Temple was represented. This all 'seemed so right and proper', commented the (Anglican) *Church Times* 'that few people probably realised how great a departure from precedent it was'.[44] And Cardinal Arthur Hinsley was laid to rest not in Kensal Green cemetery with his family but in the chapel of St Joseph in Westminster Cathedral.

---

44 Aspden, *op. cit.*, p. 255.

6

Bernard Griffin

In his much-quoted *History of English Christianity* Adrian Hastings dismissed Bernard Griffin as 'the least important Archbishop of Westminster of the century, a nice, hard-working nonentity'.[1] This seems a rather harsh judgement, especially as Griffin was succeeded by William Godfrey to whom Hastings devotes slightly more space but whose role, at least as Archbishop at Westminster, was singularly inconspicuous. Moreover, as Hastings concedes, for almost half of his episcopacy Griffin was far from well, a fact which his devoted secretary from 1945, Derek Worlock, later Archbishop of Liverpool, did his best to disguise.

Griffin was born in the Cannon Hill area of Birmingham on 21 February 1899 and baptized Bernard William after his father, who was William Bernard. He was the elder (by twenty minutes) of twin boys: his brother Walter also became a priest, and a monk of Douai Abbey. His father was the manager for a cycle manufacturer and a city councillor; his mother, Helen Swadkin, came from an agricultural background. They were a particularly devout family, close to their parish priest to whom the boys both attributed their vocations. They attended Dennis Road Primary School, but then won scholarships to King Edward Grammar School. This was not a Catholic college, and

---

1 Adrian Hastings, *A History of English Christianity, 1920–2000* (London: SCM Press, 2001), p. 478.

permission to attend had to be obtained from the Archbishop of Birmingham. They were there only from the ages of 12 to 15. Given their desire to become priests, in September 1913 they were sent to the minor seminary at Ushaw College.

They finished their schooling in 1917, and, still together, they joined the Royal Naval Air Service at Manston in Kent. While serving in the ranks Bernard caught the virulent flu which swept the country in 1918. It did him considerable damage, and he was offered an early discharge from the service on health grounds, but he refused, fearing that if he were invalided out of the forces he would not be accepted into the seminary. At the end of their time in the forces the twins separated, Walter to Douai Abbey, Bernard to the diocesan seminary at Oscott where he stood out as one of the brighter and more diligent students. In 1922, therefore, he was dispatched for further studies to the English College in Rome, where he remained until 1927, obtaining doctorates both in theology and in canon law, and where he was ordained on 1 November 1924. In 1927 he returned to the Birmingham Archdiocese. His time in Rome had marked him out for promotion, so instead of being posted as a curate in a parish he began on the lowest rung of the clerical *cursus honorum*, that of secretary to the diocesan ordinary. He rose to be chancellor of the diocese before being moved, in the summer of 1937, to the Birmingham suburb of Coleshill as parish priest.

Though the appointment was clearly intended to provide the rising star with some pastoral experience before he moved on to higher things, it was something of a challenge. An orphanage had been started there in the nineteenth century, but had been greatly expanded at the turn of the twentieth by the then parish priest Father George Vincent Hudson; the complex, which included an orthopaedic hospital, became known as Father Hudson's Homes. Griffin clearly enjoyed the challenges of his new post, not least that of building a massive new church which he dedicated to Thérèse of Lisieux, a saint to whom he had an especial devotion and to whose Carmelite convent in Lisieux he later became a frequent visitor. In more recent times there have been charges of brutality against some of the nuns, and of child abuse against some of the clergy who worked in the Homes at Coleshill, but Griffin's frequent mention of the importance of providing a 'hearth and a home' for children for one reason or another without a family to support them shows that he believed the Homes were an important service to the Catholic community. He said as much in a speech about the 1948 Children's Act: 'The aim and object of voluntary societies has been to try, as far as is humanly possible, to make up to the child its home life and the affection it should have had from its parents.'[2] Orphanages or foster homes, he believed, were better for children than a bad home.

His appointment to Westminster was unexpected. He had been created a Bishop in 1938 as an assistant to Archbishop Thomas Williams, and he became Vicar General. It was thought that he would be promoted to the role of a diocesan bishop; his elevation to Westminster came as a surprise to many, including himself.[3] He was very young, but the mood in Rome, the Apostolic Delegate told Williams, was 'that a young man should be placed at Westminster to grapple with the afterwar problems'.[4] The Foreign Office had more pressing concerns. The British Minister to the Holy See was instructed to let the pope know that they did not simply want 'an efficient administrator of a religious minority and nothing more'.[5] The

---

2 Michael de la Bedoyère, *Cardinal Bernard Griffin* (London: Rockliff, 1955), p. 66.

3 In their memoir of Archbishop Worlock, John Furnival and Anne Knowles suggest that Archbishop Joseph Masterson of Birmingham was the obvious choice, but because he was seriously ill he suggested his young assistant. Unfortunately for this theory, Masterson did not become Archbishop until 1947. It could possibly be true of Thomas Williams, who died in 1946, cf. *Archbishop Derek Worlock: His Personal Journey* (London: Geoffrey Chapman, 1998), p. 78.

4 Aspden, *op. cit.*, p. 262.

5 Owen Chadwick, *Britain and the Vatican during the Second World War* (Cambridge: Cambridge University Press, 1986), p. 257.

appointment was dated 18 December 1943, nine months after Hinsley's death – a delay which suggests that the choice was not obvious, but he had already attracted attention by publicly criticizing the situation of Catholics in Northern Ireland. He was sufficiently vociferous to have annoyed the Home Secretary, Herbert Morrison, who summoned him to Whitehall and asked if he wanted to start a civil war.

He chose his enthronement address to take on the government over the Education Bill which was just about to go through Parliament. 'Whilst others are satisfied with the proposals of the Bill,' he said, 'we Catholics are not satisfied. As loyal members of the State, and as tax payers equally with others, our parents claim they should not be allowed to suffer because of their consciences, but should be granted equal facilities with other members of the community.'[6] The issue was the level of the grant, but some bishops had other problems, such as raising the school leaving age to fifteen.

The bill was being steered through Parliament by R. A. Butler, once president of the Board of Education, but by now raised to the rank of Minister. As introduced on 15 December 1943 the bill proposed either that all schools be handed over to the local education authority with permission for the Churches to use the premises on Sundays, or that the schools be left in the hands of the Churches, with the right to appoint and dismiss the teaching staff, but in which case they would receive only half the capital costs. The grant had originally been intended only for schools which were being moved to new sites, but pressure from the Churches, especially from the Catholic Church, managed to have this provision extended to all new schools. Butler got on well with Griffin – he had found Downey of Liverpool impossible to deal with – and recognized him as he came into the House of Commons to listen to the debate.

---

6 Bedoyère, *op. cit.*, p. 45.

He records the occasion in his autobiography *The Art of the Possible*:

> I had just got to the second part of my speech, in which I anticipated playing against the wind, when Mgr Griffin, the newly appointed Archbishop of Westminster who had been enthroned the day before, was ushered into the Distinguished Strangers' Gallery. There, with the sun illuminating his red hair, he sat looking directly down on me as I outlined the provisions of the religious settlement.[7]

Griffin arrived to hear him quote from a hymn:

> Ye fearful saints, fresh courage take,
> The clouds ye so much dread
> Are big with mercy, and shall break
> In blessings on your head.[8]

The following day he received from Archbishop's House, as a gift from Griffin, a set of the Catholic classic, *Butler's Lives of the Saints*.[9]

But the Archbishop was not satisfied, and agitation to win an increase in the grant continued. There was a public meeting at the Royal Albert Hall in June 1950 attended by some 7,000 Catholics, and a rally in Trafalgar Square where Griffin addressed the large crowd from a plinth. The hierarchy submitted figures to the government to demonstrate that their financial projections in the 1944 Education Act had been wildly inaccurate: the government responded that there would be no

---

7 Furnival and Knowles, *op. cit.*, pp. 81–2.
8 Hastings, *op. cit.*, p. 422.
9 At the memorial service in March 1982 for Lord Butler, Cardinal Basil Hume read a lesson at the invitation of Lady Butler, a potent sign that, despite all the criticism at the time, the 1944 Act had worked to the benefit of the Catholic community.

renegotiation. In a speech in January 1950 he declared the Butler Education Act as 'the death sentence' for Catholic schools. Butler had suggested that there was always the possibility of an Amending Act. Griffin uttered dark words about such bills, saying that Amending Bills amended Acts only in favour of the government, nonetheless in 1959 the grant was increased to 75 per cent.[10] And as for the 1944 Act being the 'death sentence', in the event it turned out to be nothing of the sort, but that would not have been obvious at the time. The provisions of the Act did indeed do considerable harm to the Church of England's network of schools, whereas Griffin started a Central Schools Fund and Catholics rallied to the challenge to raise the large amounts of money to keep them in being, and to build new ones. Catholic schools and the funding thereof were part of the cement that held the Catholic community together in the 1950s and 1960s.[11]

It was one of Griffin's general complaints, and one not without weight, that the government should not have embarked upon such drastic social reforms in wartime because it made those who resisted some of the changes appear unpatriotic. Nothing could have been more drastic than the introduction of the Welfare State. Griffin's predecessor, Cardinal Hinsley, and his former ordinary, Archbishop Williams, had both welcomed the Beveridge Report, but the majority of the bishops had not. They were opposed to the extension of State intervention in what they saw as the responsibility of individual families. There was much talk of the growth of totalitarianism in England just as

---

10 And later, of course, to 90 per cent.
11 He also saw Catholic schools as a bulwark against totalitarianism. As he wrote in his 1951 Advent pastoral letter, 'We have only to look at what is happening in the Communist-controlled States of East Europe today, where the State is seizing Catholic schools and is compelling parents to send their children to State schools providing secular education only to realise how easily children can become mere tools in the hands of unscrupulous politicians.' Maurice Whitehead, 'A View from the Bridge' in McClelland and Hodgetts, *op. cit.*, p. 225.

it was being combated on the continent, and of the government undermining the rights of parents to care for their families. And of nothing was this more true than the establishment of the National Health Service. As a doctor said in a letter to the *Catholic Herald* in 1944, 'The public must awake and realise that the whole nation is threatened with the loss of its democratic liberties just as seriously as Germany was in 1933.'[12]

There were two major issues. One was fairly easily resolved. There were fears that Catholic doctors might find themselves involved in practices which were against their consciences, specifically with relation to contraception: the government provided an opt-out clause. More problematic was the fate of the 70 or so Catholic hospitals. The hierarchy wanted the hospitals to have their own management boards, under regional boards, which would have two-thirds of their members as Roman Catholics, with the right to hire and fire staff. Griffin established a good relationship with the minister in charge, Aneurin Bevan – the minister even visited Griffin in hospital (St John and St Elizabeth's, one of those in dispute) when the Archbishop had his tonsils removed. It seems as though the Archbishop resorted to a form of blackmail to get his way, threatening so to demonize the National Health Service that Irish nurses, upon whom the Service so heavily depended, would not come to England to fill the empty posts. In the end the decision to withdraw the hospitals was accepted by the government. Few Catholic voices were raised against the decision, though one of the critics was Michael de la Bedoyère in the pages of his *Catholic Herald* who though that they ought to have entered the state system. Grffin's view was quite different: 'It will be a sad day for England', he said, 'when charity becomes the affair of the State.'[13]

---

12 Peter Coman, *Catholics and the Welfare State* (London: Longman, 1977), p. 46.
13 Bedoyère, *op. cit.*, p. 66.

Part of the reason for Griffin's opposition to the growth of State intervention came from his own experience of his father being a councillor. In a sermon preached in 1945 in Finchley, London, he said:

> I am a firm believer in local government because it seems to me that in it we have a true expression of democracy and liberty. The bond between those who are governing and those who are governed is much more intimate, and local needs will be better understood and more easily dealt with by local authorities than by direction from Whitehall.[14]

These are words which many have echoed in more recent times.

It was perhaps his father's influence that encouraged him to take as seriously as Hinsley had done Catholic social action. He had an agenda. He wanted decent housing (for 'fair-sized' families), he wanted full employment and 'family' wages (wages to support this fair-sized family), family allowances, grants to those about to get married, parental rights over their children's welfare respected, and so on. He founded the Association of Catholic Trade Unionists in Westminster in 1945,[15] and a similar organization for managers and employers. He was a supporter of the Young Christian Worker movement[16] – the Vatican, which had not been too happy with the YCW's stance

---

14 Aspden, *op. cit.*, p. 265.
15 This was most definitely not an alternative trade union for Catholics, such as those which have existed in continental Europe, but an organization among whose aims was to encourage Catholic workers to join their appropriate trade union. Catholics became prominent in opposing the rise of Communism in some unions.
16 Clifford Longley, in *The Worlock Archive* (London: Geoffrey Chapman, 2000), p. 28, believes that the express support for the YCW that Griffin gave in his Lent pastoral letter for 1947 stemmed from Derek Worlock, though he is also of the view that it was Griffin who steered Worlock in the direction of the YCW.

on Spain, suspected it and the *Catholic Worker* newspaper of being too socialist.

Hinsley had fostered, by accident or design, a more pro-active role for lay people in the English Church of the 1940s. Griffin had his social agenda, but who was to carry it through? The Catholic Social Guild was one obvious choice, but it was now, as a consequence of the onset of the Welfare State, deeply divided. Some members of its executive saw the Welfare State as a major challenge to the principles of Catholic social teaching because the Welfare State appeared to shift responsibility for a family's well-being from the father to the government. Others were equally deeply convinced that the State needed to play a more significant role in the life of the poor and under-privileged. The result was a major crisis in the Guild, but the story of that belongs to the episcopacy of Griffin's successor.

There were of course many other Catholic lay organizations, and Griffin intended to make use of their membership. But he had very clear ideas about the extent of their independence of action. In his Lenten pastoral for 1952 he wrote:

> At no time in the past has it been more important that the laity should be conscious of their role and adequately trained for their task. Their apostolate is to be fulfilled as ever under the direction of those who have received their authority from the Church founded by Christ. It is for the laity to share in the apostolate of the hierarchy and, if their role is dependent on the hierarchy of the Church this in no way diminishes the importance of their task or the very real responsibility which is theirs.[17]

All of which sounds very like the ideology of Catholic Action to which Hinsley had at first given his attention, and then abandoned.

---

17 Bedoyère, *op. cit.*, p. 109.

Another organization to which he might have turned was the Sword of the Spirit. This still survived, but only just. It had a large number of members, but many had ceased to be active, and the movement had lost direction: a proposal to work for the reconstruction of British society, and to open itself up once again to non-Catholics, was rejected. In 1945 there was an attempted re-launch, but it failed. By 1947 the Cardinal was told that there was a financial crisis, and there was no possibility of the Sword continuing. In fact the necessary sum was raised, and the Sword stayed in business, but not before Griffin had informed the astonished executive that the Vatican wanted it shut down. One member angrily pointed out that the Vatican had in 1943 given its approval. The Vatican can change its mind, responded Griffin – though he did not want his remark minuted.

The Vatican's approval had indeed been given, in a document from the Holy Office (now the Congregation for the Doctrine of the Faith) on 4 January 1943, though the Sword executive did not learn of it until over a year later. It was a remarkable statement for the time. It said that there might be 'mixed societies or gatherings' in grave situations, and evidently in 1943 Britain was in such a grave situation. Moreover, it allowed for joint prayers of Catholics and Anglicans together. The permission was a limited one, but there is no disguising that in granting permission for both prayer in common, and for joint meetings of Catholics and Anglicans, Rome was for once at least showing itself far more open than the majority of the English bishops had been.[18]

And that was one aspect of Hinsley's episcopacy that Griffin did not foster, cordial relations with other Christian Churches. Archbishop Geoffrey Fisher invited him to tea at Lambeth Palace in May 1946, but Griffin did not reciprocate, which

---

18 See Walsh, 'Ecumenism in War-Time Britain', pp. 393–4, and *From Sword to Ploughshare*, pp. 15–16.

upset the Archbishop of Canterbury. Then there was a protocol problem about joint action. Griffin was quite prepared, on any letter to *The Times* for instance, for the Archbishop of Canterbury's signature to go first, but he thought his should then follow, whereas Fisher thought that the signature of the Archbishop of York should come second. By such pettiness, as it now seems, the good will which Hinsley had built up was dissipated.

This was not wholly Griffin's fault. As has been seen (above, p. 133), the late Cardinal had been among those founding what came to be known as the National Council of Christians and Jews, and Griffin continued this tradition as a member of its board. The Vatican, however, banned Catholics from being members of the overarching body, the International Council of Christians and Jews, on the grounds that it was promoting religious tolerance, a concept which Pope Pius XII chose to interpret as promoting indifferentism in religion. In December 1949 the Holy Office warned bishops 'against those who under false pretexts stress the points on which we agree rather than those on which we disagree'.[19] Then in June 1954 it explicitly condemned the British organization:

> Having considered the dangers arising from the questionable ideas regarding religious toleration accepted by the Protestants and Jews of the National Council of Christians and Jews of England and the equivocation found in their ideas of education, it is not desirable that Catholics in England should have part in this aforesaid National Council . . . As the matter is rather delicate it would be useful if the Catholic press in England could publish an article showing that the Catholic Church has never been wanting in its mission of charity, nor in defending the rights of the human

---

19 Aspden, *op. cit.*, p. 269.

person, whether it be a question of the Jews or any other persons suffering persecution and violence.[20]

'Spinning' bad news, it is evident, is not the prerogative of politicians alone.

The Holy Office's instruction came to Archbishop Godfrey as Apostolic Delegate, and he communicated it to Griffin, asking that he resign his vice-presidency of the Council. He agreed to do so, but only reluctantly. The Jesuit ecumenist Maurice Bévenot wrote to the Cardinal saying there was a danger that the Holy Office's views would be taken as condemning all religious toleration – something which Griffin himself had already protested to the Holy Office, though it took no notice. But that was exactly how Geoffrey Fisher understood it. 'Of course', he wrote, 'the Roman Catholics find the phrase "religious toleration" difficult because they do not believe at all in religious tolerance, choosing stupidly to equate that with religious indifferentism which is quite a different thing.'[21]

There were of course areas where collaboration was perfectly possible. Long before the D-Day landings in Normandy had occurred, a number of committed churchmen and women, including Archbishop Temple, had been working on a statement that, when it appeared in April 1944, was entitled 'The Future of Europe'. Temple had hoped that the statement would appear over the signatures of all the major British church leaders along the lines of the 1940 letter to *The Times* (see above, p. 132f). Griffin confessed himself in sympathy with the sentiments of the letter but preferred not to sign. The statement proposed a federal Europe, though what Britain's role in this federation would be was not at all clear – there were still the Empire and the Dominions to consider.

---

20 *Ibid.*, p. 270.
21 *Ibid.*, p. 271. Catholics rejoined the National Council a decade later.

Somewhat later in 1944 was founded the British League for European Freedom, the purpose of which was to support refugees from Eastern Europe, and to publicize the lack of freedom in those countries occupied by Russia. The Catholic Church obviously had a considerable interest in this, especially in Poland which Griffin visited (see below, p. 149), and he was a member of the advisory panel of the League alongside other church leaders. Similarly he was a supporter of Ernest Bevin's proposed Western Union – the Foreign Secretary consulted him, as he did Geoffrey Fisher, Archbishop of Canterbury in succession to Temple. He collaborated actively in organizing a meeting at the Albert Hall as Bevin attempted, through Frank Pakenham, the future Lord Longford, to bring the Churches behind the idea of the 'spiritual unity' of Europe. The conference, at least in terms of the numbers attending, was a huge success. The Cardinal followed it with an article for the *Westminster Cathedral Chronicle and Gazette* for September 1948 on 'The Unity of Europe': 'European unity will not come about merely by economics and politics. These are material things. Europe was united through the Faith and the nations of Europe will be re-united through the same Faith.'[22] The position of the Catholic Church, as it was outlined by Griffin in his article, differed from that espoused by Fisher: it was much more federalist than others were prepared to countenance.

Early in 1947, and inspired by Winston Churchill, the United European Movement was founded. Churchill sent Hector Amery to invite Griffin to sit on its Council, an invitation which he clearly found flattering but felt unable to accept. Instead he proposed the Bishop of Nottingham who eagerly offered his services and enthusiastically took part. The Cardinal proposed

---

22 Philip Coupland, *Britannia, Europa and Christendom: British Christians and European Integration* (Basingstoke: Palgrave Macmillan, 2006), p. 104. The article was originally a speech delivered to the Newman Association. This section on Griffin and European unity is drawn from Coupland's excellent study.

other names – John Eppstein, who by now was Director of the British Society for International Understanding, Michael de la Bedoyère, and two Conservative Members of Parliament, Christopher Hollis and William Teeling. He was invited to speak at the inaugural conference held at the Albert Hall, but was in Rome at the time. Similarly he was asked to be, with the Chief Rabbi, the Archbishop of Canterbury and others, patron of the United Kingdom Council of the European Movement, which was launched at a meeting in the House of Commons in February 1949.

The Catholic Church never joined the British Council of Churches, but when in 1950 the BCC set up the Religious Bodies Consultative Committee to promote co-operation among the denominations (it included Jews) on international affairs, the Cardinal appointed two priests to sit on the committee. One of them was the Jesuit Fr John Murray whom Barbara Ward had once believed had Fascist leanings (see above, p. 130n). One of the first acts of the Consultative Committee was to produce a declaration on 'The Spiritual Inheritance of Europe' which was followed by a conference held in London on 'Religion and European Unity'.

Griffin travelled widely in Europe, setting off not long after he was appointed to visit Pope Pius XII. With the assistance of the Foreign Office he flew to Rome in the summer of 1944, making his way there by way of Lisbon, Algiers, Rabat and Naples. After Rome he travelled up to the allied front line, which was then just south of Florence. He managed to get a message of greeting across the German lines to the Cardinal of Florence. As soon as the war was over, and with Foreign Office assistance, he travelled through France, Belgium, Holland and Germany, arriving eventually at a devastated Berlin. In Munster he met the bishops of the British Zone of Occupation, led by the redoubtable Clemens August von Galen, since beatified by Pope Benedict XVI. Von Galen was anxious about the restoration of Catholic education. 'I have fought the Germans; unless they give us our schools I will fight the British too.' When he got to Berlin, Griffin was able successfully to make the case for the schools to the British authorities.

In May 1946 he visited the United States, receiving an honorary doctorate alongside President Harry Truman (with whom he shared a bottle of Coca Cola) at Fordham University in New York. He travelled around the country and then went to visit Canada. His most significant tour, however, was to Poland in June 1947, where on one occasion his car was picked up and carried by an enthusiastic crowd. His visit was the first by any foreign prelate since the war, and as Derek Worlock later discovered when he accompanied Archbishop Heenan to a dinner given by the Polish bishops during the Vatican Council, it was much appreciated.[23] In his Advent pastoral letter the year he visited Poland he wrote that 'The forces of evil are gaining ground and threaten to destroy the soul of man, the soul or Europe.'[24] One after another leading bishops across Eastern Europe were imprisoned. The story of one was dramatized in the film – subsequently and more recently a stage play – *The Prisoner*. Griffin recommended it as 'a film which every devout Catholic should see'.[25] He directed the Sword of the Spirit to campaign for the release of the gaoled prelates, and for human rights across Europe.

Meanwhile he had been made a Cardinal. It was announced on 23 December 1946, but the telephone call to tell him of his elevation did not reach him: he was on a visit to the hospital of St John and St Elizabeth in Hampstead. His staff put a red biretta on his desk for his return, but the first formal notification came from the BBC's six o'clock news. The ceremony took place in Rome on 21 February 1947, Griffin's forty-seventh birthday. He was by far the youngest Cardinal of the 32 who had been created in December: Pope Pius called him 'My Benjamin'.

---

23 Longley, *op. cit.*, pp. 161–2.
24 Bedoyère, *op. cit.*, p. 58.
25 Tony Shaw, 'Martyrs, Miracles and Martians' in Dianne Kirby (ed.), *Religion and the Cold War* (Basingstoke: Palgrave Macmillan, 2003), p. 223.

As Archbishop of Westminster there was the standard round of visits to be performed – during one to the East End of London during the war a 'doodle-bug' fell dangerously close. The cathedral was unscathed, and Archbishop's House only mildly damaged by a piece of shrapnel. He was hesitant about spending money on the cathedral – or at least, money which he did not have. He started the 'Million Crown Fund', which eventually paid for the mosaic work in the Blessed Sacrament Chapel. The most imaginative commission was to instruct the Italian sculptor Giacomo Manzú, fresh from completing some bronze doors for St Peter's in Rome, to produce a relief of Griffin's favourite saint, Thérèse of Lisieux. He also acquired the alabaster statue now known as 'Our Lady of Westminster'. He would not, however, permit the cathedral to be used for concerts, not even concerts of sacred music. He was asked to give permission for a performance of Elgar's *Dream of Gerontius*, but refused. It was protested that the oratorio's first performance had been in the cathedral in 1903. Gordon Wheeler, the administrator, still refused. The cathedral had not then been consecrated, he said.

In February 1949 there was a protest meeting in the Albert Hall at the arrest of Cardinal Mindszenty in Hungary. Griffin was to have presided, but two weeks earlier he had been taken ill. It was put down to nervous exhaustion,[26] but in reality he had suffered a stroke which left him partly paralysed. Worlock stepped in to protect him, writing his letters and effectively running the diocese while the Cardinal recuperated. He thought the clergy of Westminster Diocese were unaware of the part he played. In fact they were well aware, and resented Worlock's role. Griffin spent his fiftieth birthday in St John and St Elizabeth's, and then went to St Leonard's to convalesce. He had a relapse in September, but by the end of the year he was, to outward appearances, back in operation. Even so, his first

---

26 This is the version in Bedoyère, written during Griffin's lifetime.

public engagement – the mass rally in the Albert Hall about Catholic schools (cf. above, p. 139f) – was not until June.

The year 1950 was particularly important, marking 100 since the restoration of the hierarchy. There was a 'Hierarchy Centenary Congress', for which Griffin was appointed papal legate. There was a celebratory Mass in Westminster Cathedral at the end of September, and at the beginning of October some 90,000 Catholics packed into Wembley Stadium. But soon after the Albert Hall gathering, the Cardinal had once again been taken ill. He had to be helped into the stadium, though the event reinvigorated him and he walked out without help. The recovery was short lived. Though he loyally went to Rome for the declaration of the dogma of the Assumption on 1 November 1950, he was too ill to attend the ceremony itself.

The definition of the dogma of the Assumption was a symbolic act. Though long part of Catholic devotion, the belief that Mary was taken up 'body and soul' into heaven has no warrant in the scriptures. The Church was asserting that its own tradition was a reliable source of true knowledge, and by the definition setting itself apart from other Christian denominations – certainly from those that had sprung from the Protestant Reformation. It was a sign of supreme self-confidence, a self-confidence that was echoed in England as Catholicism drew increasing numbers of converts, and seemed immune to the trend already visible elsewhere of declining church attendance. As Kester Aspden has put it, 'There was a swagger about the Church in the 1950s',[27] fuelled not least by its opposition to Communism and the 'martyrdom' so many Catholics were undergoing in 'the Church of silence'. Though martyrdom was far from recent English Catholic experience, it was part of the battle for human rights in Eastern Europe, and the bishops even sent £5,000 in 1948 to help the Christian Democrats defeat the Communist Party in the Italian elections. As Griffin

---

27 Aspden, *op. cit.*, p. 274.

put it to a Sword of the Spirit meeting in 1950 to mark its first decade:

> One thing that has happened since 1940 is that the English people have become increasingly conscious of the Catholic Church as a great force in the post-war world. The minds of our countrymen have changed a great deal since the 'thirties when the importance of religion, like the dangers of atheistic communism, was underrated or ignored. Today it is a commonplace to be told by non-Catholics that they fully recognise that in the strength of the Catholic Church, much more than in any material resources, lies the great hope of saving Europe, and, indeed, the world.[28]

And as he said in a sermon at Southwark Cathedral, reflecting on the centenary being celebrated in 1950, 'We have more churches, more monasteries, more convents and more schools.'[29]

There were indeed a number of major events which brought out Catholics in great numbers. Both Father Peyton's Family Rosary Crusade – a Catholic take on the revivalist rallies of Billy Graham – in July 1952, and the celebration of the Marian Year in October 1954, with the Cardinal crowning the statue of Our Lady of Willesden as its apogee, filled Wembley Stadium with devotees. In July 1953 there was a massive Vocations Exhibition at Olympia, and in the same month the Cardinal went off to Norway to celebrate the eighth centenary of the founding of that country's hierarchy by Nicholas Breakspeare, England's only pope.

Throughout all these events Griffin struggled with his health. In January 1951 he had a coronary thrombosis – the first of several – and when he recovered went off to convalesce in Torquay. In June 1956, while preaching at a service in Westminster Cathedral for Catholic holders of the Victoria Cross,

---

28 Bedoyère, *op. cit.*, p. 103.
29 *Ibid.*, p. 102.

he suffered another heart attack. He struggled on to complete his sermon, but collapsed immediately afterwards. A house was rented for him, Winwalloe, in Polzeath, Cornwall, in the hope that he would once again recover, but it was there that he died, on 20 August 1956. Derek Worlock, always in attendance, performed the last rights. The funeral service was held eight days later, and the Cardinal was interred in the crypt of his cathedral.

7

William Godfrey

Adrian Hastings in his *History of English Christianity, 1820–2000* was hardly complimentary about the role of Cardinal Griffin (see above, p. 135). He was positively rude in his assessment of Griffin's successor, William Godfrey. Godfrey was, he says, 'the dominant Catholic ecclesiastic through all these years, and no one was more sure of his own mind, or who had less to offer that [*sic*] was expected'. His time as Archbishop of Westminster was known 'rather irreverently' to the clergy of the diocese, Hastings continues, as the 'safe period'.[1] John Carmel Heenan, who succeeded Godfrey both in Liverpool and at Westminster, was equally damning, if not quite so forthright: 'William Godfrey made little mark as a bishop largely because during his robust years he was in the diplomatic service of the Holy See . . . The good diplomat is anonymous, and Dr Godfrey never had the slightest difficulty in keeping silent.'[2]

He was born in Leven Street, Kirkdale, near Liverpool, the son of George, a haulage contractor, and Maria (née Garvey),

---

1 Hastings, *op. cit.*, pp. 478–9.
2 J. C. Heenan, *A Crown of Thorns* (London: Hodder and Stoughton, 1974), p. 359. Heenan goes on to quote his own panegyric, if such it can be called, at Godfrey's funeral: 'He had a rare degree of self-control, and could not be betrayed into making angry or incautious statements. Probably he never needed to retract any words he had spoken. It is possible, of course, that sometimes prudence led him to an excessive caution. He did not take easily or kindly to new ideas. He arrived at decisions so slowly that he found it hard to yield to argument or to alter judgments he had made' (*ibid.*).

though his father had died before he was born. He went to the parish of St John's elementary school and in 1903 to Ushaw College, where he eventually became captain of the school. In 1910 he was sent to the English College in Rome. It is said that while there he became increasingly reserved, but he was nonetheless a brilliant student, and was selected as only the second English student since Wiseman (the other was George Errington) to perform the 'Public Act' (see above, p. 14). He was popular, which rather contradicts the notion of his being reserved. He was an entertaining pianist and an excellent mimic. He also played the French horn. He was ordained in October 1916, and returned to the Liverpool Diocese where he was assigned a curacy at St Michael's, West Derby Road. His stay there was brief. In 1918 he was sent back to teach Classics and Philosophy at Ushaw, where once again his powers of impersonation were much in demand. He also served as choirmaster and librarian. He progressed from philosophy to lecturing on theology in the seminary, where his teaching was thorough but uninspired. He taught by means of dictated notes, for which, according to his entry in the *Oxford Dictionary of National Biography*, he was known as 'Billy Buckets': 'Uncle Bill' was the sobriquet by which in later life he came to be known.

As well as being strict and austere, he was also particularly devout, remarked upon for the amount of time he spent in prayer in the chapel. He served as a spiritual guide to many in the college. He collected together his spiritual instructions into two books, *The Young Apostle* and *God and Ourselves* which were published in 1924 and 1927 respectively.

As early as 1918 he had been considered as a possible 'repetitor', a form of tutor, to the students at the English College, all of whom were by this time going for their studies to the Gregorian University. His bishop was again approached to free him for that role in 1928 and in 1929 he was finally freed to take over from Arthur Hinsley as rector of the Venerable English College. In effect Hinsley had been long gone (see above, p. 114), and Godfrey inherited a situation of some disorder. To reimpose discipline he insisted on the observance of a string of arbitrary rules which, in the view of the historian of the English College, Michael Williams, caused the students to suffer – sufferings which in Godfrey's mind connected those in his charge with the sufferings of the English martyrs, of whom Godfrey himself was a devotee, and of whom the college was so proud.[3] As rector, wrote Williams, Godfrey was 'never afraid of unpopularity and never compromised his principles'.[4]

Rules were his thing. He worked with Mgr Ernesto Ruffini, then secretary of the Congregation of Seminaries, on the document *Deus Scientiarum Dominus* and its appendixes which laid down the norms to be observed in training colleges for clergy around the world, and enforced them in his own institution. They were intended to bring ecclesiastical institutions more into line with secular ones, even though, as Williams says, 'Godfrey himself could sometimes scarcely conceal a contempt for English university life and learning which he considered superficial and flippant'.[5] He also demanded strict observance of such regulations as were laid down by the Congregation for the behaviour of clerics in Rome itself.[6] One of these was the prohibition of any student possessing a non-Catholic version of the Bible: Godfrey required that they be handed over. In 1934 he had printed a book of all the college rules.

Such careful toeing of the Roman line won him friends in the Vatican curia. According to Heenan, in 1935 he was chosen to replace Hinsley in Africa, but in June suffered sunstroke during the ceremony of laying the foundation stone for Liverpool's Metropolitan Cathedral and had to be ruled out.[7] In 1936 he was sent as part of a papal mission to Malta, and he

---

3 Williams, *op. cit.*, p. 164.

4 *Ibid.*

5 *Ibid.*, p. 163.

6 Later on, as Archbishop of Westminster, he demanded that all clergy wore homburgs.

7 Heenan, *Not the Whole Truth*, p. 93. Apparently he wanted Heenan to accompany him to Mombasa.

came to London as member of the entourage of the papal representative for the coronation of King George VI. He was also made visitor to the seminaries in Great Britain and in Malta, a task which enabled him to prepare the ground for a much more significant role, that of Apostolic Delegate.[8]

As has been seen (see above, p. 119), the idea of having some kind of representation of the Holy See in Britain had long been mooted, especially by those who were unhappy with the leadership of the Archbishop of Westminster, and wanted in some manner to circumvent it. Having a papal representative in London was one means of doing so.

The British Foreign Office was also having problems, but of a rather different kind. There had been a British Minister to the Holy See since 1914, but no papal equivalent in London.[9] Hence, when the pope wanted to send condolences from one head of state to another in October 1930 over the R-101 airship disaster, they were passed on to George V by Cardinal Bourne. This was a clear breach of protocol: such messages should have been relayed by way of the British Minister in Rome, but on this occasion the Foreign Office chose to ignore the diplomatic solecism. When in 1934 Pius XI's acknowledgement of the receipt of the new British Minister's letters of credence was passed on directly to the King by the Cardinal, Whitehall told the Vatican that in future it should use the proper channels. It is quite possible that the Secretary of State, Eugenio Pacelli, was perfectly aware of the breach of diplomatic etiquette, and was simply making a point. Meanwhile the British chargé at the Vatican thought that Bourne was deliberately breaching proto-

---

8 An Apostolic Delegate is not technically a diplomat. He represents the Holy See, but is 'accredited' not to the State but to the local hierarchy

9 On diplomatic relations between Great Britain and the Holy See, see Hyginus Eugene Cardinale, *The Holy See and the International Order* (Gerrards Cross: Colin Smythe, 1976), pp. 190–2. This is now out of date, however, because papal representation in Britain has since been raised to the rank of ambassador (or papal nuncio).

col by playing the role of papal nuncio in order to win favour in the Vatican where, it was believed, he was not popular.

Hinsley was unaware of the problem. Soon after he was appointed, the King and Queen celebrated their jubilee, so he sent a loyal address to the Crown from the Catholic community of Great Britain. This never got further than the Home Office. Nor did a personal letter pledging loyalty. He again ran into problems when he sent a letter of condolence to Edward VIII on the death of his father. Part of the issue was the use by Catholic bishops of territorial designations. For someone to claim to be Archbishop of Westminster, or bishop of anywhere within British territory, was technically improper,[10] and that, as far as civil servants were concerned, made receiving messages from him problematic. And as for relations with the Vatican, there was a belief that the presence of a papal nuncio in England would give ammunition to Protestant extremists, and exacerbate talk of 'papal aggression'. This might be an especial problem if the representative were to be an Italian, as many members of the papal diplomatic service were. They would be instantly suspected, rightly or wrongly, of having Fascist sympathies. If the British government wanted influence in the Vatican, Whitehall's reasoning ran, then the best way by far was to have an English cardinal in the papal administration.

The English bishops were likewise not in favour of a papal representative in London, in their case because he would come between themselves and direct communication with the Holy See. There was, however, one exception to the hierarchy's stance. Bishop Amigo, ever eager to undercut Bourne's pretensions, was actively lobbying for a nuncio. Until, that is, the appointment of Hinsley. The English bishops wrote to Rome after their October 1938 meeting when news of the possible appointment of an Apostolic Delegate was discussed. They

---

10 The Ecclesiastical Titles Act of 1851 had forbidden it, and although the penalties imposed by the Act had been abrogated in 1871 by a similarly named statute, the use of such designations had not been authorized.

were against it, and said so; so also, after the appointment of Hinsley with whom he got along, was Amigo. In July 1938 he wrote to Pacelli:

> Four centuries of separation from the See of Rome have strengthened the objection to what is not English, and with many the difficulty in becoming a Catholic is that they look upon us as foreign. There is unfortunately a very strong dislike of foreigners, and an Apostolic Delegate would have to be Italian . . . I therefore strongly feel that the interests of the Holy See are perfectly secured at present without the danger of rousing prejudice by appointing an Apostolic Delegate.[11]

By the time of the bishops' October letter, however, a decision had been taken – and without any consultation with the English and Welsh hierarchy. The Foreign Office, which had been impressed by Pius XI's defiance of Hitler during the Führer's visit to Rome in May 1938 (see above, p. 123n), was much more sympathetic to the Vatican. It had, moreover, been mollified with the assurance from the Holy See that the papal representative would not have to be a nuncio, i.e. a diplomat, and that, at least on the first appointment, the representative need not be Italian – indeed, would be British. So the way was open for the appointment of William Godfrey as Apostolic Delegate to Great Britain. It was announced on 21 November 1938: two days later Godfrey was consecrated Bishop in the chapel of the English College, and raised to the rank of Archbishop.

Hinsley was upset. As he told the bishops in August 1938 he had heard of the forthcoming appointment of Godfrey, but only by chance: the only bishop who appeared to have had prior warning was Amigo. As has been noted, the bishops decided to write a letter of protest. 'An Apostolic Delegate

---

11 Clifton, *op. cit.*, pp. 117–18.

coming to England at this juncture,' said the draft, 'even though he might be an Englishman, would be looked upon as an agent of Mussolini in the interests of the Rome–Berlin axis.'[12]

In the end, the letter was never sent, but the Delegate, who established himself in a convent in Hammersmith, then in a house in Kensington and eventually in a grand but gloomy mansion on Wimbledon Parkside,[13] was at first cold-shouldered by the bishops. He was not invited to the Low Week meetings, nor did he receive agenda papers or minutes. The Foreign Office likewise ignored him, preferring at first to deal with the Vatican through Hinsley, whom officials liked and trusted. Hinsley in turn was not disposed to trust Godfrey, and occasionally asked that sensitive papers travel to Rome in the Foreign Office's diplomatic pouch, rather than in that of the Delegate. There was an early clash. The Vatican asked Godfrey to intervene with Hinsley, and through him with the government, about the payment of allowances to soldiers' 'unmarried wives'. The Cardinal was furious. It was only natural justice, he retorted, for a man to support the women by whom he has had children, and must continue to do so after being called up for military service. As time went on, however, the Vatican used Godfrey as a channel of communication over, for example, Pius XII's peace initiative after the fall of France, an initiative which both Godfrey and Hinsley thought was a bad idea.[14]

The new Delegate's primary responsibility was to the hierarchy, which, as has been remarked, chose at first to ignore him. But until his appointment in 1953 as Archbishop of Liverpool he had considerable influence on the choice of bishops to fill the vacant sees of England and Wales. There was a joke that in

---

12 Moloney, *op. cit.*, p. 97.
13 The location of the Delegacy (now of course a nunciature) in a leafy suburb rather than in a more embassy-friendly square of Kensington or Belgravia was intentional. The Delegate felt obliged to be discreet.
14 Chadwick, *op. cit.*, pp. 138–9

order to be a bishop one had to be celibate, ordained and have attended Rome's English College. In case of necessity, it went, the first two conditions might be dispensed with, but not the third. Increasingly appointments were made from among those who had been students at the Venerabile under Hinsley. This may have caused some resentment, but it had the advantage of producing a bench of bishops who knew one another and got along together.

Godfrey was not an imaginative man and found some of Hinsley's initiatives, particularly the ecumenical aspects of the Sword of the Spirit, hard to take. 'It seems to me essential', he said in a sermon delivered in Birmingham Cathedral in 1941, 'that the use of the term "common ground" by the Holy Father should be well understood as having no connection with no surrender of dogmatic principle, or with the error of "fundamentalism".'[15] He visited prisoners of war and set up an office to search for missing persons. He met members of governments in exile (he was an excellent linguist), and was appointed the Vatican's chargé d'affaires to the Polish government in exile. After the war he busied himself with publishing English translations of papal documents.

He was intensely proud of being the pope's representative in London and was reluctant in November 1953 to accept the office of Archbishop of Liverpool. He had good reason to be hesitant. For an ordinary of a diocese he had spent remarkably little time – a parish curacy of just a matter of a few months – in any formal pastoral role. In Liverpool he devoted himself to parish visiting. He also inherited a vast and incomplete cathedral. The original design by Edward Lutyens had been abandoned. Godfrey commissioned new drawings which were a cheaper variation of Lutyen's plan and which drew a great deal of criticism from the architectural establishment. As Heenan puts it, 'William Godfrey was a man of prudence and – which is

---

15 Moloney, *op. cit.*, p. 198.

not at all the same thing – a man of great caution. Three years was not nearly long enough for him to put plans for the new cathedral into operation.'[16]

He was only three years in Liverpool because, in December 1956, he was appointed by Pius XII to succeed Griffin as Archbishop of Westminster, being enthroned on 11 February 1957, the first time such a ceremony had been televised in England. He was created Cardinal only in 1958, at the first consistory held by John XXIII, so he was not eligible to attend the conclave which elected Pope John. Nor of course was Giovanni Battista Montini, who was created Cardinal on the same occasion and succeeded Pope John as Pope Paul VI.

Bruce Kent, who was ordained by Godfrey in Westminster Cathedral, remembers him as a 'quiet, decent man'.[17] Others were less complimentary. Derek Worlock continued at Archbishop's House as secretary, and was instructed, on Godfrey's arrival, to put an end to the practice in the cathedral of having evening Masses which Griffin had very reluctantly permitted. Realizing that this would incur a good deal of wrath from regular Mass-goers, he managed to stall, and the services went on as before.

As Archbishop of Westminster, Godfrey built churches and expanded schools. He was very attached to the cathedral, and used to sit there in prayer. He continued Griffin's policy of refusing to allow concerts to be held in the cathedral, even concerts of sacred music. He raised money – £225,000 – to continue the work of putting marble on the brick pillars. He drew up a four-year catechetical course for the diocese which priests were supposed to preach from the pulpit each Sunday. Neither his own sermons nor his pastoral letters were inspiring. One year, however, when recommending the Lenten Fast to raise money for what was not then, but soon after became, the

---

16 Heenan, *op. cit.*, p. 283.
17 Bruce Kent, *Undiscovered Ends* (London: HarperCollins, 1992), p. 74.

Catholic Fund for Overseas Development (CAFOD), he wrote, 'A plump and pampered poodle might run all the more gaily after a reduced diet on simpler fare.' Unfortunately for the Cardinal, the letter coincided with Cruft's Dog Show. His words made headlines of a sort, and attracted much ire from dog lovers around the country. It also raised much more money than such appeals had done hitherto.

But without doubt the major event of his tenure at Westminster was the calling of the Second Vatican Council. This was an 'ecumenical' Council, that is to say a Council of the World-wide Catholic Church. The word 'ecumenical' had, however, gathered another meaning, namely the movement towards unity among the Christian denominations. In Liverpool, Archbishop Heenan was busy promoting the latter idea, while, on Godfrey's instructions, his faithful secretary Derek Worlock was – correctly – telling everyone that it was a *general* Council.[18] Heenan established an ecumenical office in Liverpool and gathered a committee. His enthusiasm was encouraged by the visit at the end of the 1960 of the Archbishop of Canterbury, the shortly to retire Geoffrey Fisher, to Pope John, the first by an Archbishop of Canterbury for nearly 600 years. Heenan set up a conference, and invited over the leading Vatican ecumenist, the German Jesuit Cardinal Bea. Godfrey was suspicious of the whole affair, and would not offer hospitality to his fellow cardinal at Archbishop's House. He was, moreover, upset by Bea's insistence on calling at Lambeth Palace, where Michael Ramsey had recently taken up residence as Fisher's successor. This action of Cardinal Bea's did not endear the cause of ecumenism to the majority of the English bishops.

Before the Council, however, the bishops had a task to do.

---

18 There was perhaps at first a confusion in Pope John's own mind about the purpose of the Council, cf. Michael Walsh, 'The Religious Ferment of the '60s' in Hugh McCleod (ed.), *The Cambridge History of Christianity* (Cambridge: Cambridge University Press, 2006), vol. 9, pp. 308–9.

They had to propose possible items for the agenda. Godfrey drew up notes on his pet topic, the discipline of the clergy, and then had to stimulate the rest of the bishops to send in their responses. They were not inspired – but that was true of the majority of responses from around the world.[19] Rather to his alarm, it would seem, Godfrey was appointed to the Council's Central Preparatory Committee. Despite Worlock's urgings, he was reluctant to go to Rome, partly because he would have to stay at the Venerabile which was having problems Godfrey wanted to steer clear of, and partly because he was suffering from cancer. He had an operation which failed to resolve the problem, and left a wound which failed to heal properly. He finally agreed to go to Rome only in March 1961.

When the Council finally opened in October the following year, the English bishops stayed at the Venerabile. They plotted their strategy. Much to his surprise, Godfrey was made the unofficial spokesman for the Americans, Canadians, Australians, Irish and Scots, as well as the English and Welsh, a fact which may have less to do with the esteem in which he was held than with his fluency in Latin. Nonetheless, after the Council had opened, various conservative groups sought his support. He had indeed been shocked by the bitterness of the attack by several of the Council fathers on Cardinal Ottaviani and the Holy Office, and was willing to come to Ottaviani's defence. The arch-conservative Marcel Lefebvre, who ended his life excommunicate, looked for his support, and so did his old friend Ernesto Ruffini, now Cardinal of Palermo. There was a meeting between Ruffini and Godfrey in the residence of the Italian bishops (unlike the English bishops at the Venerabile, they were living there rent free, Worlock could not help

---

19 The present writer heard the Archbishop of Birmingham, Joseph Grimshaw, speak about the Council after the first session. All he ever wanted from the Council, he said, was that the name of St Joseph should be added to the canon of the Mass – and that had been achieved.

noting),[20] and another one was planned but did not happen because Godfrey had been double-booked.

The English bishops meanwhile had drawn up their own plan of campaign. They decided which of their number they would propose for the various committees of the Council, and distributed the lists to friendly episcopal conferences whose votes they felt they might rely upon. Some were indeed elected to the chosen committee, but not Godfrey, who had been proposed for the committee on the sacraments. There had been a degree of confusion about whether Pope John was himself going to appoint those of the rank of cardinal to the different groups, and when the list of names was first drawn up, Godfrey's name was omitted. It was then decided to add it on, so there were in existence two lists – one with Godfrey's name, one without. Heenan distributed the one without the Cardinal's name on it. It may have been a genuine mistake: Derek Worlock, as ever intensely loyal to his boss, thought Heenan had done it on purpose. Nevertheless Godfrey played a small part in the Council. His theology was of the variety which he had studied at the Gregorian many years before and which was fast being supplanted, but he was clear, fluent and, thought Worlock, very commonsensical.

Cardinal Godfrey returned to London in December 1962. While in Rome he had been making regular visits to the Salvator Mundi hospital for treatment. Shortly after he got back home he went into the Westminster Hospital for what was his fourth operation. He survived the operation, but on 19 January 1963 he had a mild heart attack. He died still in the hospital on 22 January, just as the Archbishop of Canterbury had come to call.

---

20 The English bishops were required each to pay the Venerabile a rent for their room. After some discussion they agreed that the price being charged was quite reasonable.

8

John Carmel Heenan

From Wiseman to Griffin, each Archbishop of Westminster has found a biographer. No one has ever written a biography of Cardinal William Godfrey, and it is highly unlikely that anyone ever will. It is much more surprising that no one has chosen to compile a study of John Carmel Heenan. He was the best-known churchman of his day, at least equalling in popularity his well-loved contemporary across the river at Lambeth, Michael Ramsey. Perhaps it is that the audience for archiepiscopal lives is a declining one, though Basil Hume, who was to succeed Heenan at Westminster, has attracted the interest of several authors. And so, for that matter, has Derek Worlock, who was Heenan's successor-but-one as Archbishop of Liverpool.

There is one rather obvious reason for the lack of a biographer. Cardinal Heenan penned his own life story in two substantial volumes to which reference has already been made, *Not the Whole Truth* and *A Crown of Thorns*. In these, Heenan relates the events of his life in some considerable detail up to the point of his appointment to Westminster. They are astonishing works of self-justification, in which he comments sententiously on every topic from the Jews to the Irish, and reveals himself as a remarkably patriotic Englishman.

This last is surprising, because he was born, on 26 January 1905, to thoroughly Irish parents. His father, James Carmel Heenan of the small town of Clareen, not far from Lough Derg, married the girl next door, Anne Pilkington, and they both came to London. They lived first in Fulham, then moved, before any of the children were born, to 33 Ripley Road in Ilford. There were four sons and one daughter: John's brother James also became a priest. He was a twin: the second twin, christened George, died 12 hours after his birth. The family was not particularly well off – James worked in the Patent Office as a clerk – and they struggled to get the children educated. His mother even tried to win John a place at Westminster Cathedral Choir School, but Sir Richard Terry, who auditioned him, turned him down. It is perhaps ironic that it was when Heenan was at Westminster that the Choir School came closest to being closed down.

Heenan therefore went to the Catholic elementary school which served his parish of SS Peter and Paul: the parish priest, Paddy Palmer, was Heenan's great hero and supporter in his wish to become a priest. At the end of the elementary school there was a scholarship on offer for the Jesuit college of St Ignatius at Stamford Hill in north London. Heenan sat for the scholarship, though it was given to another boy – but he was sent to a boarding school and the place at St Ignatius was offered to Heenan instead. He studied there until he was 17 when, still certain of the vocation he had felt as a young boy, he went to Ushaw to train for the priesthood. Ilford lay within the Diocese of Brentwood, and candidates for ordination might have expected to be sent to the nearest seminary, St Edmund's at Ware in Hertfordshire. But the Bishop of Brentwood, Bernard Ward, was at odds with Cardinal Bourne over the latter's decision in a bout of patriotic fervour to introduce the Officer Training Corps into St Edmund's.

So Bishop Ward sent Heenan to Ushaw, which John did not like at all. The food he found practically inedible, the study undemanding. There was one incident, however, which stood out, and which he records in some detail. He fell ill, and after he recovered he was allowed out for a short period of sick leave. During this break from the seminary he met a girl and fell in love with her, only determining to return to Ushaw after a considerable amount of soul-searching.

He was not there for long. At the end of October 1924 his bishop rescued him from Ushaw and sent him to the English College in Rome. There, under the tutelage of the rector Arthur Hinsley he flourished. He studied philosophy and theology at the Gregorian University, being rather more attracted to the former than the latter. He was allowed to be ordained in his home parish, on 6 July 1930, and after a final year in Rome as a priest, a year of study which qualified him, by the regulations of the day, to entitle himself 'Doctor' Heenan, he came back to the East End of London as a curate in the parish of St Ethelburga's, Barking, after first taking a holiday in the United States.

He arrived in his new parish to discover himself in charge, the parish priest being away. He immediately had to deal with a delicate problem. There had been a famous medieval convent in Barking, of which St Ethelburga had been the first abbess. The town was celebrating the 1,300th anniversary of its foundation with a pageant. There were Catholics playing leading roles in the pageant but they had been instructed, according to the Church's rules, that they might not attend the church service with which the pageant was to close. It was then revealed that a real Anglican bishop, in full episcopal dress, mitre and crosier, was intending to walk in the procession. In the view of the young Fr Heenan this turned the procession into a liturgical event from which Catholics had to be banned. In 1931 Barking the erstwhile Catholic participants meekly obeyed, and laid aside their costumes. It was Heenan's first major brush with the niceties of inter-Church relations.

He found his parish priest at Barking – a shy and timid man – rather difficult to get along with at first, but gradually grew to like him. Heenan readily made friends and became involved in local issues. He records with pride his collaboration with the anti-contraception pressure group the League of National Life – which was concerned not so much about the morality of birth control as the falling birth rate in Britain – to prevent the establishment in Barking of a Marie Stopes

clinic.[1] He was an enterprising young man. In 1936 he conceived of the idea of visiting the USSR, a courageous, indeed
foolhardy thing to do. He was encouraged by Hinsley, now at
Westminster, who gave him permission to leave behind his
clerical collar and breviary, but was discouraged by almost
everyone else. He tried to go as a journalist, but the newspapers he approached thought the adventure far too risky.
Finally he disguised himself as a psychologist ('There is no
more fertile field than psychology for the charlatan', he later
wrote)[2] and arrived in Leningrad, with a good deal of trepida-
tion, on 11 October 1936. Dressed as he was in a 'natty gent's
suit in slate blue twill' as he recalled with obvious relish 40
years later,[3] he launched himself on his fact-finding mission.
His disguise was never penetrated, not even by Lola, a student
who was clearly attracted to him, and continued to write to
him after his return to England until he revealed his identity
as a Catholic priest. Back in London, and at Hinsley's suggestion, he organized a meeting at the Albert Hall in which he
was to describe his experiences. Unfortunately the other
speakers he brought in for the occasion so overran their time
that in the end he could manage no more than ten minutes.

Though not a member of the Westminster Diocese, Heenan
was close to Hinsley. The new Archbishop of Westminster was a
stranger to the diocese he had been appointed to run, especially so because Bourne had sent few clergy to Rome for their
studies. Hinsley recruited a Northampton priest as his secretary, Valentine Elwes, later chaplain at Oxford University, and,
particularly after the fiasco of his Golders Green sermon (see
above, p. 119), tried to recruit Heenan. Bishop Doubleday flatly
refused to release him, and did so again in 1937. Doubleday did

---

1 At the Lambeth Conference of 1930 the Church of England had changed its
 stance, and had adopted a position of greater tolerance towards contraception.
2 J. C. Heenan, *Not the Whole Truth* (London: Hodder and Stoughton, 1971),
 p. 105.
3 *Ibid.*, p. 110.

not get on well with the energetic young curate, but even when the Cardinal went directly to him to ask that Heenan might be transferred to Westminster, he refused. But at least he recognized Heenan's talent. He was not allowed to go to Archbishop's House but instead, in April 1937 at the (then) remarkably early age of 32, he was appointed parish priest of the church of St Nicholas at Manor Park.

He remained at Manor Park throughout the war, visiting the bomb sites and the hospitals, hurrying people into air-raid shelters, and still saying the morning Mass – which required him to be fasting from midnight. He was so tired that, on one occasion, he fell asleep while driving and woke up to find the car on its side. He was rushed to hospital, but had not been badly injured. Sitting in the air-raid shelters he found time to write *Letters from Rush Green*. He had already produced *Priest and Penitent* in 1936, a response to a Catholic Truth Society pamphlet entitled *Pitfalls of the Confessional* to which he took exception. In 1940 he volunteered himself to the BBC as a contributor to 'Britain Speaks', a series of broadcasts to the USA, which were published as *Were You Listening*. A sequence of broadcasts to the armed forces became *Untruisms*. He also wrote scripts for beaming to South America, and features for the *Sunday Graphic* which, he boasts, he could dictate in half an hour.

The position of the Irish Republic, which remained neutral during the war even though thousands of Irishmen joined the British forces, caused a degree of hostility to Ireland, not least among Catholics. Michael de la Bedoyère, the editor of the *Catholic Herald*, invited him to make an extended visit to Dublin, ostensibly in the guise of spiritual director to the Legion of Mary. While there he met all the leading politicians, and on his return was able to write persuasively in defence of the Irish stance on the war. He also visited Belfast, and in his articles graphically highlighted the discrimination shown to Catholics in Northern Ireland, which he contrasted with the toleration shown by the Dublin government to non-Roman Catholics. They have not even, he said, tried to recover the two once-Catholic cathedrals 'now being used by dwindling Protestant congregations while the teeming millions [*sic*] of Dublin's Catholic have no cathedral of their own'.[4] It was not all praise. He drew attention to the amount of poverty he encountered in Dublin, and he also commented, presciently, on deteriorating relations between the clergy and the local youth:

> It is remarkable that not only the priest but also Protestant ministers were at one in naming dances as one of the great crises of modern Ireland. I therefore lost no time in seeking the views of the young people themselves. I found, as I had suspected, that they were sullen and resentful at the attitude of the clergy.[5]

There was much else to occupy him. The *Jewish Chronicle* charged him with anti-Semitism, against which he vigorously defended himself, in the process demonstrating that he had not yet risen entirely above the attitudes towards Jews prevalent in the 1930s Catholic community in England. He also took H. G. Wells publicly to task over remarks he made about the Church, but Wells refused the offer of a public debate. But it was the debate about education that took up most of his time before the 1944 Act. Eventually his bishop forbade him to accept any more speaking engagements outside his parish, and required him to resign from the local education authority, appointing a priest from elsewhere in his place. 'From Bishop Doubleday I learned how to suffer injustice from a Father-in-God', he wrote in *Not the Whole Truth*, 'without developing a grudge against the Church of God.'[6]

Doubleday, who had twice refused him permission to work for Hinsley, in 1947 released him to become superior of the Catholic Missionary Society. The debate about allowing the

---

4 *Ibid.*, p. 240.
5 *Ibid.*, p. 242.
6 *Ibid.*, p. 272.

CMS to die – it had been founded by Vaughan in 1901 – or attempting to revive it had taken place at the Low Week meeting. The majority of the bishops were in favour of letting it fade away, but Godfrey warned them that such an obvious failure in the spirit of evangelism would not go down well in Rome, so instead they turned their attention to finding new staff. Heenan believed that Doubleday agreed to his appointment only because he was too deaf to notice what was going on until the vote had been taken. Heenan agreed only if he was allowed to select the remaining missioners, which he did. From then on, comments Adrian Hastings, 'Heenan became a national figure, leader of the Church's pastoral renewal.'[7] With his usual energy he founded a new headquarters, in West Heath Road, Hampstead, and went off to the USA to visit his relatives and to find out how similar organizations were run across the Atlantic. He did not, he comments, learn very much about the activities of missioners, but he encountered the notion of a Catholic enquiry centre, a model which the CMS established in Britain.

A year was spent preparing the clergy for mission work, then, in the summer of 1948, the CMS launched a mission right across Oxfordshire using volunteer priests. This appeared to be so successful that the bishops decided, in the run-up to the Holy Year of 1950, to embark upon a countrywide mission in 1949. Again the volunteers had to be prepared: Heenan produced *Hints for Missioners*. In addition to the missions, he preached; Heenan was much in demand for one-off talks and as a retreat giver. His retreat talks appeared as *The People's Priest*.

He served as superior of the CMS for only three years. 'The year 1951 did not begin auspiciously', he wrote at the start of *A Crown of Thorns*. 'My brother died in January, my sister lay dying of leukaemia, and I was nominated bishop of Leeds.'[8] When

---

7 *Ibid.*, p. 480.
8 *Ibid.*, p. 9. His sister did not, however, die. Despite her illness she insisted on attending his consecration as Bishop, and while there was blessed by Archbishop Godfrey with a relic of Pius X. This, Heenan records, brought about her cure.

the call came from the Apostolic Delegate, Heenan was preaching a mission in County Durham. 'I did not doubt my ability to organize a diocese, nor was I lacking in pastoral expertise', he wrote. 'It was my spiritual qualifications which were wanting.'[9] He confessed all to the Delegate, an old friend from Roman days, who reassured him. He was consecrated Bishop in St Anne's Cathedral, Leeds, on 12 March 1957.

There was a lot to do. Heenan's predecessor in Leeds, a convert Anglican vicar, had been a quiet, gentle man, interested in bees and goats – he was president of the society of Yorkshire goat-keepers – and unwilling to disturb the even tenor of the lives of his clergy. He had, moreover, died more than a year before Heenan took over. The new Bishop sent for the Vicar General and asked for a list of all priests who wanted to move parishes, or who ought to move parishes. Wholesale changes followed. Heenan tells the story against himself, that for a time the Diocese of Leeds was known as 'the cruel see', and that the clergy when meeting one another would ask not how are you, but where are you. He does not mention the other story, that he even tried to move clergy who were not in his diocese. 'I have no doubt', he remarked in the second volume of his autobiography, 'that I acted imprudently.'[10] He instituted an 'open day'. Every Friday anyone with a problem, priest or lay person, could come to see him.

He had been appointed in a general election year. As the October date approached, he preached a sermon on the choice facing the electorate. He was not prepared, he said, to reveal his own preferences, but warned Catholics that within the Labour Party there were Marxists who did not have at heart the country's best interests. Shortly afterwards he received a letter from an agitated Harold Wilson. There were Catholics among his party workers in his Huyton constituency who were

---

9 *Ibid.*, p. 324.
10 J. C. Heenan, *A Crown of Thorns* (London: Hodder and Stoughton, 1974), p. 27.

refusing to work for him on the strength of Heenan's remarks, and Wilson wanted clarification: was he included in the bishop's condemnation? He was not, replied Heenan in a letter, and added that he could make the letter public should he so wish. He later congratulated himself on saving the seat of the future Prime Minister who won in 1951 with only a small majority.

The following year there was a Eucharistic Congress in Barcelona which he attended, he said, because no other member of the hierarchy was going: 'The English do not find congresses attractive.'[11] And nor did he, but he made the most of his time in Barcelona, visiting whatever took his fancy, from prisons to the abbey of Montserrat. His views of Franco's Spain were naive. He remarked on the prevalence of the Catalan language, but not on the fact that the Caudillo had banned its use. While in Barcelona he was invited to Australia to lecture. He went in the spring of 1953, his fare paid for by the War Office as he made pastoral visits to British troops in Singapore, Korea, Japan and Hong Kong. He went by way of Rome, and dropped in on the Regina Coeli prison, and Karachi, which he reached by a Comet plane. The aircraft he travelled on was one of those which later crashed. He was absent from his diocese for three months after being in post for only two years.

Though constantly expressing the wish that he were at home, he obviously enjoyed foreign travel. In 1956, on the slim excuse of growing immigration from the West Indies – 'slim' because there were then few immigrants within his diocesan boundaries – he set off for a prolonged tour of the Caribbean, his pastoral antennae as ever on high alert. 'The expression "living in sin" would be meaningless here', he wrote of Jamaica. 'They are not living in sin but usually living in hope of saving enough money to have champagne with their wedding breakfast.'[12]

---

11 *Ibid.*, p. 42.
12 *Ibid.*, p. 180.

Heenan was still the best-known priest in Britain. He 'seemed to epitomize the self-confident new Catholicism of the post-war period,' Adrian Hastings wrote of him, 'a Catholicism which yielded intellectually not an inch but which appeared quite at home and seldom out-marshalled in the debating hall and on the television screens of the 1950s'.[13] The Bishop of Leeds was undoubtedly at home in both venues. In January 1954 he presided at a televised pontifical High Mass from St Anne's Cathedral, the first such Mass ever on British television. Given his fame, it is not surprising that, even after so short a time in Leeds, he was asked to move to Liverpool. It was announced on 7 May 1957, and he was enthroned in Liverpool's pro-cathedral on 16 July the following year. 'As Bishop of Leeds I had asked many priests to move', he wrote in *A Crown of Thorns.* 'I could hardly complain when asked to move myself.'[14] This time, apparently, there was no soul-searching.

In Liverpool, as in Leeds, his regime was much the same, a continuous round of parish visiting and hospital visiting. But there were a number of unique features to his new archiepiscopal office. For one thing, he had no proper cathedral. The crypt which Edward Lutyens had designed was massive and lying empty. He swiftly got it up and running, but then turned his thoughts to its completion. He decided on a competition run under the auspices of the Royal Institute of British Architects, of which Sir Basil Spence, the architect of Coventry Cathedral, was then the president. Spence himself undertook be be one of the assessors, along with Heenan and a Catholic architect. In a rare moment of self-doubt he wondered what would happen if he did not agree with the professionals. They persuaded him that the winner would be obvious – which indeed proved to be the case. The commission was awarded to Congregationalist Frank Gibberd, who was busy designing Harlow New Town and who had only entered as an after-

---

13 *Ibid.*, p. 480.
14 *Ibid.*, p. 207.

thought, having attended the opening of a Catholic church in Harlow designed by one of his partners, and being impressed by his first experience of the liturgy.

One major difference between Leeds and Liverpool was the degree of sectarianism still rife in the latter. Although Catholics were commonly on the receiving end of intolerance, successive archbishops had done little to mitigate the hostility of Protestants towards Catholics, not least over the issue of mixed marriages. Dispensations for Catholics to marry non-Catholics were difficult to get, and under some regimes impossible. The only choice was to go across the border to set up a quasi-domicile in a neighbouring diocese. Even when a dispensation was granted, the restrictions on mixed marriages took a great deal of pleasure out of the event. Such weddings were allowed to take place only in a side chapel, there was no Nuptial Mass, and it was forbidden to play the organ. One of Heenan's first acts in his new diocese was to remove these disabilities. The wedding might take place at the high altar of a church, and there could be music. He also asked for his CTS pamphlet *Mixed Marriages: A Letter to a Non-Catholic*, published in 1957, to be withdrawn.[15]

Heenan had always cultivated good relations with clergy of other denominations, at least since his time at Manor Park. At Leeds he counted Michael Ramsey, then Archbishop of York, among his friends (York fell within the Leeds Diocese) and they appeared together at the 1957 Oxford Conference on the Four Gospels. But his views on ecumenism could scarcely be called advanced. As he said in a lecture he gave at Sheffield University for the Student Christian Movement: 'To a Protestant the Catholic attitude is insufferable and wrong. In a short talk I cannot prove that it is not wrong, but I hope to show that it is not insufferable. The fact that my theology is true will not take me to heaven, but I would lose my soul if I were to pretend it is false.' He quotes this speech in *A Crown of Thorns*, and adds

---

15 He had also published *They Made Me Sign: A Series of Talks to a Non-Catholic about to Marry a Catholic* (London: Sheed and Ward, 1949).

that he would no longer speak in that fashion. But nonetheless, 'The Catholic ecumenist believes that reunion will come about in God's good time and in God's own way without any dogma of the Church being discarded.'[16]

He attended the funeral of Pius XII in 1958, and as he waited for the service to begin looked along the row of cardinals. 'The superlative qualities of Pope Pius made all the cardinals look undistinguished', he remarked.[17] But Cardinal Roncalli of Venice, shortly to become John XXIII, was about to change the Catholic Church for good. He summoned a Council of the Church, and after doing so, established a number of commissions to prepare the agenda. One of these commissions, though with a separate life of its own, was the Secretariat for Promoting Christian Unity. At its head was Cardinal Bea, and Archbishop Heenan was appointed a member – he later became Vice-President. It was his role, as he saw it, to make ecumenism acceptable to the Church in Britain, a task which was made somewhat easier by the visit of a rather nervous Geoffrey Fisher to an almost equally nervous John XIII, at the end of 1960, shortly before Fisher resigned from Canterbury. But the size the of task was vividly demonstrated when, on the day of the very first meeting of the Secretariat, Protestants in Liverpool presented a petition with a thousand signatures to the city council against Catholic schoolchildren being allowed to used an empty county school while their own was being rebuilt. The council gave in to the Protestants.

As has been seen (above, p. 164), Heenan promptly set up an ecumenical secretariat in Liverpool, and, to the irritation of Derek Worlock, tended to present the forthcoming Ecumenical Council as one of reunion. In the August before the Council was due to begin, Heenan organized a major conference at Heythrop College, the Jesuit house of studies then in the

---

16 Heenan, *op. cit.*, p. 203.
17 *Ibid.*, p. 255.

Oxfordshire countryside. His chief speaker was Cardinal Bea, for whom Godfrey failed to find a bed at Archbishop's House. Bea insisted on visiting Lambeth Palace, to call upon the new, much more ecumenically minded, Archbishop of Canterbury, Michael Ramsey. Bea's action did nothing to reassure the English bishops, commented Heenan.[18] Nevertheless it was perhaps their sensitivity to ecumenical concerns that among their otherwise rather banal responses to the Vatican request for suggestions for the conciliar agenda they added that there was no need for a further Marian dogma. (The idea had been mooted that the Council might declare formally Mary to be the Mediatrix of All Graces.)

The English bishops, Heenan remarks, were psychologically unprepared for the Council – one presumes he excludes himself from that judgement. He was certainly busy. Longley, following Worlock's reminiscences, presents him as scurrying about in a conspiratorial manner[19] and, as has been seen (cf. p. 176) , sabotaging efforts by the English and Welsh hierarchy to raise Cardinal Godfrey's profile. The profile of the English and Welsh hierarchy as a whole was not very high. In the history of the Council the name of Christopher Butler, who was there as an abbot (of Downside) rather than as a bishop, though he became one shortly after the Council ended, is mentioned more often than that of any of the bishops, Heenan included. Heenan spoke on religious liberty, directly opposing Cardinal Cardinal Ruffini who claimed that religious tolerance was all that could be justified theologically, and he spoke critically on what was known as 'Schema 13', about its treatment of the laity. When the Council moved on to mixed marriages, he was against the proposal that it should no longer be required of the non-Catholic partner to promise to bring up children of the marriage as Catholics. When it came to discussing the clergy,

---

18 Heenan notes in passing that Ramsey had invited him to stay at Lambeth, but Godfrey tried to dissuade him.

19 Longley, *op. cit.*, pp. 51–2.

Heenan made a remarkable intervention extolling the virtues of golf.[20] Above all, he was worried about liturgical reform. He wrote to Evelyn Waugh in November 1962, in a letter which displayed his distrust of intellectuals, and especially of foreign intellectuals:

> What a pity the voice of the laity was not heard sooner. The enthusiasts who write in *The Tablet* and the *Catholic Herald* are so easily mistaken for the intelligent and alive Catholics. The real difficulty (I think) is that Continentals are twisting themselves inside out to make us look as like as possible to the Protestants.[21]

Naturally he made a speech on ecumenism. By this time he was Archbishop of Westminster and had inherited Derek Worlock as his secretary. Worlock had fought his corner on behalf of Cardinal Godfrey, but managed a seamless change to suit the more progressive style of Heenan. He discovered that one Bishop, George Andrew Beck, was planning to make a speech on Christian unity which would upset his new boss, and warned him of it. Heenan took it upon himself to make the speech – doing so, he insisted, on behalf of the whole hierarchy. 'The Archbishop declared that we were prepared to do anything, short of denying the faith, to obtain the union of Christians', Worlock noted in his diary, and added that Heenan's speech was greeted with 'a tremendous burst of applause.'[22]

Not that Worlock, in retrospect, judged kindly Heenan's role during the Council. When speaking in the debates, he said, he resorted to the tactics he had used when working for the CMS, or at Speakers' Corner in Hyde Park, of 'destroying one's oppo-

20 Michael Walsh, 'The History of the Council' in Adrian Hastings (ed.), *Modern Catholicism* (London: SPCK; New York: Oxford University Press, 1991), pp. 35–47.

21 Scott M. P. Reid (ed.), *A Bitter Trial* (London: The Saint Austin Press, 2000), p. 31.

22 Longley, *op. cit.*, pp. 162–3.

nents. In this he alienated many who had admired his brilliance and pastoral zeal. By the end of the Council I did not dare to put him up at the weekly Press Conference. Those who turned up were hostile to him for the sweetly paternalistic way in which he could turn a question to make the questioner [look] naive or ridiculous.'[23] One need not take this criticism too seriously. Worlock desperately wanted to have a role at the Council, rather than simply be secretary and press officer to the English and Welsh hierarchy. Eventually he was made a *peritus*, a theological expert, but Heenan had little time for the theologians at the Council, and said so in one of the debates.[24]

He was appointed Archbishop of Westminster in succession to Cardinal Godfrey on 2 September 1963, and was made a cardinal in February 1965. Worlock claimed in his diary to welcome the appointment:

> The Archbishop had made a most spectacular take-over of the diocese and the appointment has been widely acclaimed throughout the Press and in all national circles. What was more important was that the priests welcomed it and for the first time we had an Archbishop coming to Westminster who is already well known . . . He met the priests in the Cathedral Hall on Friday afternoon, spoke with them very frankly, giving them in general a go-ahead to do what is best for the flock and not to worry with asking too many permissions. It was all rather like a breath of fresh air . . .'[25]

One of the priests who welcomed the choice of John Carmel Heenan was Bruce Kent, who soon replaced Worlock as Heenan's secretary. Worlock had been used to running the man who ran the diocese and, although he did not seem to

---

23 *Ibid.*, p. 212.
24 'Timeo peritos, adnexa ferentes', he said, with a distant reference to Virgil: 'I fear experts bearing appendices [to conciliar texts]', see Peter Hebblethwaite, *Pope Paul VI* (London: HarperCollins, 1993), p. 378.
25 Longley, *op. cit.*, p. 154.

realize it, had consequently upset many of the clergy. In any case, Heenan was certainly not going to take directions from his secretary, and sent him off to Stepney, a parish in London's East End. Worlock thought, not unreasonably, that this was a step towards making him a bishop, which indeed happened, but not as he had imagined. He saw himself as an assistant bishop to the Cardinal; instead in the autumn of 1965 he was appointed to the Diocese of Portsmouth (Heenan had first tried to send him to Wales). 'After the next session of the Council', Heenan said to him, 'you will not be returning to Stepney. You are likely to be a bishop, but you need not imagine that you are going to be one of my auxiliaries here. You will be much further away.'[26]

Kent agrees with Worlock that Heenan's appointment was welcome. He was 'a popular choice with the rank and file'.[27] His was a no-nonsense approach. He thought that nearly every problem could be dealt with in fifteen minutes, and had Kent organize his appointments accordingly. He gave short shrift to problematic priests, but set up retirement homes for the retired ones, and brought in a pension scheme for priests' housekeepers. He had a packed schedule, as in Leeds and Liverpool, of parish visiting which took in convents, hospitals, old people's homes. He asked curates whether they had any problems with their parish priests, perhaps remembering his own first difficult years. 'His generosity and compassion were, it must be said, outstanding', concludes Kent. 'Perhaps he never really realized how much I admired the way in which he took on the Augean stables of Westminster.'[28] He took his new secretary with him when he went, as did Pope Paul VI, to the Eucharistic Congress in Bombay in 1964. This journey was typical of Heenan's travels. Though on his way to India for the

---

26 *Ibid.*, p. 207. It must be remembered, however, that this is Worlock's own recollection of the conversation.
27 Kent, *op. cit.*, p. 93.
28 *Ibid.*, p. 97.

Congress, he stopped off in Rome and then Beirut, where he lived in luxury but visited refugee camps, then on to Karachi and from Karachi to Bombay, and from Bombay down to Kerala. He came back to London by way of Moscow, where he stayed at the British embassy.[29]

These were heady days, but the excitement of the Council soon receded as it was interpreted for the people in the parish. Although *A Crown of Thorns* does not for the most part continue into Heenan's time at Westminster, the sense of the Cardinal's disillusionment is palpable. It makes depressing reading. 'The joy of Pope John's Church soon gave way to the misery of the early years of Pope Paul's', he wrote.[30] The most pressing issue was liturgical reform, which he did not like. He had voted against the *Missa Normativa* but he loyally attempted to implement it despite his better judgement. He did not like it. At the 1967 Synod of bishops he said:

At home it is not only women and children but also fathers of families and young men who come regularly to Mass. If we were to offer them the kind of ceremony we saw yesterday in the Sistine Chapel [a demonstration of the Normative Mass] we would soon be left with a congregation of mostly women and children. Our people love the Mass but it is Low Mass without psalm-singing and other embellishments to which they are chiefly attached.[31]

He prepared the parishioners of his diocese for the changes by briefing the clergy, and then instructing them to hold meetings in their churches. He also instructed that at least one Sunday Mass in each church should be in Latin, though not in

---

29 The trip led to Kent's dismissal as Heenan's secretary. There were two reasons. 'When in India [I] laughed at an anti-Irish joke, and in Moscow I had left him to find his own way home' after a party (Kent, *op. cit.*, p. 105). Kent reckoned that most secretaries only lasted two years.

30 *Op. cit.*, p. 380.

31 Reid, *A Bitter Trial*, p. 70.

the old, or 'Tridentine' rite, but according to the new form of the ritual. In October 1971 he asked the pope directly to allow the occasional service to be held in the Tridentine rite. He had not consulted his fellow bishops, and they were far from enthusiastic, so although the indult existed, it was used very rarely, partly because it seemed to align those asking for this form of the liturgy with the schismatic followers of Archbishop Marcel Lefebvre. Alan McClelland writes that Heenan was not in favour of having one single English-language translation for the English-speaking world. He was opposed, in other words, to the programme of the International Commission for English in the Liturgy (ICEL). He thought the resulting translation too American in style, composed in a too over-simplified syntax. 'If Heenan's view had prevailed, some of the opposition to the clinical translations over the next twenty years would have been obviated', McClelland comments.[32]

If the English and Welsh bishops had been psychologically unprepared for the Council, as Heenan suggested, they were at least as unprepared theologically. The theology of the Council had immense impact and not simply on the Catholic Church, but many seminary courses had to be rethought in the light of the conciliar documents. One step to raising the standard of theological literacy among ordinands and others was the proposed development of the Jesuit house of studies at Heythrop, near Chipping Norton in Oxfordshire. In 1965 the Jesuits, with the support of the bishops, opened up the courses in the college to non-Jesuits. It was raised in rank to a 'pontifical athenaeum' (not quite a pontifical university because there were only two faculties), and houses were built in the college grounds to house members of other religious orders. Cardinal Heenan became the athenaeum's first and only Chancellor, and a particularly splendid set of robes was commissioned for him in this role. He also sent to the college to teach perhaps

---

32 V. A. McClelland, 'Great Britain and Ireland' in Hastings (ed.), *Modern Catholicism*, p. 366.

the best Catholic theologian in England at the time, Charles Davis.

The athenaeum did not, however, flourish. This was for a variety of reasons, but certainly one of them was that pontifical degrees, excellent though they might be in themselves, did not quite fit within the British educational system. It was decided therefore to move the college into a British university. London was decided upon, and Heythrop College, University of London, opened its doors in the autumn of 1970. The Cardinal was again supportive. Westminster diocesan students were re-located at Allen Hall, in Chelsea, so that those appropriately qualified for a university education might study at Heythrop.

His experience with Corpus Christi, a catechetical college he helped to create in Bayswater, west London, was much less happy. He appointed as its principal Hubert Richards, a lec-turer in Scripture in the diocesan seminary, and his colleague at the seminary, Peter de Rosa, became vice principal. There were complaints about its teaching, regarded as far too theo-logically radical, well within twelve months of its establishment in 1965. Heenan was disturbed, too, by the evening lectures that were being mounted, attracting large audiences. The vice principal resigned in 1971, the rest of the staff later in the year after Heenan had refused to approve the list of proposed visit-ing lecturers. A new principal was appointed, but the college closed in 1975.

There were other woes. Charles Davis left the priesthood and left the Church in December 1966. 'I have come to see that the Church as it exists and works at present is an obstacle in the lives of committed Christians', said his press statement.[33] So high-profile a defection was bad enough in itself, but in an editorial in the Dominican monthly *New Blackfriars* which he edited, Fr Herbert McCabe wrote, about Davis's action, the fact that the Church is 'quite plainly corrupt' was no good reason

---

33 Charles Davis, *A Question of Conscience* (London: Hodder and Stoughton, 1967), p. 16.

for abandoning it. The 'quite plainly corrupt' was seized upon, McCabe was sacked from his job, and for a time he was even suspended by his superiors from his priestly ministry. There was a huge outcry, and after some three years McCabe was given his job back. Heenan was not directly involved, the issue being one for the Dominican Order, and he tried to steer something of a middle course, even on one occasion presiding at a 'teach-in' ('teach-ins' being then much in vogue), but he succeeded in pleasing neither side, certainly not the pro-McCabe group.

In *A Crown of Thorns* he comments about radical theologians: 'Anti-papal theologians abounded, but most of the laity regarded them with contempt. The publishers of their works soon went out of business.'[34] One may doubt the accuracy of the second sentence, but Heenan was probably half right. The vast majority of the laity did not so much regard radical theologians with contempt as with disinterest. Issues such as the McCabe affair affected only a fairly small number of Catholic intellectuals. But birth control was a different matter entirely: it affected the lives of every Catholic couple.

Heenan's active involvement with this controversial issue began with an intervention at the Council by Archbishop Thomas d'Esterre Roberts in April 1964. He also wrote an article which originally appeared in a newsletter called *Search*, edited by Michael de la Bedoyère, which in turn was reported in *The Times* on 19 April. Tommy Roberts was an English Jesuit who had in 1937 been appointed Archbishop of Bombay. He had consecrated Valerian Gracias as his Assistant Bishop in 1946, and simply resigned to make way for him to succeed as Diocesan Bishop in 1950: Gracias became a Cardinal in January 1953. Roberts then returned to London and spent the rest of his life – he died in 1976 – at the Jesuit headquarters in Mayfair. He was an Archbishop on the loose, not a member of the

---

34 Heenan, *op. cit.*, p. 382.

bishops' conference, and a man of controversial views on peace and war as well as on birth control.[35]

These last had been forged in Bombay. The debate, when it broke, was not directly about the morality of the contraceptive pill: Roberts was questioning the notion of contraception itself: 'The Protestant missionary [in India] offers a contraceptive not as an ideal solution but as a lesser evil than sterilization, than abortion, than the hunger of his children, than the death of his wife or the death of their married love.'[36] Heenan was distinctly put out. He wanted to make it clear that talk of the Council changing the ruling on contraception was mistaken. The teaching of the Church, he argued, had been constant. As long ago as the early fifth century St Augustine had written that intercourse was unlawful where 'the conception of offspring is prevented'. Unfortunately Heenan had got St Augustine wrong. What the saint had really said, it was swiftly pointed out to him, was 'where the conception of offspring is avoided'. If that were to be the Church's official line, then it would rule out even the 'rhythm method', which had been expressly approved. Heenan was also taken to task by one of the Church's leading moral theologians, Bernard Häring, a *peritus* at the Council, who argued that the Pill presented an entirely different problem from other means of artificial birth control. He seemed to suggest that the English bishops had erred in more ways than their use of St Augustine. Finally Cardinal Ottaviani intervened. He would have no truck with any change, but he did not want any old bishops' conference apparently

---

35 Roberts, who had been a headmaster before being sent to Bombay, always claimed that the appointment was a mistake by some Vatican functionary not discovered until he had been consecrated, at which point it was too late. Roberts tended to be frozen out by many bishops, even in his former Diocese of Bombay. Bruce Kent records seeing him on the fringes of the crowd, rather than part of the welcoming party of bishops, when Paul VI arrived in Bombay for the Eucharistic Congress Kent attended as secretary to Heenan.

36 Robert Blair Kaiser, *The Encyclical that Never Was* (London: Sheed and Ward, 1987), p. 79.

legislating on this matter. It was to be left to the Holy See, which effectively meant him, at the head of the Holy Office. Derek Worlock had to get on the phone to Häring and the Holy Office to ensure that the Archbishop was not in the dock over his remarks.

The issue of birth control had been removed from the Council agenda by Pope John XXIII and given to a small commission. Paul VI had expanded this commission until it numbered over 70 – theologians, population experts, doctors, laymen and laywomen. There was an executive committee of nine bishops and seven cardinals, and Heenan was a vice president alongside Cardinal Doepfner of Munich. Cardinal Ottaviani was the president. Karol Wojtyla, Archbishop of Cracow, was also a member, but could not attend: the Communist authorities would not grant him a visa. Heenan was not often present but was kept informed by a lay member, Dr John Marshall, a consultant neurologist at University College Hospital, London.

By the spring of 1966 Heenan had become alarmed at what he was hearing from Marshall, and thought he ought to listen to the debates himself. In early June, just before he went off to Rome, he decided to write a pastoral letter. It was all rather ambiguous.[37] Clearly he had come to the conclusion that the Church's teaching on birth control might change, just as it had changed on other topics – after all, he wrote, at one time children in England had been put to death for stealing – but the pope would listen to all the views and then give his verdict, which loyal Catholics would accept.

In Rome he found himself presiding at the crucial penultimate session of the commission. The spokesman against change was the American Jesuit John C. Ford. A German Jesuit, Josef Fuchs, put the opposite point of view. As Kaiser puts it,

---

37 'Although truth remains the same', he wrote in the pastoral letter, 'our knowledge of it is always increasing. Some of our notions of right and wrong have also undergone change.'

'Ford was scathing, bombastic, rhetorical, almost savage in his attack on those who wanted change. The princely Fuchs was cool, brief, quiet in his defence of an intelligent, reasoned approach.'[38] Heenan was shaken, and began to change his mind. But he wanted decisive, clear answers, and he felt that the theologians were not providing them. He had a rant against theologians – as has been seen, never his favourite people – before adjourning the meeting. The following day he apologized. It is clear from the discussions in the final session of the commission which happened later that month that Heenan had become more sympathetic to the argument for change, though without becoming a proponent of it. When he returned to London he let editors of Catholic papers and moral theologians know that they might have to prepare for a change. It was an uncomfortable time for the Cardinal, not made any easier by Pope Paul VI's claim that, on this issue, the Church was not in a state of doubt. It was this claim, that Charles Davis categorized as a straight lie, that provided the occasion for his leaving the Church. 'One who claims to be the moral leader of mankind should not tell lies', he said.[39]

When the encyclical *Humanae Vitae* was published in July 1968 banning all artificial means of contraception, the Pill included, there was an outcry. The British press was full of it. Peter de Rosa, at Corpus Christi College, organized a letter of protest to *The Times*. Many clergy signed it, or otherwise expressed their strong disagreement with the papal ukase. A good number of them were suspended by their bishops, though most were reinstated. Heenan's attitude was, as Kaiser describes it, 'one of peaceful coexistence'.[40]

The Cardinal's most significant contribution to the debate in Britain came in December, when he was interviewed on television by David Frost. He fell back on the argument he had

---

38 *Ibid.*, p. 192.
39 *Ibid.*, p. 232.
40 *Ibid.*, p. 258.

used in the penultimate session of the Birth Control Commission, reported above, that science would eventually sort the matter out – it never became clear what exactly he had in mind. But in the meantime, Frost pressed him. 'The teaching of the Church is very clear,' the Cardinal replied, 'for the man is bound to follow his conscience, and that is true even if his conscience is in error, but this is a basic teaching of the Church.' Of course, Heenan went on, individuals have a duty to inform their consciences, but when there has been a long period of dispute, he appeared to suggest, then informing one's conscience might bring one to a different conclusion from that proposed by the Church. So, said Frost, if a couple were to tell their priest they are following their consciences, what should the priest say? 'There was a tense pause – everybody was holding their breath – and then Cardinal Heenan said, "God bless you".' A couple using contraception, he went on to say, should not give up going to the sacraments. Frost speculated that he might one day be Pope. 'I hope not,' he replied, 'but if so I'll be very careful about writing Encyclicals.'[41] This was Heenan at his best, allowing his pastoral instincts, his compassion, to overcome his otherwise fundamentally conservative convictions.[42]

Along with the Archbishopric of Westminster, Heenan inherited the presidency of the Sword of the Spirit, founded under Hinsley (see above, pp. 124ff). The Cardinal remembered it well. He had turned to the Sword for help in housing some of his families made homeless by the wartime bombing, and had himself spoken from its platforms. He remembered it, however, as an ecumenical organization, which it never was, except by accident, and describes it as such in *A Crown of Thorns*.[43] In

---

41 The interview can be found in David Frost, *An Autobiography, Part One – From Congregations to Audiences* (London: HarperCollins, 1993), pp. 396–401. The quotations are on pp. 399 and 400.

42 'Do let me know when you are likely to be coming to London', he wrote to Evelyn Waugh in January 1966. 'I would like to have you here for a nice anti-progressive dinner.' See Reid, *op. cit.*, p. 62.

43 Heenan, *op. cit.*, pp. 311–14.

March 1965 the chairman of Sword, Tom Burns, and its general secretary Margaret Feeney paid a courtesy call on Heenan, and explained that, given the range of activities in which Sword was now involved, including sending volunteers overseas, the executive wanted to change its name: the military tone of 'Sword of the Spirit' no longer seemed appropriate. They wanted to call it the 'Catholic Association for International Relations'. Heenan preferred the 'Catholic Institute for International Relations', and so CIIR replaced Sword. It engaged in a wide variety of activities, among which educating the laity on moral issues in world politics, such as justice and development, ranked high.

There was a particular instance of this when in 1973 England and Portugal celebrated 600 years as allies. The president of Portugal was to visit Britain, and CIIR organized a meeting to draw attention to some of the failures of the regime, effectively a fairly benign dictatorship, both in Portugal and especially in its overseas territories. One of the speakers, Adrian Hastings, drew attention to a massacre of the indigenous population carried out by Portuguese troops at a place called Wiriyamu in Mozambique[44] on 16 December 1972. CIIR kept the massacre before the public, holding a memorial service on the anniversary. Heenan was leaned upon by the Portuguese ambassador, and wrote to Mildred Nevile, now CIIR's General Secretary, so say that the organization was criticizing a Catholic country (Portugal under Salazar, who had recently died, had often been held up as an exemplar of Catholic social doctrine in practice) but never a Communist one. He was going, he said, to bring the matter up at the hierarchy's Low Week meeting.[45]

---

44 Adrian Hastings, *Wiriyamu* (London: Search Press, 1974).

45 The Archbishop of Westminster had been *ipso facto* president of the bishops' conference from 1850 onwards, but with the more collegial, democratic structures after Vatican II, Heenan asked that this be changed, and the president elected annually. This was agreed. Heenan was invariably elected.

Miss Nevile wrote to the bishops. CIIR had, as Sword, a long history of drawing attention to the abuses of Communist regimes, she said, but it had changed its focus onto the developing world in response to a papal encyclical. Moreover, the criticism of the Portuguese regime had largely come from within the country, and information about it had been received from Catholic sources. The letter was received *nem. con.*, Heenan reported, which is not quite the same as saying that it was overwhelmingly approved. But then, almost immediately after the bishops' meeting, came the peaceful Portuguese revolution when the soldiers marched with carnations in the barrels of their rifles, and the regime which CIIR had been attacking suddenly crumbled. Heenan, who had once been so critical, hastened to make amends. Less than two months later he came, unusually, to the Annual General Meeting of CIIR. 'It is very good indeed', he said, 'to have an unofficial voice and a voice of the laity which is not stamped with the official approval of the Church; most valuable to the public; most valuable to the Church at large, and so therefore I pay tribute to the CIIR.'[46] It was a handsome apology.

He was a complex personality. *A Crown of Thorns* displays his deep disappointment with the developments within the Church, with the challenge to traditional authority, to the number of clergy resigning from the priesthood, with the shedding of religious habits and clerical dress,[47] with the reformulation of the liturgy. And yet he had instructed that Liverpool Metropolitan Cathedral, whose opening he attended as papal legate after his move to London, be designed for the efficient functioning of the post-Vatican II rite. He was angered by the radicals, but he was equally angered by the traditionalists who wished to reject the Vatican Council.

---

46 Walsh, *From Sword to Ploughshare*, p. 32.
47 He was particularly upset when a Jesuit lecturer from Heythrop College, by this time in London, appeared on television in a collar and tie.

Although he had commissioned Liverpool Metropolitan Cathedral, he seems to have been far less happy with the one at Westminster. There were enormous financial problems, and at a meeting of the senate of priests he wondered out loud whether a cathedral was needed at all. As has been mentioned, the cathedral choir school was also struggling financially, and he thought that it, too, might have to close. In any case he was impatient with the way the liturgy was performed. He gave instructions that High Mass should take no more than an hour, and that sermons should last only five minutes. To speed things up, he said there should be less time spent on incensing everyone. He also wondered, as the cathedral's founder Herbert Vaughan had done, whether instead of the cathedral's clergy, monks could not be brought in to sing the daily offices. He had gone so far as approaching the abbot of Ampleforth to discuss his proposal.

His health declined rapidly. He had heart attacks, and suffered from encephalitis. He could not sleep. Running the diocese was becoming too much for him, and he offered his resignation in September 1975. But before Rome could make up his mind, he had died, in the Westminster Hospital, on 7 November. He was buried in Westminster Cathedral.

9

George Basil Hume

As he left the service of solemn vespers in Westminster Abbey which followed Basil Hume's installation as ninth Archbishop of Westminster, the BBC's religion correspondent, the late Douglas Brown, remarked to a friend,[1] 'There's no question who is now Mr Religion No. 1, is there?' His judgement was confirmed when, not long afterwards, six people were stopped on the street by a television company to be asked the name of the then Archbishop of Canterbury. Five did not know. The last, an old lady according to the usual version, replied, 'Isn't it that nice Cardinal Hume?'[2] Such fame was a strange outcome for someone who might reasonably have expected to live out his life in the relative obscurity of a Benedictine monastery.

He was one of five children, and was born at 4 Ellison Place, Newcastle upon Tyne, on 2 March 1923. His father, William Errington Hume, was a doctor, a consultant at the Newcastle Royal Infirmary and, eventually, professor of medicine at King's College in the city. He was knighted for services to medicine in 1952. His mother was French, the daughter of an army officer who had served as military attaché in Madrid. William Hume and Marie Elizabeth Tisseyre – known as Mimi – met

---

1 The present author.
2 Clifford Longley, 'Ten Years and Westminster' in Tony Castle (ed.), *Basil Hume: A Portrait* (London: Collins, 1986), p. 136. Longley does not, however, provide a source for this much-quoted story.

when William was serving as a major in the Royal Army Medical Corps. They married in November 1918.

There were five children, of whom George – the future Basil – was the middle one, and the elder son: all had names which were equally usable either in English or French, and the children grew up speaking both languages – always French with their mother and, when they went on holiday to France, also with their French cousins at Wimereaux, on the Channel coast, where Mimi's parents had settled. Their father rarely attended these family gatherings. Nor, as a non-Catholic, did he attend church when Mimi led her brood off to Mass on Sundays, much preferring the golf course. He was present at the baptism of his youngest child, Madeleine, but that apparently was the limit of his churchgoing.

George was sent not to a Catholic elementary school but to the kindergarten attached to Newcastle's Central High School, and then to the Newcastle Preparatory School, where he was not happy. It was there, however, that he learned to play rugby, a game which became an abiding passion, though his father also took him to see Newcastle United play at home, and turned him into a lifelong supporter. In September 1933 he was sent to Gillingham Castle, the preparatory school for Ampleforth where he spent a year before moving on to the main college. As a pupil he was unproblematic, though he excelled on the sports field – he was captain first of the under-16s XV, and then of the First XV in what was said to be a particularly successful season – and in the debating chamber rather than in things academic.

He also rose to be Company Sergeant Major in the cadet force. But with that there came a problem. He was leaving school in 1941, early in the Second World War, and was clearly officer material. He had to make a choice – the armed forces or the monastery. He chose the latter, entering Ampleforth as a novice in September 1941. Some of his school fellows thought he was letting down the country in a time of crisis, and said so. Much later in life Basil confessed that, had he his time again, he would choose differently.

Novices are not expected to enjoy the noviciate. It is a time of trials and petty humiliations designed to test the vocation, the determination and the endurance of the neophyte, cut off as novices are not just from their families but, rather oddly, from the community of monks which they are asking to join. So rigorous was the isolation that Basil, the name he was given as a monk, was not even allowed to associate with his brother John (then a pupil in the school), except very occasionally, and only with special permission. Not surprisingly he suffered from depression. In religious circles this state of mind is dignified with the term 'accidie', or spiritual torpor, but depression is how it affects the individual. Basil thought of leaving the monastery, but decided to stay, and took his first vows after a year, and then was solemnly professed as a monk of Ampleforth in September 1945. The year before, he had begun a degree in history at the Benedictine house of studies in Oxford, St Benet's Hall, played rugby, and came away with Second Class honours.

When Benedictines make their solemn profession they take a vow of stability, that is to say they commit themselves to their community for the rest of their lives – unlike, say Jesuits, Dominicans[3] or Franciscans who can expect to live at a series of different addresses in the course of their careers. Basil might have expected to return to Ampleforth after Oxford in order to study Theology in preparation for ordination, but instead his abbot sent him to the University of Fribourg in Switzerland: he noted on 19 October 1949 as he took the ferry to France en route to Fribourg that this was the thirty-fifth time he had crossed the Channel. After Oxford, Fribourg was something of a shock. For one thing, lectures were mainly in Latin, as were the (oral) examinations. It was not different from clerical education elsewhere in the Catholic world, still dominated as it was by the apostolic constitution *Deus Scientiarum Dominus* which

---

3 The Catholic Humes had sometimes attended a Dominican parish in Newcastle, and were close to one of the priests. George briefly considered becoming a member of that Order.

William Godfrey had helped to draft (see above, p. 157). The fact that this old-fashioned structure was more or less universal did not make it any more palatable than the food, which he also did not find to his taste. Ecclesiastical history was far more interesting to him than theology itself: he had, after all, studied history at Oxford. Its chief attraction, however, was that the lectures were delivered in French.[4] Despite these difficulties he succeeded fairly well at his studies, graduating as an STL (Licentiate in Sacred Theology) with a *magna cum laude* – a *summa cum laude*, the grade above, being the equivalent of a First. He also made the most of the opportunity provided by living in Switzerland to tour Europe during vacations.

In the meantime, however, he had become a priest. He was ordained at Ampleforth on 23 July 1950 and on his return to the monastery was assigned to work in the local parish as a curate. But this was only a part-time job. Most of his time was spent in the school. He taught History, in which of course he had taken his Oxford degree, but given his fluency in French and in German he was asked also to teach modern languages. It was this which proved to be his greater skill – that and rugby: he became head of modern languages and coach of the First XV. In 1955 he was put in charge of St Bede's House, which meant not just having pastoral care of a large number of boys, but living with them in close proximity: as a housemaster, he enjoyed little privacy. He was given further responsibilities that same year, being elected by his fellow monks to become a member of the Abbot's Council, and being appointed by the abbot to serve as teacher of theology in the community. This last was a significant position. At Fribourg he had evinced no great passion for theology and, despite his STL, it may have seemed an odd choice, but it brought him into contact with the

---

4 For an account of what it was like to study in an ecclesiastical university (admittedly at a slightly later date than Basil Hume, but little had changed), see Anthony Kenny's *A Path from Rome* (London: Sidgwick and Jackson, 1985) pp. 45–9.

younger monks within what was, by Benedictine standards, a very large community. If he was to rise through the ranks, then he needed to be better known.

He was, however, becoming well known, even outside the confines of his own abbey. Benedictine houses are organized into 'Congregations', each Congregation having a distinctive interpretation of the Rule of St Benedict. Most of those in Britain and a couple in the United States are members of the English Benedictine Congregation (EBC). In 1957 Basil was elected to the chapter of the EBC, and was given charge of the education of the young monks in the EBC.

Then, in the middle of the Second Vatican Council, he was elected abbot. The date of his election was 17 April 1963, though he did not receive the formal abbatial blessing, the local bishop investing him with the accoutrements of his office (including a mitre, which his mother made), for another two months. It was a period of tension in the monastery (as it was in the Church at large), as the community tried to come to terms with the changes brought in by the Council. The life of a monk is one of prayer and worship largely in a community context, and nothing tested the cohesion of the monastery more, as of the Church, than liturgical reform. Abbot Basil was judged to be particularly adept at managing the changes, showing under-standing for those who found them problematic. For instance, though much of the recitation of divine office was translated into English, the traditionalists were mollified by his keeping the old form of Latin Vespers. He established a liturgical com-mission to advise on public worship, which long laboured on the production of a new version of the divine office for the Abbey. It did not complete its work until Basil had moved to Westminster. He was ready to seek advice, but he commonly did so by talking to individuals in the community and then passing off his decisions as if they had been arrived at collec-tively. But evidently the community did not mind: he was re-elected as abbot in 1971. By now he was taking an active part in shaping the fortunes of the wider Benedictine family. He became a friend of the Abbot President of the Confederation of Benedictine Congregations, the American monk Rembert Weakland, and Weakland made him visitor to houses outside Britain. He was put in charge of both the Commission on Monastic Renewal, and the Ecumenical Commission. He began to travel more widely abroad, though at the cost, he himself felt, of his commitment to his home community.

In the summer of 1975 it became evident that Cardinal Heenan would soon have to be replaced. A *Sunday Times* journalist profiled the six most likely candidates, and included Basil Hume. When she learned of this from her son, Mimi is reported to have laughed, which, according to his biographer Anthony Howard, rather upset the abbot.[5] But there were others who took the proposal more seriously, not least Archbishop Donald Coggan, now at Canterbury, who had come to know Hume when he was Archbishop of York. He had other support, too, including the weekly *The Economist*, which took a surprising interest in the succession to Westminster. The fact that its editor was a former pupil at Ampleforth presumably had something to do with it. It is commonly thought that the deciding voice, at least outside Rome, was the surprisingly radical Miles, Duke of Norfolk. The Duke had at first favoured Michael Hollings, then a parish priest in west London, but when it became evident that there was no chance of Hollings being appointed, he switched his support to Hume. Presiding over all this was the rotund figure of the Apostolic Delegate, the Swiss-born Bruno Heim, who had visited Ampleforth soon after his arrival in Britain. He took soundings from well-known Catholics and even from the Archbishop of Canterbury. In December 1975 he went to Rome and talked to the pope and to the head of the Congregation of Bishops, and the announcement was made on 17 February 1976.

Hume himself had heard the news a few days earlier, while attending a course on church leadership at St George's House,

---

5 *Basil Hume: The Monk Cardinal* (London: Headline, 2005), p. 82.

Windsor. He had, however, abandoned the course for the evening to have dinner with an old school friend who lived nearby, and it was there that Heim rang him. He knew where to find him because he had consulted Hume's sister who was married to John Hunt, a senior civil servant, and a neighbour of the Apostolic Delegate in Wimbledon. Heim, who could not resist a gossip, had told Hume's sister of his news, so she was the first to know, even before her brother. Hume was summoned to Wimbledon to see the Delegate, and on entering the house glanced at the visitors' book. The last name before his was that of Derek Worlock, so when Heim rather disingenuously asked Hume who should fill the vacant see of Liverpool, he replied 'Bishop Worlock of course.' Heim was reported to have been somewhat thrown by Hume's perspicacity.

Soon after the appointment was made public, Hume went off to Rome on a scheduled visit to chair the Commission on Monastic Renewal. But while in Rome he made a round of calls in keeping with his new office. He went to the famous clerical tailors, Gammarelli's, to be fitted for his purple cassock. He paid a call on Archbishop Agostino Casaroli, the future Cardinal Secretary of State but then Secretary for Extraordinary Ecclesiastical Affairs, in other words the papal foreign minister. He was also granted an audience by Pope Paul VI, a meeting which had a profound effect on him. The Pope's parting words were, 'Always remain a monk.'[6]

Hume's first formal engagement was three weeks before he was consecrated Bishop. He had to preside at a concert in the cathedral on 4 March as part of an appeal to raise one million pounds, half for the cathedral itself, and half for the choir school. The appeal had been launched under Cardinal Heenan, and counted the Archbishop of Canterbury and the Moderator of the General Assembly of the United Reform Church among its patrons. There were also a number of political figures and prominent composers and conductors, and the

6 *Ibid.*, p. 97.

concert on 4 March was to be held in the presence of the Duke of Edinburgh. It was an introduction to the echelons of the London Establishment with which Hume was to become familiar. The appeal, followed by a smaller one specifically for the choir school, was a success, reaching its target in eighteen months, helped by a generous £100,000 donation by the Greater London Council, and ensured the continuance of the school. Not surprisingly, Hume, as a former schoolmaster, took a considerable interest in the choir school and proposed various changes – including the acceptance of day pupils and of non-Catholics, as well as bringing in a lay headmaster – which made the school's future secure.

The service at which Basil Hume was consecrated Bishop took place in the cathedral on 25 March, and was televised. The cathedral was packed with a congregation of 2,500, four cardinals, eight archbishops, 36 bishops and 130 monks from Ampleforth, as well as the Archbishop of York and sundry other Anglican prelates. Six hundred clergy concelebrated the Mass. In the late afternoon, as has been mentioned, the monks sang solemn vespers in Westminster Abbey at the other end of Victoria Street,[7] and then attended a reception in the hall of Westminster School. Hume was made a Cardinal in remarkably short order, in a consistory on 24 May. This time he emerged from his papal audience in tears.

From the rambling and draughty Ampleforth to the rambling and draughty Archbishop's House, memorably described by the journalist Peter Stanford as 'huge, very dark, and about as welcoming as a north country station hotel during a period of national mourning',[8] cannot have been too much of a shock,

---

7 'Worlock was the only English Catholic bishop present. It was not scene-stealing; it was magnanimity. He had come to offer his full public support to the man who had beaten him to the prize [of the Westminster archbishopric]; and to do so in a striking ecumenical context', Longley, *The Worlock Archive*, p. 210.

8 Peter Stanford, *Cardinal Hume and the Changing Face of English Catholicism* (London: Geoffrey Chapman, 1993), p. 7.

but mindful of Paul VI's advice to remain a monk, he established a 'cell' in a small room at the top of the house, and would often dress in his monastic habit. His manner was much more informal than his predecessor's. If he was at home of an evening he was happiest with a couple of boiled eggs and a choc ice for his supper, followed by the BBC's *Match of the Day*. He played squash at the RAC Club not far away in Pall Mall, and went running on the rather more distant Wimbledon Common, at least until he had his left hip replaced in 1983, an operation which had to be repeated a decade later. To keep fit from then on he had a mini-gym installed next to his bedroom. When on occasional holidays he enjoyed fishing.

It is remarkable how swiftly he became an accepted part of British national life. After only a couple of years in office the then Labour Prime Minister, James Callaghan, offered him a life peerage, and thus a seat in the House of Lords alongside the Anglican 'Lords Spiritual'.[9] The Conservative Prime Minister, Margaret Thatcher, repeated the offer in 1987. Hume refused on both occasions, though on the first his response to Callaghan was not a straightforward 'No, never.' 'I would ask you not to put my name forward,' he wrote, 'at least at this stage.'[10] He might have been firmer in his refusal: the notion of Catholic clergy holding public office was anathema, especially under Pope John Paul II.

Hume took part in the 1978 conclave which elected Pope John Paul II and, of course, the conclave a few weeks earlier which had elected Albino Luciani as the short-lived John Paul I. 'God's candidate', Hume said of Luciani as he emerged from the conclave, which, in the circumstances, proved to have been a rather unfortunate remark. He was more careful the second time round. In the second conclave, in October, Hume

---

9 There were other examples of major religious figures offered peerages, including Donald Soper, the leading Methodist who accepted a barony under Harold Wilson in 1965, and Immanuel Jakobvits, the Chief Rabbi, who became a life peer in 1987.

10 Howard, *op. cit.*, p. 113.

received one vote in the first ballot.[11] After the election of Karol Wojtyla, the new pope appointed him as his own replacement on the fifteen-man secretariat of the Synod of Bishops. The following year he accepted the presidency of the episcopal conference of England and Wales which he had at first refused while he learned his job,[12] and also the presidency of the Council of European Bishops' Conferences. He had rapidly become a highly respected figure among the College of Cardinals, and also in the offices of the Roman curia. But this reputation was shortly to be put under strain.

The problem was of Derek Worlock's making. Worlock had earned a reputation as a champion of the laity, and soon after his appointment to Liverpool he conceived the idea of asking the laity their opinions on a whole variety of issues. The venue for this was to be a National Pastoral Congress, held in Liverpool in May 1980. There were 2,000 delegates, representing parishes, Catholic organizations and so on. It was prepared with great care, with papers on a variety of topics – justice and peace, family life, and so on, though it was contraception, which Archbishop Dwyer of Birmingham, when he, rather than Hume, had chaired the Bishops' Conference, had wanted kept off the agenda, which attracted all the media attention. The number two at the Apostolic Delegation, Mario Oliveri, was opposed to the whole idea of anything as democratic as a Congress and, in the absence of the Delegate himself who had been generally supportive, forwarded to Rome the complaints of those conservative Catholics who wanted the Congress stopped, or at least brought firmly under episcopal control.

---

11 Francis A. Burkle, *Passing the Keys*, 2nd edn (Lanham, MD: Madison Books, 2001), p. 278.

12 *Si qua est* of 1911 (see above, p. 90) gave the Archbishop of Westminster leadership of the conference, but Heenan asked that this provision be waived in favour of an elected chairman from among the bishops. Heenan was, however, always elected. Hume had as his vice president Derek Worlock, 'a very equal, fruitful but never easy relationship' (Longley, *The Worlock Archive*, p. 2).

The debates in Liverpool were in the end uninhibited by episcopal pressure, but they proved to be intelligent and responsible. It was judged a great success by clergy and laity alike. Archbishop Worlock then organized the writing of the Congress Report together with the hierarchy's response. Entitled *The Easter People*, it came out the same year, and was, or so he claimed, largely written by Worlock himself. It was an upbeat, hopeful document, and Hume and Worlock set out for Rome to present it to Pope John Paul II. They did so, drawing the Pope's attention to what had been said on contraception (namely, not that the Church's teaching was wrong – those taking part in the Congress were too level-headed for that – but that it ought to 'develop'). John Paul simply waved it away, no doubt having been forewarned of its unpalatable message. Then either the Cardinal or the Archbishop invited John Paul to visit England and Wales.[13] He agreed on the spot: 'It is inevitable' he is reported to have said.[14] Much to the surprise of the Cardinal, the date was promptly fixed for the summer of 1982. He had expected a longer delay, more time to prepare. John Paul, however, wanted to bring the hierarchy into line and, by his presence, take attention away from the message of *The Easter People*.

Hume and Worlock had one more chance to put their case. There was scheduled to begin in September a Synod of Bishops devoted to the topic of 'The Family'. The two English prelates, representing the bishops of England and Wales, divided out their tasks. Worlock was to speak on the predicament of divorced and remarried Catholics, the Cardinal on contraception. He spoke of those who

> . . . cannot accept the total prohibition of the use of artificial means of contraception where circumstances seemed to make this necessary or even desirable. Natural methods of

---

13 The invitation was not off the cuff. The Scottish hierarchy had earlier been approached to see if they wanted to be associated with it, which they did. Hence the papal visit was to Britain as a whole.

14 Howard, *op. cit.*, p. 125.

birth control do not seem to them to be the definitive and only solution. It cannot just be said that these persons have failed to overcome their human frailty and weakness. The problem is far more complex than that. Indeed, such persons are often good, conscientious and faithful sons and daughters of the Church. They just cannot accept that the use of artificial means of contraception in some circumstances is *intrinsice inhonestum* as this latter has been generally understood.

He concluded his intervention in the Synod by saying

I have not come to this synod with solutions to the difficult pastoral problems created by the controversy. But, as a pastor, I, like you, am much concerned for the spiritual welfare of all the people about whom I have spoken. I hope and pray that as a result of this synod, and with the help of the synod fathers, I shall be able to give better guidance to those married people who are looking to the Church for help.

This was his prepared speech. Much more media attention was, however, given to one delivered off the cuff, in which he spoke of the dream he had when dropping off to sleep in the middle of the synod debates. In the first part of it he saw the Church as a fortress, where every stranger approaching it was a threat. Then he spoke of the Church as a pilgrim towards truth:

The leaders, too, of the pilgrimage are often themselves not always clear, and that can be painful. They may sometimes co-agonize with the other pilgrims. Co-responsibility will always involve co-agonizing. The fortress was a temple, but the pilgrim lived in a tent. It is sometimes better to know the uncertainties of Abraham's tent than to sit secure in Solomon's temple.[15]

---

15 Longley, *The Worlock Archive*, pp. 291–2.

On the outcome of the Synod the speech made little or no difference. Worlock and Hume both believed that the outcome had been decided long before the bishops met. They were not alone in that conclusion. The papal response to the Synod was the apostolic exhortation *Familiaris Consortio*. As Jan Grootaers and Joseph Selling remark towards the end of their detailed study of the Synod and the pope's document:

> It appears to us that [*Familiaris Consortio*] could have been written even if the Synod had not taken place . . . what the bishops had sought was an adequate response to genuine pastoral needs. In reading the apostolic exhortation, virtually none of these requests are fulfilled, nor are the suggestions for further study given credibility. In the end, while the event itself focused attention on the topic and provided a display of unity and collegiality among the hierarchy of the Church, the impact of the 1980 Synod on papal teaching was negligible.[16]

Reports from the Synod had disturbed members of the National Conference of Priests. They had expected the two bishops to be more forceful in putting the views of the National Pastoral Congress, and so organized a meeting between representatives of the National Conference and Cardinal Hume and Archbishop Worlock. A minute of the meeting was produced, which read in part:

> The National Conference had some problems with the bishops' message for they felt that the bishops had moved away from some of the resolutions of the Congress. The bishops appeared to give up their right as a local Church and to be too willing to give way to the Roman curia.

---

16 Jan Grootaers and Joseph A. Selling, *The 1980 Synod of Bishops 'On the Role of the Family'* (Louvain: Louvain University Press; Peeters, 1983), pp. 337–8.

The Cardinal replied that he considered that conservatism was succeeding in many parts of the world and was also rising in Rome. We had to remember that Western Europe was now a minority in the Church and places like Africa and South America were very conservative. Our local Church has to find its way in the present circumstances and it is not always clear how it should proceed.

The Cardinal was sure that it would not help to have public calls on our bishops to act by themselves. There were some conservatives in this country who were attacking what had already been done by himself and Archbishop Worlock.[17]

This was all very true, and no doubt an accurate summary of what Hume said to the delegation from the Conference of Priests, but when Worlock saw a draft of the minute he was horrified, and immediately contacted Westminster. It would have undoubtedly been disastrous for the Catholic Church in England and Wales had such a frank assessment of the situation in the Church at large, and of the obvious disaffection of the leader of the Bishops' Conference, been circulated. It would have aroused a flurry of complaints from the many conservative groups, and could easily have led to greater Roman control over the leadership of the Church in this country. The bishops' concern was given substance when, the following year, these groups came together under an umbrella organization, 'Pro Ecclesia et Pontifice' ('For Church and Pope') to give voice, it claimed, to the 'silent majority' of Catholics who were alarmed by developments in the Church, and especially by contemporary catechesis. It organized five massive conferences (1996–2000) under the title of 'Faith of Our Fathers'. The first featured Mother Angelica, the Poor Clare nun who, rather curiously, runs the EWTN Global Catholic Network, and was addressed by Cardinal Hume. His message was that, obviously within limits,

17 Longley, *op. cit.*, p. 294.

Catholics should be free to hold to their own interpretation of the Faith, but that they should not call those who disagreed with them heretics. William Oddie, the former Anglican priest who at the time edited the *Catholic Herald*, was chairing the meeting, and said that he hoped the Cardinal's speech would be published. 'Not at our expense', someone called from the back of the hall.[18]

One of the most powerful of the right-wing movements was Opus Dei. Hume had received complaints from anxious parents about Opus's methods of recruitment, and his own anxieties were no doubt increased by a feature-length article, highly critical of the organization, in *The Times* in January 1981. He therefore issued, on 2 December 1981, four guidelines to be observed by Opus within the Diocese of Westminster. They were essentially concerned with the transparency of the organization's activities, especially in recruitment of young people, though the fourth added that 'initiatives and activities of Opus Dei, within the Diocese of Westminster, should carry a clear indication of their sponsorship and management'.[19] Given the influence that Opus was said to be able to exercise in Rome, this was a brave thing to have done.However cordially phrased by Archbishop's House, the guidelines were also an implied rebuke.

Given all this background, it was essential that the papal visit to Britain at the end of May and the beginning of June 1982 should go off without any major glitch. It was prepared with great care, structured around the administration of the seven sacraments, and was regarded, not least in Rome, as having been a considerable success. Even the sun shone, at least for most of the time. The visit, however, was not as Hume had wanted it. He had asked the Pope to include in his itinerary lunch with the Queen and her family on the day of his arrival,

---

18 Heard by the present author.
19 For the full list, see Michael Walsh, *The Secret World of Opus Dei* (London: Grafton Books, 1989), pp. 164–5.

28 May, and lunch with the leaders of the Church of England and of the Free Churches at Canterbury the following day. Both proposals were rejected, though a courtesy meeting with the Queen was inevitable, and there was also a meeting with the leaders of other Churches, even if not a lunch. He also wanted the Pope to stay at Archbishop's House, but he insisted on retreating to the Nunciature (the representation of the papacy in Britain had been raised to ambassadorial level not long before John Paul's arrival) in Wimbledon during his stay in London. He did, however, agree to the suggestion that he should visit both cathedrals in Liverpool, Anglican and Catholic, situated at each end of Hope Street.

But then, in the midst of all the preparation, there occurred the Falklands War. Hume was intensely patriotic (the Pope's refusal to lunch with the Queen had upset him greatly), and he was a supporter of Prime Minister Thatcher's decision to send troops to the South Atlantic.[20] Nonetheless it was evident that, with Britain at war with Argentina, the Pope was in a difficult position, and it seemed for a long few days that he would not come at all. Worlock and Hume went off to Rome to try to persuade him. When John Paul finally agreed, it was because of a deal struck by Worlock, rather than by the Cardinal. He went to Rome and concelebrated in a Mass of reconciliation with two Argentine cardinals, rather against his better judgement. It was also decided that the Pope would pay a brief visit to Argentina soon after his trip to Britain. With that, the visit went ahead.

There was an unexpected coda to the whole affair. Hume helped to plan the thanksgiving service at St Paul's to mark the end of the Falklands War. It was he who was behind the controversial decision to remember the Argentine, as well as the British dead. That much might have been expected. What was more surprising was the action of the Dean of St Paul's, Alan Webster, when the Ministry of Defence approached him over

---

20 He was later to support the 1991 Gulf War, even though the pope, and many Roman Catholics, took a different view.

their wish to have a memorial to the fallen soldiers in his cathedral. Webster asked the advice of the Cardinal before he sought the advice of the Archbishop of Canterbury.

That was a reflection not just of his involvement in the memorial service, but his general engagement with the ecumenical movement as a whole. As Abbot of Ampleforth he had taken part in meetings of the local council of churches; in 1974 he had attended, along with Rembert Weakland and Archbishops Michael Ramsey and Donald Coggan, the inaugural meeting of the Anglican Conference of Religion; in 1979 he had addressed the General Synod of the Church of England and afterwards told Douglas Brown that *Apostolicae Curae* (see above, p. 80) needed 'careful reconsideration';[21] he had attended the enthronement of Robert Runcie as Archbishop of Canterbury in 1980. He was, however, resistant to the idea that the Catholic Church in England should ever join the British Council of Churches (BCC), and had told the General Synod so, although several members of the bishops' conference were in favour of such a move, and it had been urged by the delegates to the National Pastoral Congress. Ecumenical relations were given a fillip by the visit of John Paul II to Canterbury and the agreement with Runcie to breathe new life into the Anglican–Roman Catholic International Commission (ARCIC). He had tried to persuade the Congregation for the Doctrine of the Faith, under Cardinal Ratzinger, to respond positively to ARCIC's 'Final Report', but Ratzinger proved less than enthusiastic. He tried to do the same again in 1990, writing this time to the Apostolic Nuncio, but the decision of the Church of England soon afterwards to ordain women priests brought an end to substantive talks.

Although not a member of the BCC, the Catholic Church kept close contact. There were talks in 1984 which led to a conference held at Swanick in September 1987, attended by Hume. None of his episcopal colleagues was clear about what Hume was going to

---

21 Stanford, *op. cit.*, p. 87.

say. What he told the conference was that the time had come for the Catholic Church to move from co-operation to commitment. This was not, however, to be commitment to the old BCC. A new body was to be set up, the Council of Churches in Britain and Ireland (CCBI, later renamed Churches Together in Britain and Ireland) which was to facilitate ecumenical encounter rather than be an agent of it. Nor was it a subsidiary body of the World Council of Churches as the BCC had been: the Catholic Church is not a member of the WCC, which might have made membership of the BCC somewhat problematic. According to one senior ecumenist, despite approving of entering the CCBI, Hume was never really happy with the arrangement. 'He always remained an Abbot,' he said, 'and he didn't like an organization where he could not see clear lines of command.'[22]

Relations between the Catholic Church and the other Churches in Britain at the end of the 1980s appeared to be flourishing. In September 1989 Archbishop Runcie went to Rome to see the pope on a visit organized by Hume. He saw the pope a remarkable five times in four days, and then preached a sermon in the presence of the pope in which he called upon all Christians to acknowledge papal primacy, no doubt sweet music to the Congregation for the Doctrine of the Faith and to the Pontiff himself, but rather less well received back home by fellow Anglicans.

All such ecumenical initiative were, in any event, to come to nothing when in 1992 the General Synod of the Church of England voted to ordain women to the priesthood. Hume himself was, it seems, not unwilling to entertain the notion of women's ordination. In a response to a phone-in on the BBC's World Service in 1978 he said,

> I accept the authority of my Church, which does not advocate the ordination of women to the priesthood. The answer given is 'This is not part of our tradition' – and that may be a

---

22 Private conversation.

good argument and that may be a bad argument. I personally, if the authorities of my Church agreed to the ordination of women, would have no problem about it. But I am a man under authority and I would not be in the Catholic Church if I did not accept that.[23]

There was no likelihood of the ordination of women in the Roman Catholic Church under the pontificate of John Paul II – nor, indeed, was it likely to happen in any foreseeable pontificate. The ordination of married men is another matter, but that, too, was ruled out under Pope John Paul. There was, however, the issue of what to do about the *c.* 400 Church of England clergy who chose to leave their own Communion over the issue of women's ordination.

Hume was ready to accept them and, indeed, accept them as candidates for ordination, which is what about half of them wanted. Rome made it clear that there was no problem about this,[24] but the Cardinal was concerned to avoid any hint of triumphalism.[25] This was not simply a matter of maintaining good ecumenical relations with the Church of England: there was the Catholic Church's own faithful to consider, some at least of whom thought that women's ordination was a good thing, and that receiving conservatives, as they saw them, into Catholicism was a betrayal. There was also the obvious paradox that the Church was embracing married clergy while at the same time rejecting from the active priesthood those Catholic clergy who wanted to marry. In the end there was relatively little fuss, even when as high a profile a figure as Graham Leonard, Bishop of London from 1981 to 1991, and a good friend of the Cardinal, became a Catholic, and a priest, soon after his retirement.

If there was relatively little fuss over the reception of the Church of England clergy, there was almost more over one

---

23 Howard, *op. cit.*, p. 233.
24 It is accepted that clerical celibacy is a matter of discipline, certainly not one of doctrine.
25 Needless to say, the traffic in converts was not all one way.

Catholic priest with a penchant for campaigning. As Bruce Kent wrote in his autobiography *Undiscovered Ends*:

> Much as I enjoyed the experience of being a parish priest and much as I tried to concentrate on parish affairs, by 1979 it was clear to me that I could not both do justice to St Aloysius [his parish, not far from London's Euston Station] and fulfil the many demands made on me, and willingly accepted, by Pax Christi, War on Want, CND, PROP (the national prisoners' movement) and the many other groups with which I was connected.[26]

Kent had been chairman of CND, but there was about to be a vacancy as General Secretary of CND, a full-time post. He therefore went to see his Bishop, Cardinal Hume, and asked if he might take up the post. 'I can't say that he thought this a wonderful idea',[27] Kent remarks, but he gave his permission.

There was no question of his ceasing to be a priest, and he found a home on a north London parish where he could fulfil the role of a curate in whatever time there was to spare from CND activities. This situation lasted for some half-dozen years, but he felt a growing sense of isolation from the institutional Church whose priorities and preoccupations were not necessarily his. He traces this back to the failure fully to implement *The Easter People*, but the catalyst for his eventual resignation was the general elections of 1983 and 1987. In 1983 Hume came under considerable pressure from right-wing Catholics to force Kent to withdraw from CND. He was, wrote one, 'doing the work of the Kremlin', another called his position 'a grave scandal'. A more alarming intervention was that of the papal nuncio who included him 'with the "useful idiots" who serve the interests of the Soviet Union'.[28] Hume certainly had his

---

26 Kent, *op. cit.*, p. 168.
27 *Ibid.*, p. 169.
28 *Ibid.*, p. 202.

doubts about Kent's increasingly political stance, but nonetheless continued to support him, even arranging a meeting at Archbishop's House with Kent and Bishop Thomas Gumbleton, a leading Catholic peace campaigner from the USA.

As the 1987 election approached, the controversy around Kent's role broke out afresh. Hume had imagined that by this time Kent would have got over his enthusiasm, but the opposite was the case. He reflected that, had the Cardinal told him to retire from the priesthood or resign from CND, he would have felt obliged to choose the former; he therefore decided to go of his own accord, and told the Vicar General of the diocese so in December 1986. In February 1987 he had a final interview with the Cardinal, and he and the diocese parted company. As Anthony Howard points out in his biography, Hume himself was uncertain of his position on the nuclear issue about which Kent felt so strongly. John Paul II in 1982 had told the United Nations that nuclear deterrence was acceptable insofar as it was a step on the way to general disarmament. The Church of England produced a report which called for unilateral disarmament,[29] but then the General Synod refused to endorse it. The Scottish Catholic Church declared itself unilateralist. It was a debate which waged in the British Catholic press, often with the heavyweights Michael Quinlan, a senior civil servant at the Ministry of Defence, and Gerard Hughes, a Jesuit moral philosopher, ranged against one another. Hume saw the issue which Hughes highlighted: 'To condemn all use and yet to accept deterrence, places us in a seemingly contradictory position', he wrote in *The Times* in November 1983.[30]

There is a touching coda to the story of Bruce Kent and the Cardinal. When Kent heard from the Cardinal's secretary that he was gravely ill, and had only a few days to live, he wrote him a letter which he delivered personally to the hospital. The Cardinal dictated a reply. 'I have received a great many letters,'

---

29 One of its authors was the late Fr Brendan Soane, a moral theologian and priest of the Diocese of Westminster.

30 Howard, *op. cit.*, p. 155.

he wrote, 'but none gave me more pleasure than yours.'[31] It was the last letter the Cardinal ever wrote.

Hume had backed Kent, albeit a mite reluctantly, in his campaigning, and was himself something of a campaigner for causes about which he felt strongly. One of these was the case of Patrick Joseph – known as Giuseppe – Conlon, a prisoner in Wormwood Scrubs. The Cardinal visited him just before Christmas 1978 and came to the conclusion that Conlon, together with other members of his family, the 'Maguire Seven', were innocent of the charge of bomb-making for the IRA for which they had been found guilty in 1976. Their case was related directly to that of the 'Guildford Four', who had been found guilty in 1975 of having planted the bombs and, though less directly, to that of the 'Birmingham Six', who had been tried and found guilty, also in 1975, for bombings in Birmingham. Hume's interest, however, was at first simply in gaining the release of Conlon because he was very seriously ill – he did indeed die still as a prisoner.

Hume at first attempted to avoid publicity. He approached the Home Secretary, and was furious when, three months after the meeting with William Whitelaw and his senior civil servants, an account of the conversations got into the press. When he failed to make any headway he wrote to the Prime Minister, but Margaret Thatcher simply passed his letter back to the Home Secretary. That was in July 1984. In October 1986 the Cardinal, with others, reopened the debate in the columns of *The Times*. He also formed a small committee – himself, two former Home Secretaries and two former Lords of Appeal – which produced a dossier that was handed to the Home Office in July 1987. The Home Secretary, Douglas Hurd, agreed to consider the dossier, but then said he would take no further action – though he had the decency to inform Hume personally of his decision. But then, after more pressure from Hume and his committee, it was agreed to take the case of the Guildford Four to the Court

---

31 *Ibid.*, p. 167.

of Appeal. In October 1989, just two days before the case was to be heard, the Crown announced that it was not going to defend the case. The day the appeal court met, the Home Secretary announced in the House of Commons that there would be a judicial enquiry into the Maguire trial and the police handling of it. Similarly, in 1991, the conviction of the Birmingham Six was overturned, and a Royal Commission on Criminal Justice was established, out of whose report the Criminal Cases Review Commission was set up. Hume had won his battle, but the victory gave him little consolation. He was dismayed at the miscarriages of justice, the behaviour of the police, and the length of time it had taken to free those who had been wrongly convicted. His faith in the criminal justice system was severely shaken.

Not all his campaigns took so long. In 1978 he persuaded the Prime Minister, James Callaghan, and the Foreign Secretary, David Owen, not to sell arms to Pinochet's Chile. His visit to the starving in Ethiopia in 1984, together with the BBC's Michael Buerk's compassionate reporting, helped to focus British, and the world's, attention on that disastrous country. But then he did not always win his campaigns. One of his most public defeats, almost a humiliation, was over a school in his diocese, the Cardinal Vaughan Memorial School, 'patronized', Peter Stanford writes, 'by the offspring of the quieter sort of aristocrat and the arts establishment who congregate in Holland Park'.[32] Strictly speaking, it was over two schools, but one of the two, the Oratory, was not technically a diocesan school but under the governance of the Fathers of Brompton Oratory who had no problem about making their authority felt when the diocesan education authorities tried to close all the sixth forms in the schools, and send the pupils to a new sixth-form college, St Charles. The Vaughan governors also protested. There was an additional complication. Secondary schools were being encouraged, under the Education Reform Act of 1988,

---

32 Stanford, *op. cit.*, p. 137.

to apply for grant-maintained status which, in simple terms, made them self-governing. The Catholic bishops objected to this. The schools had been built by the Catholic community for the Catholic community, and grant-maintained status, it seemed, would at least in theory allow them to break their links with the diocese.

As Trustee of the school, the Cardinal sacked the governors who would not follow his instructions, and he refused to name the governors on the application form for grant-maintained status. He was threatened with court action by one of the sacked governors, and rather grandly announced that he would go to gaol rather than give in. In the end he was forced to concede, the Secretary of State instructing him to name the governors. He was in a difficult position. He could not argue that independent schools were wrong because, as many of his critics were not slow to point out, he had spent most of his life in one. He argued instead that though 'opting out', as grant-maintained status was often called, was not wrong in itself, it was wrong for the Catholic community. He also commented on the discrepancy of funding that would ensue: 'The choice that should exist should never have to be between a school providing a decent education and one providing a poor one'.[33]

Nor did he have a great deal of success on some of the other major moral issues that were addressed by Parliament during his episcopacy. As has been seen, he was sympathetic to those Catholics who did not accept the teaching on contraception, and largely kept silent about it while endorsing the Vatican's line against the use of condoms. The English Catholics in 1979 produced a statement on homosexuality which is described by Stanford as 'one of the most tolerant and compassionate in the Catholic world'.[34] This tolerance had its limits. Quest is an association of gay Catholics. For many years it was listed in the *National*

---

33 *Ibid.*, p. 144. Tony Pellegrini, the headmaster who lead the rebellion against the diocese, after his retirement became a priest of the diocese.
34 *Ibid.*, p. 171.

Catholic Directory, but when the Cardinal learned that its constitution spoke of homosexual relationships – implying sexual relationships – he asked for that clause to be withdrawn. After considerable discussion among its members, and with the Cardinal, Quest refused to change its constitution. Hume then had it banned from the pages of the *Directory*. Hume personally wrote to the then Cardinal Ratzinger protesting against the Vatican document of 1992 on homosexuality, which suggested that the law was right to discriminate against homosexuals, but it is unclear whether the letter, with Hume's reflections, was ever sent.

He was, on the other hand, as utterly opposed to the 1984 Warnock Report which permitted experimentation on embryos as he was to abortion. He wrote to every member of Parliament in support of Enoch Powell's private member's bill which would have, if it had been passed (it was talked out), banned all experiments on embryos produced by *in vitro* fertilization. 'Innocent life is to be protected by the criminal law and public policy; no law should countenance discrimination by the strong against the weak', he said.[35] He presented the Church as defending the rights of the weak, the unborn children, against the strong. He again opposed the 1990 Human Fertilisation and Embryology Bill, saying in a piece in *The Times* that experimentation on embryos would lead to the destruction of society. But this bill, too, became law. Britain could no longer call itself a Christian country, he said. On these, and similar issues such as euthanasia, the Catholic Church, under his leadership, appeared a vociferous minority, which is perhaps no bad thing to be, but it also appeared anti-progress.

There was, however, something of a coup for the English bishops in the run-up to the general election of 1997, when they produced their document 'The Common Good'. It was a well-argued survey of the major issues, presenting them from a moral perspective, and it was remarkably well received, selling out time and again. Anthony Howard suggests that Hume

---

35 *Ibid.*, p. 177.

himself was not too happy with it, believing it all a bit too much of an endorsement of New Labour.[36] But it certainly reflected one of Hume's deepest convictions, that Catholics should not approach the election as if it were a single-issue vote. The Catholic pro-life lobby felt let down.

As has been noted above on homosexuality, Cardinal Hume did not always find himself in agreement with the line taken by the Vatican. But he was nonetheless a powerful and much respected figure in Rome. No one would call the English and Welsh bishops radicals, but under Hume those appointed showed themselves for the most part fairly liberal-minded men. Hume is thought to have prevented Rome, in 1993, appointing a member of Opus Dei to an English diocese. When Lavinia Byrne, a member of a religious order, was condemned by the Vatican for her book *Woman at the Altar*, the Cardinal came sturdily to her defence because he thought she had been unjustly treated – though in the end she left the order anyway.[37] He did not want Rome interfering in the affairs of the English Church. As Howard puts it, 'He saw himself . . . as an experienced housemaster who, provided he kept his own house in order and under control, did not need (and certainly did not welcome) interference from the headmaster.'[38]

Within his own diocese, however, he seemed at times a trifle grand and rather remote. The remoteness was of his own making. Early on he divided Westminster into pastoral areas, each with its area bishop, and each area bishop responsible for the administration of his own area, so one could choose to emphasize one aspect of pastoral strategy, and another something quite different. In the East End of London the much-loved Victor Guazzelli was particularly radical, and particularly successful. That he did not agree with Hume on the use of condoms, or

---

36 Howard, *op. cit.*, p. 254.
37 Ms Byrne tells her story, as do others who have similarly incurred the Vatican's displeasure, in Paul Collins (ed.), *From Inquisition to Freedom* (London: Continuum, 2001), pp. 162–88.
38 Howard, *op. cit.*, p. 320.

the justice of the Falklands War, was something the Cardinal coped with happily enough. But there was always the possibility that disgruntled parishioners, or, for that matter, parish priests, could go over the head of their area bishop to the man at the top who perhaps should not have listened, but he did.

The claim is often made that, under Hume, the Catholic Church entered the mainstream of British life. Anthony Howard claims that he – despite his French mother – was the most English of English cardinals. 'Basil', he says, 'in effect annexed the English Catholic Church to the British establishment.'[39] That his brother-in-law, Sir John, later Lord, Hunt was a senior civil servant and from 1973 to 1979 secretary to the Cabinet, certainly helped. He had close relations with the 'Establishment'. An invitation to stay at Windsor Castle arrived only a week after his installation as Archbishop of Westminster, and the Queen not only visited a flower festival organized by the Duchess of Norfolk to raise funds for the cathedral, but came back again for the cathedral's centenary, on 30 November 1995. He corresponded with Prince Charles, he received the Duchess of Kent into the Church. He ordered a Requiem Mass for Princess Diana after her death. He was not particularly close to Prime Minister Tony Blair – when Blair was still leader of the Opposition he had banned him from receiving Communion at the church in Highbury, North London, which he attended with his wife and children – but Blair as Prime Minister still came frequently to the cathedral. It was not on Hume's watch, however, that he converted to Catholicism.

But it is easy to make too much of this. He was not as close to the Establishment as Manning, say, or as much part of it as Vaughan, or as overtly patriotic as Hinsley. And perhaps more than any of his predecessors – even Manning – he has been involved in providing services for the dispossessed. When he arrived at Westminster, the piazza in front of the cathedral was a favourite gathering place for down-and-outs. The Passage,

---

39 *Ibid.*, p. 318.

based close to the Cathedral in Carlisle Place, looks after some 300 such people a day, providing medical services, temporary accommodation, meals, and assisting those who come to it towards rehabilitation. In a nice ecumenical touch, one of the funders has been Westminster Abbey. Younger people in difficulties are assisted at the Cardinal Hume Centre, set up in 1986, again not far from the cathedral, in Horseferry Road.

Basil Hume learned he was suffering from cancer, and that it was in an advanced stage, on 13 April 1999. He wrote to tell the priests of the diocese, and to inform his fellow bishops. He wanted, he said, no fuss, and he intended to keep on working for as long as he could. On 1 May he learned that the Queen intended to bestow on him the Order of Merit: the news was made public on 26 May and the Cardinal rose from his hospital bed and made a last trip to Buckingham Palace to receive the award from the Queen on 2 June. It was to be his last journey. He died in the Hospital of St John and St Elizabeth in the late afternoon of 17 June, and his requiem, attended by the Prime Ministers of both Britain and the Republic of Ireland, took place on 25 June. The pall-bearers were drawn from the altar servers whom he had trained in the Ampleforth parish, where he served his pastoral apprenticeship after his ordination.

He had been scheduled to visit the United States to speak to the US Catholic bishops at their annual conference. As he could not go, he recorded a video message, which was played on the day after his death. His last message was forthright. He had been surprised, he said, by the form and tone of letters received from the Vatican; he found some episcopal appointments, and the time it took to make them, unsatisfactory; he was uneasy about the way the Vatican chose to treat some theologians. The pope, he said, should meet heads of all national conferences of bishops at least every other year. And in another address to American Catholics gathered in conference, this time read out on the day of his funeral, he said, 'It is important always to be strict concerning principles, and endlessly compassionate and understanding of persons.'

10

Cormac Murphy-O'Connor

In his 1993 account of the episcopate of Basil Hume, Peter Stanford ruminates on the then 'rising stars' of the bench of bishops. He finds it on the whole encouraging: 'Men like Crispian Hollis in Portsmouth, Christopher Budd in Plymouth and the long-serving and underrated Cormac Murphy-O'Connor in Arundel and Brighton are very much in the Hume mould, friendly, unfrightening, patently men of God, above politics but with a vocal concern for injustices in the society around them.'[1] When Bishop Murphy-O'Connor's appointment to succeed Hume at Westminster was announced in February 2000, the Catholic weekly *The Tablet* was almost ecstatic in his praise: 'He may well turn out to be more ready than Hume to chance his arm ecumenically and pastorally . . . Inside Cormac Murphy-O'Connor is a prophet waiting to get out.'[2] And Ruth Gledhill, *The Times*'s religion correspondent but on this occasion writing in the issue of *The Tablet* in which the editorial just quoted appeared, seems to have found that the appointment confirmed her (Anglican) faith:

> Anyone who doubts the existence of God must surely now come to believe. It had seemed almost impossible that a Vatican said to be dominated by conservatives with an ailing

---

1 Stanford, *op. cit.*, p. 60.
2 *The Tablet*, 19 February 2000, p. 223.

Pope at the helm could come up with this ultimate 'dream ticket' of Murphy-O'Connor and Vincent Nichols.[3]

Such expectations would take a great deal of living up to.

Cormac was born in Reading, where his father George was a general practitioner, on 24 August 1932. Both George and Ellen, his mother, came from Cloyne in County Cork. George had qualified as a doctor at Cork, and was 31 before he married: Ellen was ten years his junior. They travelled over from Ireland originally to Liverpool, where George was a locum, before acquiring his own practice in Reading. Ellen gave birth to five sons, of whom Cormac was the last, and then, somewhat belatedly, a daughter. Two of Cormac's brothers became priests in the Diocese of Portsmouth along with Cormac, one became a doctor, and the other joined the Royal Artillery, but died young in a tragic accident.

It was a close-knit family, and unusually devout – the less friendly might say priest-ridden: Cormac had three uncles who were priests, and three first cousins. Cormac's father and mother were daily Mass-goers, and each evening before surgery they knelt for a family rosary. Both parents were activist: Dr Murphy-O'Connor founded the Society of St Vincent de Paul in his local parish, Ellen established the Union of Catholic Mothers. Perhaps more significantly, George persuaded the Irish Presentation Brothers to come to England and open a school in Reading, which all his sons attended. His mother had studied for a degree in French at Cork, and this opened her to the European tradition. She tried to get her children to speak French over meals, though with little success (they tended quickly to dissolve in giggles). She was more adventurous than George, and a member of Cardinal Hinsley's pioneering Sword of the Spirit. The children were all encouraged to learn a musi-

---

3 *Ibid.*, p. 233. Vincent Nichols was appointed Archbishop of Birmingham at the same time as Murphy-O'Connor was translated to Westminster. Archbishop Nichols had been an Assistant Bishop in Westminster.

cal instrument, but only Cormac persevered. So much so that, when it came to choosing a career, he was sufficiently competent to be able to consider a life as a concert pianist, but instead opted for the Church.

After the Presentation College the boys were sent to Prior Park, near Bath. Cormac was there for the five years immediately after the Second World War. 'They were tough years', he has written. 'Food was pretty rotten, and I remember the bitterly cold winter of 1946–7.'[4] He does, however, seem to have been happy there. All the brothers excelled at sports (one eventually played rugby for Ireland) and there was ample opportunity for such activities. In an odd similarity with Basil Hume, Cormac joined the cadet force and rose to the rank of sergeant.

After school, the seminary. Two of his brothers were already at Rome's English College, as candidates for the priesthood in the Diocese of Portsmouth. Perhaps to get out from under their shadow, Cormac wanted to offer himself to the Diocese of Westminster, but his father insisted he first got the permission of Archbishop King, the Bishop of Portsmouth (the 'Archbishop' was in this instance an honorary title, bestowed by the pope), and King laid claim to all three of the Murphy-O'Connors. But there was a problem. The English College's long-serving Rector, Mgr John Macmillan, thought two Murphy-O'Connors enough, and had to be persuaded to take a third: all three were, however, together in the College for only a year. When in October 1950 Cormac made the journey to Rome, it was the first time he had been out of England, apart from family holidays in Ardmore, County Waterford. On the train he had his very first taste of spaghetti. He arrived just in time for the solemn proclamation of the dogma of the Assumption.

He was seven years in Rome, studying at the Gregorian University – he was a slightly younger contemporary of Anthony Kenny, whose description of the regime at the 'Greg' was

---

4 Cormac Murphy-O'Connor, *At the Heart of the World* (London: Darton, Longman and Todd, 2004), p. 20.

mentioned above (p. 198). He was in St Peter's Square with Kenny for the proclamation of the dogma of the Assumption, and they wheedled their way into the basilica itself by claiming to be secretaries to a couple of cardinals. He also, in the course of his stay in Rome, made his way to San Giovanni Rotondo to meet Padre Pio – but he did not, he records, go to confession. He also met by chance in a coffee bar one Mgr Giovanni Battista Montini, the future Pope Paul VI. Rome was not all religion. There was also rugby – the English College once played the Italian national side, and won. Cormac's ability as a rugby player was spotted, and he was offered a place in a professional team. There were concerts, at which he played the piano, and a performance of *The Mikado* in which he played Nanki-Poo: another future archbishop played the Mikado himself, and a future bishop the 'daughter-in-law elect'.[5]

He was ordained in Rome on 28 October 1956, and the following year sent as a curate to the parish of Corpus Christi, North End, Portsmouth. In 1962 he went to the Sacred Heart, Fareham, a parish which he describes as occupying most of the space between Portsmouth and Southampton. It was Fareham which seems to have provided him with his most formative experiences. It was there he realized the value of bringing people together to pray in small groups, such groups helped, he says in his autobiographical *At the Heart of the World*, to create a vibrant parish. He spent a good deal of his time working with the young people of the parish – though he remarks he was not particularly good at it. While there, he won a competition for writing a Gospel song – 'Come ye blessed of my Father' – which he played on a guitar (in the 1960s every young clergyman's musical instrument of choice). He attributes his victory to the vociferous support he got from members of the parish's youth club.

He was in Fareham little more than three years before he was made secretary to the Bishop of Portsmouth, Derek Wor-

---

5 At six feet four inches, commented one of his contemporaries, Cormac was far too big to play female roles.

lock. With Worlock he helped in 1968 to create Park Place, a particularly flourishing diocesan pastoral centre, in a grade II listed building that had formerly been a convent school. He also found himself part of the team of priests organizing the first meeting of the National Conference of Priests. It was perhaps this event that framed his later career. The idea of this gathering of clergy, which was held at Wood Hall Pastoral Centre at Wetherby in Yorkshire in May 1970, had come from Cardinal Heenan, who was aware of the considerable unrest and disillusionment among the clergy of England and Wales in the aftermath of *Humanae Vitae*. Beneath the gaze of Heenan, Murphy-O'Connor proved himself to be a remarkably able mediator and peacemaker.

In 1970 Worlock appointed him to his first – and only as parish priest – parish, that of the Immaculate Conception in Portswood, Southampton. He was not there long. In 1971 he was summoned to replace Mgr Leo Alston as Rector of the Venerable English College in Rome. It had not been a happy time at the Venerabile. The unrest which had afflicted the clergy in Britain had also affected the British seminarians in Rome. One of those present at the time has claimed that Cormac saved the College from collapse. He succeeded in restoring discipline among the students, as well as imbuing a deeper commitment to study, yet he did so always in a manner which carried them with him. But he was equally good on conviviality. He was, indeed, renowned as a host: he once told the interviewer Sue Lawley on the BBC's *Desert Island Discs* that he was a dab hand at mixing cocktails, a skill learnt as Rector of the English College. One of those who enjoyed his hospitality was Donald Coggan, when, as Archbishop of Canterbury, he visited Pope Paul VI. Another, at the time less eminent guest was the future Archbishop of Canterbury, Rowan Williams. Cormac set up a series of exchanges between the Venerabile and Anglican theological colleges, and Williams, then a student for the Anglican ministry at Westcott House in Cambridge, was one of those who took advantage of the chance of spending time in Rome.

He enjoyed being back in Rome, but it did not last long. In March 1977 Bishop Michael Bowen of Arundel and Brighton was appointed Archbishop of Southwark, and Cormac was chosen to replace him. He was ordained Bishop on 21 December 1977, and took up residence at St Joseph's Hall, Storrington – a house, and a location, which he loved. As his episcopal motto he took the opening words of Vatican II's Constitution on the Church in the Modern World, 'Gaudium et Spes': 'Joy and Hope'.

It was no surprise that in 1982 he was selected to be the co-chairman of ARCIC II. When, years later, he was installed at Westminster, he repeated his conviction that 'I do not think you can be a proper Catholic without being an ecumenicist. My ecumenical work has made me more convinced of my Catholicity.'[6] This may not have been the most politic way of putting it, but there has never been any doubt of his commitment to Christian unity – as exemplified by the exchange scheme at the Venerabile. As he said to the Anglican Synod at Chichester in 1978, 'The scope of ecumenism is not like a merger of companies, with limits on how far the merger will go. It is rather like a road on which someone enters, and from which he discovers there is no going back.'[7]

It was a difficult time to attempt to foster relations with the Anglican Communion. Soon after the first women priests had been ordained in Bristol Cathedral for the Church of England, Cormac wrote in an article in the Catholic weekly *The Universe*:

Clearly the decision of the General Synod in 1992 to admit women to the priesthood has had considerable repercussions throughout the Church. It is very important to understand that the basic question is not about whether or not women can be ordained but about the authority of the Church of England to make such a decision.[8]

---

6 Baty, *op. cit.*, p. 8.
7 *Ibid.*, pp. 30–1.
8 *Ibid.*, p. 91.

That was certainly the position of many of those who felt obliged to leave the Church of England and enter the Roman Communion. They believed that their Church lacked the authority, on its own, to make such a break with the past. It is not, however, the view of the Vatican, which regards the ordination of women not as a matter of tradition but as something metaphysically impossible. When, at a press conference alongside his Anglican co-chairman Bishop Mark Santer, Bishop Murphy-O'Connor had to present the exchange of letters between Lambeth Palace and the Holy See on the ordination of women, he looked, and sounded, distinctly uneasy.

Perhaps as a consequence he proved very sympathetic to those clergy who moved to Rome and wished to continue their ministry as Catholic priests. He said of them:

> We have been asked by the Holy Father to be generous in our response to those of the Church of England who find themselves in difficulties of conscience. As bishops we are confident that such generosity will be forthcoming and we will be ready not only to welcome our new priests, their wives and families, but also to be enriched by the experiences and insights which they will bring to us all.[9]

Perhaps it was as an acknowledgement of such sensitivity that Archbishop George Carey awarded him the Lambeth degree of Doctor of Divinity in 1999, the first time it had been granted to a Catholic prelate.

It was at Fareham, he has written (see above, p. 226), that he became convinced of the value of small groups. It was no doubt this conviction that encouraged Bishop Murphy-O'Connor to launch the RENEW programme in his diocese, a programme conceived originally for the Diocese of Newark in the USA. The two-and-a-half-year enterprise, which began in 1988, was

---

9 *Ibid.*, pp. 32–3.

studied by a group of sociologists, though they lightly disguised their subject by hiding 'Arundel and Brighton' under the name 'Downlands', and renaming Bishop Cormac as Bishop Patrick. Their findings were published as *The Politics of Spirituality*.[10] It was claimed – though not by the authors of this study – that some 50 per cent of the Mass-going population of 'Downlands' participated in the small-group prayer and study sessions.[11] The conclusions of the sociologists were not favourable. For one thing, the organization and materials proved quite expensive. They point out that, as it came to an end, the diocese found itself in a financial crisis – though they admit that this may not have been directly as a result of RENEW. They also questioned whether it empowered the laity: 'In spite of all the rhetoric about lay empowerment, in fact, RENEW was imposed by the religious leadership in the diocese from the top down.'[12] And while the group discussions were for many 'a welcome opportunity to meet and befriend other parishioners',[13] they did not find that these small groups continued to meet after the end of the programme, as Bishop 'Patrick' had wished. Although the authors of *The Politics of Spirituality* – all of whom themselves took part in the process of RENEW – attempt to present an academically respectable neutrality, it is clear they were far from impressed. They came to the conclusion that certain diocesan activities were, oddly, more clericalized after RENEW than before it. They were also clearly disappointed that the discussions did not sufficiently alert participants to issues of justice and peace.[14]

---

10 Michael Hornsby-Smith, John Fulton and Margaret I. Norris, *The Politics of Spirituality: The Study of a Renewal Process in an English Diocese* (Oxford: Clarendon Press, 1995).

11 Bishop Victor Guazzelli, Bishop in east London in Hume's episcopate, also considered using RENEW in his pastoral area. He finally decided against it, and instead devised his own.

12 Hornsby-Smith et. al, *op. cit.*, p. 116.

13 *Ibid.*, p. 148.

14 It was indeed the lack of adequate emphasis on social issues, at least on social issues confronting those in east London, that decided Bishop Guazzelli against importing the programme (see above, footnote 11).

In a sense this programme was intended only as a beginning. Hoping to build on the sense of community that he believed RENEW had engendered, in April 1991 Bishop Cormac sent out a questionnaire asking the people of the diocese to identify the needs of the diocese as a basis for formulating a pastoral plan. Slightly under 3,000 of these were returned, but it was calculated that more than 8,500, or roughly a fifth of those who regularly attended Mass, were involved one way or another in responding. As a result, seven areas were highlighted, including adult education, ecumenism and small communities.

This overall vision of a pastoral plan was not well received by the clergy of the diocese. The diagnosis of the hostility was that it arose because the clergy (and the people) did not 'own' the plan. Despite the consultation it seemed as if it were being imposed from the top down. At the end of 1998, therefore, when Cormac proposed holding a Diocesan Synod to deal with reforming and reshaping the diocese to respond to the declining numbers of clergy, he tried to get everyone to take part, visiting each of the deaneries personally to meet priests and people and to urge their involvement. The date for the Synod was to be 2002. By that time, however, he had been moved to Westminster.

The news of his appointment was broken by the *Sunday Telegraph* on 13 February 2000: the formal announcement came two days later. Cormac Murphy-O'Connor moved from the hacienda-style St Joseph's Hall in Storrington to Archbishop's House, bringing with him his grand piano, but leaving behind Max, his Golden Labrador. Much as he admired him (see above, p. 223), Peter Stanford clearly had not been persuaded that he was likely to make it to the top:

Bishop Cormac Murphy-O'Connor of Arundel and Brighton [he wrote], who rivals Cardinal Hume for sheer niceness and has a way of putting a human face on even the thorniest of Church teaching, is considered by some of his fellows to have let his doubts on *Humanae Vitae* show through.[15]

Was he then a liberal, he was asked after his appointment:

> If by a liberal you mean someone who is open to all new things that come along, then I am not. I am a Catholic bishop who respects the tradition of the Church. If by conservative you mean someone who is a rigid fundamentalist, then I am not that either. I am a man of the Church.[16]

Those who welcomed him so warmly to Westminster, on the other hand, rather put him, as Stanford had done, among the liberals. But both sides of the Catholic divide were cheered shortly after his appointment was announced when he told David Frost in a television interview that he thought the Act of Settlement, which forbids anyone in line for the throne to marry a Catholic, was discriminatory, and ought to be abolished. If this was a case of *lèse-majesté*, the Queen did not seem to mind. He was invited to preach to the Royal Family at Sandringham early in January 2002.

He was installed as the tenth Archbishop of Westminster on 22 March 2000. In his homily he mentioned a stone he had come across in the Outer Hebrides. On it was inscribed 'Pilgrim Cormac: He went beyond what was deemed possible.' Which may be what he thought he himself was being asked to do when there blew up, in July 2000, renewed criticism of his handling of the case of the child abuser, Fr Michael Hill. The charge was that he had moved Hill from one parish to another, knowing that he was a child abuser, and had eventually sent him to Gatwick airport as chaplain, where he again offended. Murphy-O'Connor was accused of attempting to cover up Hill's crimes, presumably to save the good name of the Church.

---

15 Stanford, *op. cit.*, p. 213.
16 Baty, *op. cit.*, p. 2.

The story was, however, much more complicated. Hill had indeed once been moved from one parish to another, but that first instance had nothing to do with any sexual misdemeanour. When his sexual abuse was discovered he was suspended from active ministry and retrained at the diocese's expense as an accountant – though he never practised as such. He was sent to Stroud, to a clinic which specializes in priests who offend (though not only in matters of child abuse). He discharged himself from there after four months, claiming that further treatment would be counterproductive. Cormac was advised that he might re-offend, but decided to send him to Gatwick on the mistaken assumption that he would not there come into contact with children. He was arrested in 1996, and convicted for offences stretching back over twenty years.

In a letter to *The Tablet* in January 1995 – when of course he was still at Arundel and Brighton – he wrote not so much to defend himself, but to deny the association which was often made between clerical celibacy and child abuse, a canard he had no difficulty disposing of. He then went on:

> Until recently most bishops, like many other people, were not fully aware of all the facts concerning paedophilia or of its compulsive nature for some men. This, in some way, explains what can now be seen as an inadequate pastoral and professional response . . . All efforts are being taken to ensure that any accusations reaching Church authorities are being heard in a responsible and appropriate manner and in accordance with the law, and with particular concern for the victims of such abuse.[17]

Portsmouth Diocese had issued guidelines on how to deal with charges of sex abuse as early as June 1993, and it was these which became the model for *Child Abuse: Pastoral and Procedural Guidelines* issued by the Bishops' Conference the following year.

---

17 *The Tablet*, 17 January 1995, p. 15.

Among other things, it committed the bishops to supporting police investigations. There were complaints that the guidelines dealt with the abuser, but not with the abuse. This issue was addressed in 1996 by the bishops' document *Healing the Wound.* In 1999 Arundel and Brighton collaborated with Southwark and with Portsmouth Dioceses in drawing up a policy for child protection.

It was always Cormac's defence that he had not, any more than others, understood the nature of paedophilia, and that when he did so he acted accordingly. He also complained that many of his critics took no notice of the guidelines in place since 1994. But the accusations did not stop. At the end of September 2002 the BBC's *Today* programme returned to the attack, claiming that the Cardinal (as he now was) had failed to report the abuse to the police, which might be construed as perverting the course of justice, and early in November devoted half an hour to allegations against him without giving him opportunity to answer. Then the Sunday newspaper the *News of the World* carried a story that an assistant bishop in Southwark had offered Hill £50,000 to keep quiet about the Cardinal. This time Cormac complained to the Press Complaints Commission. The paper said it had a transcript of the conversation, but this turned out to have been faked. The *News of the World* was instructed to print an apology, which it did, under the headline 'Sorry, Cardinal', but not until seven months after the original allegations, and then only on page 6.

That proved to be more or less the end of the affair, but those close to the Cardinal reported that he had been shaken by it all. As *The Tablet* remarked at one point, he might not unreasonably have thought he was being got at, that the BBC in particular was conducting a campaign against him. There were calls for his resignation, and he considered it, but stayed, and appointed Lord Nolan, who had headed the enquiry into standards in public life, to chair a high-powered committee to review the 1994 guidelines. The outcome was a much more rigorous set of guidelines and system of child protection, but some at least among the clergy were left feeling they had been stripped of their natural rights to self-defence.

All the while there was a long series of other issues to engage him. One which made the headlines was the case of the conjoined twins. Their parents had brought them to England from Malta for treatment, but would not accept an operation if one of them would be bound to die in the course of it. They thought such an action would be contrary to the will of God. The case came to court, and in September 2000 the Cardinal produced a twelve-page submission, arguing that the rights of the parents should be respected. In the end the case went against the parents, and one of the babies did indeed die. In October 2004 he met the surviving twin, Grace Attard, on Gozo.

He also gave thought to the reorganization of the Diocese of Westminster, as he had of Arundel and Brighton. A year and a half after coming to the diocese he decided to abolish the geographical pastoral areas and replace them with 'four keys areas of pastoral outreach', with greater emphasis on the deanery as part of diocesan structure. Even earlier he had announced that he wanted more permanent deacons. Hume had been lukewarm on this innovation, believing that they had no clear role to play in the diocese, and could be said to 'clericalize' the laity. Now a number of men were recruited and trained for ordination to the deaconate. He also, he said, wanted more catechists and greater collaboration in parishes between priests and lay people. And, rather against the trend that was coming from Rome, he wanted Communion under both kinds to be common practice. And despite the criticism of RENEW in Arundel and Brighton, he launched it in the Diocese of Westminster in November 2002, under the title of 'At Your Word, Lord'. It was announced with a series of thirteen meetings around the diocese, and a gathering of priests (an 'away day' at Bognor Regis) to brief them. He once again embarked upon RENEW because he had heard, he said, from some in his former diocese how greatly the programme had helped them.

It ran until 2005, and some 20,000 are said to have taken part – a rather smaller proportion of the Mass-going public of Westminster than had been involved in Arundel and Brighton.

He also began a consultation on the future of diocese. In May 2005 there was published *Graced by the Spirit – Planning Our Future Together,* known as 'the Green Paper'. This analysed responses from the parishes about the pastoral needs and future strategy of the diocese. The Cardinal's response was 'the White Paper', *Communion and Mission: Pastoral Priorities for the Diocese of Westminster,* which appeared in February 2006. The Cardinal identified five pastoral priorities, which contained no surprises – an emphasis on the diocese as a 'community of communities' and a stress on the need for small groups. As part of the strategy to meet a declining number of clergy, it was very weak. It did, however, call for an 'audit' of the needs of the diocese:

I will ask the Deans with the Auxiliary Bishops to conduct an audit in consultation with the parish councils/teams and the priests of the deanery. This audit will profile the life and mission of each parish so as to assess its needs and resources and to help develop its relationships with neighbouring parishes and within the deanery. In order to assist this reflection an audit document will be provided to guide the evaluation. This will contain questions about the size of congregations and the number of Masses celebrated in the area, the number of church buildings, their capacity, parish halls, demographic changes, the availability of staff and the training and formation needed for ministers. Such an audit will have important implications for each parish and deanery in the Diocese and should take place between September and December 2006.

Such local conversations will enormously assist future decisions that need to be taken with regard to the clustering and merging of parishes where necessary in some areas. These decisions will not be taken centrally and imposed. They will be taken gradually, at different times, as the circumstances arise, and only after the evaluation and contribution of each local community is assessed.

So there was to be reorganization – but not just yet. Although cast in rather vague language, *Communion and Mission* displayed a greater awareness of the problems facing the Diocese of Westminster than has so far been evinced by other bishops about their own patch. The audit, incidentally, included the seminary. Given the decrease in number of candidates for the priesthood, he proposed an amalgamation between Wonersh, the Southwark diocesan seminary, and Allen Hall in Westminster, but could get no agreement.

He was made a Cardinal at a consistory on 21 February 2001. In May he attended an extraordinary consistory (a meeting of cardinals with the pope) at which he addressed the need for great collegiality in the Church. He wanted representatives of bishops' conferences to meet in Rome every three years, and he argued that the Synod of Bishops should have the same standing in the Roman curia as the Congregation for the Doctrine of the Faith. He also called for renewed efforts to progress ecumenical dialogue, which has all but stalled in Britain since the ordination of women in the Church of England. This ecumenical pause has not, however, stopped regular collaboration between Lambeth and Westminster: Cormac Murphy O'Connor and Rowan Williams are very good friends, and the Archbishop of Canterbury was appreciative of the support the Cardinal gave over the Jeffrey John affair, when Williams had to persuade the openly gay John, then canon theologian at the Anglican cathedral in Southwark, not to accept a bishopric.

At a meeting of Churches Together in England in November 2004 the Cardinal mused about the future of the Catholic Church under the next pope. He listed four challenges: the secularization of Europe, dialogue with Muslims, the gulf between rich and poor, and greater collegiality. All these had to be addressed, he said, if the Church was to be credible. In the conclave of April 2005 Murphy-O'Connor might therefore have been expected to vote for a candidate who was committed to greater collegiality among the bishops of the Church. Joseph Ratzinger, who emerged from the conclave as Pope Benedict XVI, was not that man, and there is a suggestion that the Cardinal of Westminster did not cast his vote in favour of the former head of the Congregation for the Doctrine of the Faith. Talking to reporters afterwards he said, 'When *they* chose this man . . .' only to draw attention to his slip by correcting himself to 'When *we* chose . . .' It was a short conclave: Murphy-O'Connor had been expecting a long one: 'He planned on packing a Victorian novel or two. "It'll be a sort of Brontë. Or Jane Austen".'[18]

It almost seems as if, the papacy having failed to live up to the challenges he has set it, Murphy-O'Connor has taken them on himself. He is a considerable Europhile (as Bishop he chaired the episcopal conference's committee on Europe), and in April and May 2005 put on a series of lectures under the title of 'Faith in Europe' – the ambiguity is intentional – which he has since edited and published. He has called for greater collegiality and has tried, though with mixed results, to implement it within his own diocese through consultation with clergy and laity, and he has urged the establishment of councils in each parish to advise the priest.

On the other hand, he has perhaps not been as active as other church leaders in engaging with Islam. He has expressed reservations about Muslim schools. He would not, he said, want Catholic children to attend such schools (there are sometimes Muslims in Catholic institutions), but did not think they ought to be denied them. But it would be right, he said, to have 'certain hesitations because if Muslim schools were not going to actively inculcate the kind of civic values that are given in Christian schools, then that would be dangerous.'[19]

---

18 David Gibson, *The Rule of Benedict* (San Francisco: HarperSanFrancisco, 2006), p. 99. Gibson's account of the events of the conclave is thought to be a fairly accurate reflection of what happened.
19 *The Tablet,* 1 October 2005. The remark was made in a BBC 2 programme, *God and the Politicians.*

It is, perhaps, on the divisions between rich and poor that he has been most active. He spoke at the Fighting Economic Injustice Conference in November 2003, and early the following year addressed a Treasury Conference on globalization, backing the then Chancellor, Gordon Brown, in his proposal of an International Finance Facility which could double aid to the developing world. He also got the Vatican not only to lend its support, but to hold a conference on the IFF, which Gordon Brown addressed. He has tried to show his support for the poor in more direct ways, travelling to Sri Lanka the year after the tsunami to visit CAFOD relief projects (his original intention had to be there over Christmas, but this raised protests among the cathedral staff), and the year after visiting Bethlehem in the company of other church leaders to demonstrate solidarity with the Palestinians. More recently he has backed the London Citizens' Campaign for a living wage, and held in the cathedral a Mass for migrant workers, also orchestrated by London Citizens. 'You know that here, in the Church in London, you have a home', he told them.

There have been gaffes. He appointed an Opus Dei priest to a parish in Swiss Cottage. The press, not usually concerned with the movement of parochial clergy, took an interest. He was carefully briefed for a television interview, but then appeared to say, despite his talk of collaborating with the laity, that the appointment of a parish priest was none of their business. There was also a public, and acrimonious exchange when two fairly prominent gay Catholics celebrated their long-standing partnership. Cardinal Hume would have handled it with more finesse.

In the quotation above (see p. 232) just after his appointment, he refused to identify himself as either liberal or conservative. On many of the moral issues of the day – abortion, research on embryos – he has spoken out for what many would judge as a conservative position. In an interview with *The Independent* in July 2004 he appeared more firmly opposed to women priests than had his predecessor, but certainly appeared to approve of the ordination of married men after they had raised their family. He thought it possible 'any time in the next papacy', a view he has had to revise. He clearly broke ranks with the Vatican when he told the interviewer that, in certain circumstances, the use of condoms could be legitimate. He may have presided at a Mass for the founder of Opus Dei (though he did not preach), but when in June 2008 Cardinal Dario Castrillon Hoyos celebrated a Tridentine High Mass at the cathedral, decked out in all the panoply of cardinatial grandeur, Cardinal Murphy-O'Connor and his assistant bishops were elsewhere. At least one commentator saw their absence as a direct snub to the pope himself, who had authorized the more frequent use of this rite.

One of the rather odd things about Cormac Murphy-O'Connor is that he has a slight Irish accent. It is odd because he was born in England and raised in England. But he was the son of Irish immigrants, and he has risen to the top (well, almost to the top) of the Catholic hierarchy, and holds a respected position in the State – he has consulted the Vatican about what they would think if English Catholic bishops were to be offered seats in a reformed House of Lords – as well as in the Church. He may dislike the dark, echoing spaces of Archbishop's House, and regret having had to leave Storrington, but he does not seem, as he approaches retirement, to be too weighed down by the cares of his office.

It used to be that cardinals who were not diocesan bishops had to live in Rome. He likes Rome, and knows how the system works, so would no doubt welcome the occasional meeting of a Congregation or two. He has served on a variety of them, including the Council for Promoting Christian Unity. But he does not seem to expect to live in the Eternal City. He enjoys the occasional lunch at London's Garrick Club, and has become a member. The Club waived its fee.

Bibliography

Aspden, Kester, *Fortress Church* (Leominster: Gracewing, 2002)

Baty, Nick, *Archbishop Cormac and the 21st Century* (London: Fount, 2000)

Beck, George Andrew (ed.), *The English Catholics 1850–1950* (London: Burns and Oates, 1950)

Bedoyère, Michael de la, *Cardinal Bernard Griffin* (London: Rockliff, 1955)

Bellenger, Dominic Aidan and Fletcher, Stella, *Princes of the Church* (Stroud: Sutton Publishing, 2001)

Bennett, John, 'The Care of the Poor' in G. A. Beck (ed.), *The English Catholics 1850–1950* (London: Burns and Oates, 1950)

Burkle, Francis A., *Passing the Keys*, 2nd edn (Lanham, MD: Madison Books, 2001)

Burns, Tom, *The Use of Memory* (London: Sheed and Ward, 1993)

Cardinale, Hyginus Eugene, *The Holy See and the International Order* (Gerrards Cross: Colin Smythe, 1976)

Castle, Tony (ed.), *Basil Hume: A Portrait* (London: Collins, 1986)

Chadwick, Owen, *Britain and the Vatican During the Second World War* (Cambridge: Cambridge University Press, 1986)

Clifton, Michael, *Amigo: Friend of the Poor* (Leominster: Fowler Wright, 1987)

Collins, Paul (ed.), *From Inquisition to Freedom* (London: Continuum, 2001)

Coman, Peter, *Catholics and the Welfare State* (London: Longman, 1977)

Cornwell, John, *Hitler's Pope* (London: Viking, 1999)

Coupland, Philip, *Britannia, Europa and Christendom: British Christians and European Integration* (Basingstoke: Palgrave Macmillan, 2006)

Davis, Charles, *A Question of Conscience* (London: Hodder and Stoughton, 1967)

Dick, J. A., *The Malines Conversations Revisited* (Louvain: Leuven University Press, 1989)

Doyle, Peter, *Westminster Cathedral, 1895–1995* (London: Geoffrey Chapman, 1995)

241

Bibliography

Drumm, Walter, *The Old Palace* (Dublin: Veritas, 1991)

Dwyer, J. J., 'The Catholic Press, 1850–1950', in George Andrew Beck (ed.), *The English Catholics 1850–1950* (London: Burns and Oates, 1950)

Frost, David, *An Autobiography, Part One – From Congregations to Audiences* (London: HarperCollins, 1993)

Furnival, John and Knowles, Anne, *Archbishop Derek Worlock: His Personal Journey* (London: Geoffrey Chapman, 1998)

Gibson, David, *The Rule of Benedict* (San Francisco: HarperSanFrancisco, 2006)

Gilley, Sheridan, 'The Years of Equipoise' in V. Alan McClelland and M. Hodgetts, *From Without the Flaminian Gate* (London: Darton, Longman and Todd, 1999)

Gray, Robert, *Cardinal Manning: A Biography* (London: Weidenfeld and Nicolson, 1985)

Grootaers, Jan and Selling, Joseph A., *The 1980 Synod of Bishops 'On the Role of the Family'* (Louvain: Louvain University Press; Peeters, 1983)

Hasler, A. B., *How the Pope Became Infallible* (New York: Doubleday, 1981)

Hastings, Adrian, *A History of English Christianity, 1920–2000* (London: SCM Press, 2001)

—— (ed.), *Modern Catholicism* (London: SPCK; New York: Oxford University Press, 1991)

——, *Wiriyamu* (London: Search Press, 1974)

Hebblethwaite, Peter, *Pope Paul VI* (London: HarperCollins, 1993)

Heenan, John C., *Cardinal Hinsley* (London: Burns, Oates and Washbourne, 1944)

——, *A Crown of Thorns* (London: Hodder and Stoughton, 1974)

——, *Not the Whole Truth* (London: Hodder and Stoughton, 1971)

——, *They Made Me Sign: A Series of Talks to a Non-Catholic about to Marry a Catholic* (London: Sheed and Ward, 1949)

Heimann, Mary, *Catholic Devotion in Victorian England* (Oxford: Clarendon Press, 1995)

Hornsby-Smith, Michael, Fulton, John and Norris, Margaret I., *The Politics of Spirituality: The Study of a Renewal Process in an English Diocese* (Oxford: Clarendon Press, 1995)

Howard, Anthony, *Basil Hume: The Monk Cardinal* (London: Headline, 2005)

Hughes, John Jay, *Absolutely Null and Utterly Void: The Papal Condemnation of Anglican Orders 1896* (London: Sheed and Ward, 1968)

Ivereigh, Austen (ed.), *Unfinished Journey* (London: Continuum, 2003)

Izquierdo, César, 'La reforma de los studios eclesiasticos' in *Anuario de la Historia de la Iglesia* x (2001)

Kaiser, Robert Blair, *The Encyclical that Never Was* (London: Sheed and Ward, 1987)

Bibliography

Kenny, Anthony, *A Path from Rome* (London: Sidgwick and Jackson, 1985)

Kent, Bruce, *Undiscovered Ends* (London: HarperCollins, 1992)

Ker, Ian, *John Henry Newman: A Biography* (Oxford: Clarendon Press, 1988)

Kirby, Dianne (ed.), *Religion and the Cold War* (Basingstoke: Palgrave Macmillan, 2003)

Kollar, Rene, *The Return of the Benedictines to London* (Tunbridge Wells: Burns and Oates, 1989)

Lamberts, Emiel, 'L'Internationale noire; une organisation secrète au service du Saint-Siège' in Emiel Lamberts (ed.), *The Black International* (Louvain: Leuven University Press, 2002)

Longley, Clifford, 'Ten Years at Westminster' in Tony Castle (ed.), *Basil Hume: A Portrait* (London: Collins, 1986)

——, *The Worlock Archive* (London: Geoffrey Chapman, 2000)

McClelland, V. Alan and Hodgetts, Michael (eds), *From Without the Flaminian Gate* (London: Darton, Longman and Todd, 1999)

—— (ed.), *By Whose Authority?* (Bath: Downside Abbey, 1996)

——, *Cardinal Manning* (Oxford: Oxford University Press, 1962)

——, 'Great Britain and Ireland' in Adrian Hastings (ed.), *Modern Catholicism* (London: SPCK; New York: Oxford University Press, 1991)

McCleod, Hugh (ed.), *The Cambridge History of the Church*, vol. 9 (Cambridge: Cambridge University Press, 2006)

Moloney, Thomas, *Westminster, Whitehall and the Vatican* (Tunbridge Wells: Burns and Oates, 1985)

Murphy-O'Connor, Cormac, *At the Heart of the World* (London: Darton, Longman and Todd, 2004)

O'Neill, Robert, *Cardinal Herbert Vaughan* (London: Burns and Oates, 1995)

Pereiro, James, *Cardinal Manning: An Intellectual Biography* (Oxford: Clarendon Press, 1998)

Quinn, Dermot, *Patronage and Piety* (Stanford, CA: Stanford University Press, 1993)

Reid, Scott M. P. (ed.), *A Bitter Trial* (London: The Saint Austin Press, 2000)

Schiefen, R., *Nicholas Wiseman and the Transformation of English Catholicism* (Shepherdstown: Patmos, 1984)

Schofield, Nicholas and Skinner, Gerard, *The English Cardinals* (Oxford: Family Publications, 2007)

Schultenover, David, *The View From Rome* (New York: Fordham University Press, 1993)

Shaw, Tony, 'Martyrs, Miracles and Martians' in Dianne Kirby (ed.), *Religion and the Cold War* (Basingstoke: Palgrave Macmillan, 2003), p. 223

Bibliography

Speaight, Robert, *The Property Basket* (London: Collins and Harvill Press, 1970)

Stanford, Peter, *Cardinal Hume and the Changing Face of English Catholicism* (London: Geoffrey Chapman, 1993)

The Easter People: A Message from the Roman Catholic Bishops of England and Wales in Light of the National Pastoral Congress (Slough: St Paul Publications, 1980)

The Oxford Dictionary of National Biography (online version)

Walsh, Michael, 'Ecumenism in War-Time Britain' in the *Heythrop Journal* XXIII (1982), pp. 243–58 and 377–94

——, *From Sword to Ploughshare* (London: Catholic Institute for International Relations, 1980)

——, 'The History of the Council' in Adrian Hastings (ed.), *Modern Catholicism* (London: SPCK; New York: Oxford University Press, 1991)

——, 'The Religious Ferment of the '60s' in Hugh McCleod (ed.), *The Cambridge History of Christianity* (Cambridge: Cambridge University Press, 2006), vol. 9, pp. 304–22

——, *The Secret World of Opus Dei* (London: Grafton Books, 1989)

——, *St Edmund's College Cambridge* (Cambridge: St Edmund's, 1996)

——, *The Tablet: A Commemorative History* (London: The Tablet Publishing Co., 1990)

Waugh, Evelyn, *Ronald Knox* (London: Chapman and Hall, 1959)

Wheeler, Gordon, 'The Archdiocese of Westminster' in George Andrew Beck (ed.), *The English Catholics 1850–1950* (London: Burns and Oates, 1950)

Whitehead, Maurice, 'A View from the Bridge' in V. Alan McClelland and Michael Hodgetts (eds), *From Without the Flaminian Gate* (London: Darton, Longman and Todd, 1999)

Williams, Michael E., *The Venerable English College, Rome* (London: Associated Catholic Publications, 1979)

Index

Index

Index

Index

Index